Making Learning Happen

Praise for the first edition

'... an abundant supply of a quality that is often lacking in such books: thoughtful originality, backed up by meaningful experience on the part of the author. The book as a whole is mercifully free of unnecessary jargon, and is accessible and friendly in tone ...' – *ESCalate*

'Race ... is without a doubt a master of intelligent simplicity ... a serious understanding of the needs of learners is clear behind every page ... There is an enormous amount of practical, useful material. I will not be in the least surprised if this book is a runaway success.' – *Anita Pincas, Lifelong Education and International Development, Institute of Education, London*

'Phil Race freely shares his experience and his wise counsel in a text where he emerges from the pages as a clear thinking, clear writing, expert in this field, with much to offer.' – *John Cowan, Emeritus Professor of Learning Development, the Open University*

Making Learning Happen

A Guide for Post-Compulsory Education

Second Edition

Phil Race

Los Angeles | London | New Delhi
Singapore | Washington DC

First published 2005
Reprinted 2006, 2007, 2008, 2009 (twice)
Second edition published 2010

SAGE Publications Ltd
1 Oliver's Yard
55 City Road
London EC1Y 1SP

SAGE Publications Inc.
2455 Teller Road
Thousand Oaks, California 91320

SAGE Publications India Pvt Ltd
B 1/I 1 Mohan Cooperative Industrial Area
Mathura Road
New Delhi 110 044

SAGE Publications Asia-Pacific Pte Ltd
33 Pekin Street #02-01
Far East Square
Singapore 048763

Library of Congress Control Number: 2009940512

British Library Cataloguing in Publication data

A catalogue record for this book is available from the
British Library

ISBN 978-1-84920-113-1
ISBN 978-1-84920-114-8 (pbk)

Typeset by C&M Digitals (P) Ltd, Chennai, India
Printed and bound in Great Britain by TJ International Ltd, Padstow, Cornwall
Printed on paper from sustainable resources

Mixed Sources
Product group from well-managed
forests and other controlled sources
www.fsc.org Cert no. SGS-COC-2482
© 1996 Forest Stewardship Council
FSC

Contents

Preface to the
Second Edition

What's new?

The principal differences between this edition and its predecessor arise from my having spent most of the years between them running hundreds of workshops on assessment, learning and teaching around the UK and in various other parts of the world, talking to thousands of teachers and learners, continuing to reflect on what makes learning happen. This second edition is, in my view, not only expanded, but substantially improved, for example:

- The discussion in Chapter 2 now leads to seven, rather than five, factors underpinning successful learning, and the seven factors are now linked much more directly to different teaching/learning contexts in most of the remaining chapters.

- I've added Chapter 3 on 'Designing the curriculum for learning', an important topic missing from the first edition, replacing the previous Chapter 3 which was essentially a questionnaire limited to the original five factors underpinning learning.

- I've extended Chapter 4 on 'Assessment driving learning' not least by incorporating a tool to enable readers to interrogate their own assessment design in terms of how well it links to the seven factors underpinning successful learning, as well as in terms of validity, reliability, transparency, and so on.

- I've added new elements to Chapter 5 on 'Learning through feedback', in particular regarding the importance of helping learners to get feedback quickly enough.

- There is a new Chapter 10, 'What can I do when...?', which provides some creative tactics for addressing some of the common problems colleagues experience in teaching in post-compulsory education.

- There is a new final Chapter 11 entitled 'Reflective observation', which explores the nature of reflection, and advocates the benefits to be gained from peer observation of teaching and from reflecting actively on one's own teaching.

- I've added comments and suggestions linking various topics in the book to what we are finding out from students about their higher education experience in the UK. Using the National Student Survey, which has been published annually since 2005, I point towards things we can do to address their concerns and increase their satisfaction.

To make room for all of these additions to the book, some things had to go! In particular, I have sadly discarded the chapter on 'Making workshops work'. However, this is covered even more fully in materials I wrote for JISC TechDis (www.techdis.ac.uk) as 'Designing Effective Training Workshops', which can be downloaded from the TechDis website (and also from my own website: phil-race.co.uk). I also felt it time to discard the original chapter on 'Putting the learning into e-learning', not because e-learning is any less important now, but rather the opposite, making the topic far too big to do justice to it in a single chapter in a book of this size.

Putting the book in context

People have been trying to make learning happen throughout the recorded development of the human species – and no doubt for some time before any-one tried to describe it in words. There is now a vast literature about learn-ing and teaching. Some of it is scholarly. There is also an abundant 'how to do it' literature, spanning learning, teaching and assessment. It sometimes feels as though there is a gulf between the two kinds of literature, with some academics climbing ever higher up their ivory towers, and some practice-based writers ignoring the wisdom which emanates from those towers. This book is my attempt to bridge the gap. In some chapters I have referred to some of what I believe to be the most important scholarship underpinning best practice. However, this book does not set out to be a scholarly text, but rather an attempt to integrate how best we can make learning happen in post-compulsory education by focusing on learners themselves, and on key factors underpinning successful learning. However, as can be seen in vari-ous parts of this book, my problem with at least some of the scholarship is that I think it is adrift!

Essentially, this book is rooted in my own experience during the last four decades, where I have been working on four fronts of the interface between teaching, learning and assessment.

- Working with learners, both in subject-related contexts and learning strategy development, has helped me to get closer to how best we can talk with learners about their learning, and help them to prepare for our ways of trying to measure their progress.

- Working with lecturers and tutors in universities and colleges has helped me to work out how to help them to make learning happen with their students, and how to go about the difficult tasks of measuring learners' achievement, and getting feedback to them to aid their learning.

- Working with learning resource designers has helped me to see the necessary processes which learning resources (electronic or print-based) need to have in place to play their part in making learning happen.

- Most importantly, perhaps, continuing to work with experienced and skilled trainers on training design has helped me to 'keep my feet on the ground' and pick out the useful processes from the spurious theories or artefacts.

During this time I have come to believe that the best way forward on all of these fronts is to address, quite deliberately and consciously, seven factors which underpin effective learning:

- *wanting* to learn – often referred to as 'intrinsic motivation' by others.

- taking ownership of the *need* to learn – perhaps what others call 'extrinsic motivation'.

- *learning by doing* – practice, repetition, trial and error, learning through experience.

- learning through *feedback* – from fellow learners, from tutors, from learning resources, from results.

- *making sense* of what has been learned – getting one's head round ideas, concepts and theories. This is something we can't do for our learners, our job as teachers is to increase the probability that *they* do it successfully.

- *explaining, or teaching or coaching* – purposefully using these processes to help people (and indeed ourselves) to deepen learning, in other words to intensify the *making sense* part of it.

- *making informed judgements* – *assessing*: this is to enable learners to fully deepen their learning, and *making sense* process, and also allows a great deal more 'learning through feedback' to occur, especially in the context of student self-assessment and peer-assessment.

These factors may look obvious – indeed simple. Yet Einstein suggested that 'everything should be made as simple as possible – but not simpler'. *How* these seven factors interact with each other is indeed complex, as is how best we can set out consciously to address these factors in our bid to make learning happen for our students. My aim in this book is to tackle some of these complexities, based on the experience of many thousands of learners, teachers and trainers, as well as on my own experience.

I was first alerted to these factors through my work with students on study-skills development. Since then, and in the last fifteen years in particular, I have continued to develop the links between these factors and just about everything we try to achieve in post-compulsory education, and this book summarizes this work. I have become ever more convinced that addressing the seven factors works in practice. I have to date got several thousands of people arguing, debating and extrapolating from the factors at staff development workshops in several countries and cultures, and this book owes much to the wisdom which has been shared and the insights which have developed through these discussions.

Summary of the content

In Chapter 1, 'Setting the scene', I start with a brief look at some of the problems we have got ourselves into with the language that is commonly used about learning. Chapter 2, 'Seven factors underpinning successful learning', is an informal unpacking of the seven factors, and the way they continuously affect each other (like 'ripples on a pond') rather than function consecutively in a cycle. Chapter 2 is the heart of this edition, and many of the later chapters link to ways that the seven factors can be addressed purposefully in various teaching/learning contexts in our bid to make learning happen effectively, efficiently and enjoyably for our students (and indeed for ourselves).

Chapter 3, 'Designing the curriculum for learning', is new to this edition, and starts with a detailed discussion of the design of learning outcomes, and their place in learning. Next follows a case study, illustrating the kinds of activities which can help colleagues to align the curriculum constructively, so that learning outcomes and assessment criteria align fluently with evidence of achievement produced by students, and with assessment and feedback processes. The chapter concludes with some thinking about 'learning incomes' and 'learning outgoings', and '*emergent* learning outcomes' as worthy of consideration in the overall process of curriculum design and development.

Chapter 4, 'Assessment driving learning', is the biggest chapter in the book. I now start by asserting that assessment is presently 'broken' in post-compulsory education, in the context that for most learners, learning is largely driven by assessment ('when's the deadline?', 'what's the pass mark?', 'what standard is expected?' and so on) and that we over-assess greatly. I continue by discussing the need to make assessment valid, reliable, transparent and authentic, and then look at some of the things that are presently wrong with assessment in general in post-compulsory education. Two commonly used assessment formats (time-constrained unseen written exams and essays) are analysed in some detail against the factors underpinning successful learning. The chapter now leads into 'Towards assessment *as* learning', providing a tool to enable you to interrogate your assessment design against a range of factors linked to learning as well as in terms of reliability, validity, and so on. In Chapter 5, 'Learning through feedback', I go into more detail about the various ways that learners can be given formative feedback on their own work by lecturers, tutors, teachers and, most importantly, by each other, and how this feedback links to the other factors underpinning successful learning.

In Chapter 6, 'Making learning happen in large groups', I relate the seven factors to large-group teaching contexts such as lectures, large classes and so on, exploring what we can get our learners to do to maximize their learning pay-off in such contexts, but also analysing what lecturers and teachers can do to *cause* learners to increase their learning pay-off. Similarly, in Chapter 7, 'Making learning happen in small groups', I aim to get you thinking about your tutorial or seminar groups, and on what we can cause learners to do while working together to increase their learning pay-off.

In Chapter 8, 'Responding to diversity and widening participation', I look at how we can put more energy into addressing special educational needs. I analyse some of these needs in terms of which of the seven underpinning factors are 'damaged' or 'restricted' by particular contexts. I then go on to explore what we can do to compensate for this in our teaching and learner support. A key premise for this chapter is that 'good practice for special needs learners should be good practice for everyone'. In Chapter 9, 'Addressing employability', I use the work of Knight and Yorke (2003) as a starting point for analysing how the various skills and attributes which they have linked to employability can be related to the seven factors underpinning successful learning developed in Chapter 2.

Chapter 10, 'What can I do when...?', confronts several frequently occurring problems experienced by teachers in post-compulsory education, offering short, sharp suggestions for tactics to try out when facing such problems. The book now concludes with Chapter 11, 'Reflective observation', which is partly about reflection in broad terms, but mostly about using peer observation of teaching to aid reflection. This chapter contains a range of suggestions for designing peer observation schemes to get the most out of the processes involved, and a checklist you can adapt to help you to reflect on your own teaching.

Acknowledgements

I am grateful to countless workshop participants for their permission to share the products of our combined thinking and discussion. I remain indebted to my better half, Sally Brown, for innumerable relevant day-to-day discussions about formative feedback, assessment design, and fit-for-purpose approaches to teaching and learning in universities, and for encouraging feedback about some of the new additions present in this edition. I am grateful to Katie Metzler, who gathered and analysed feedback about the first edition, paving the way for me to build on its strengths and to address things missing there, not least curriculum design and reflection. Thanks also to John Cowan, who over the years has helped me to think deeper into the substance of what is now this book, especially about what we can do as teachers to make learning happen. I dedicate this book to all the students who have helped me to learn about learning, and continue to inspire me to work towards making learning happen successfully.

Phil Race
October 2009

Setting the Scene

Why this book?

There is a massive literature about teaching, learning and assessment, referring to all levels of education and training. Some of this literature is about scholarship and research into how human beings learn, and how best to cause them to learn more effectively. Some of this literature is more practical in nature, advocating ways to go about designing our teaching and monitoring how learning is happening. So what is intended to be different in *this* book?

Perhaps the main difference is that this book aims to get back to straightforward language about teaching and learning, and avoid some of the jargon which so often gets in the way of helping teachers in post-compulsory education reflect on their work. Also, at the time of writing, robust and well-argued criticism is appearing in the scholarly literature, questioning many of the ideas, concepts, theories and models which have been around for many years, some of which have been found to arise from limited studies in specific contexts, then been extended beyond reason to broader contexts where they cease to be useful. The reviews published by Coffield et al. (2004) have been, in my view, among the most significant critical analyses made to date of factors relating to how learning happens in post-compulsory education (and, indeed, help us to question how learning happens at all stages of life).

In short, the approach I am using in this book is to leave aside most of the questionable thinking about learning styles, and theories and models of learning, and probe much deeper into the factors underpinning *all* learning. It can be argued that these factors are actually quite easy to identify. Moreover, once identified, they are relatively straightforward to address in the design of all manner of teaching–learning contexts and environments. 'Learning styles' can then simply be regarded as the different ways that individuals respond to the main factors underpinning successful learning, and learners themselves can be liberated from the threat of being trapped in some sort of predetermined mould regarding how their brains go about the processes of making sense of themselves and the world around us.

Starting with Einstein

Einstein is reported to have said: 'Everything should be made as simple as possible, but not *too* simple.' It can be argued that much of what has been written about learning in the last half-century or more has not been as simple as possible in the words and language used, but at the same time has been *too* simple in terms of many of the models proposed.

Another Einstein maxim is 'Knowledge is experience – everything else is just information'. We are now in an age where information is more abundant than could ever have been imagined. It is also easily obtained – in other words, it is plentiful and cheap. When I myself was a student, most students left most lectures with about as much *information* as they could write in an hour or so, a few hundred words or equivalent, from what the lecturer said, did and showed. Nowadays, students are likely to emerge from an hour's learning with many thousands of words or equivalent in handout materials, downloadable files from an intranet or the web, but it is all still just *information* until they have done things with it to turn it into the start of their own *knowledge* about the subject concerned, and link it up to other things they already know about that subject and about the rest of the universe.

So perhaps at one level the quest to make learning happen in post-compulsory education boils down to how best can we help our learners to turn information into their own knowledge. I argue in this book that we can go a long way towards achieving this mission by carefully and systematically addressing the seven factors underpinning successful learning identified in Chapter 2. But first, I would like you to think a little more about the problems we've made for ourselves with the over-complex language that is so endemic at present about the meaning of learning (and, indeed, the learning of meaning).

Yet another Einstein maxim is: 'It is simply madness to keep doing the same things, and to expect different results.' We know, for example, from feedback over the last five years from UK students in the National Student Survey, that assessment and feedback are weak links in our attempts to make learning happen for them. Therefore, in many parts of this book I pose the question 'What *else* may work better?'

Minding our language

Learning? Knowing? Understanding?

In a book with the words 'making learning happen' in the title it is probably useful to stop and reflect upon what we really *mean* by 'learning' and, since the words 'knowing' and 'understanding' (among others) naturally creep into any such reflections, to try to work out what we're really about when we attempt to 'make learning happen'.

For a start it is, of course, *learners* who learn; we can't do it to them, we can't do it for them. One way or another, they have to do it themselves. We can, however, structure the environment – let's call it a 'learning environment' – so that learning becomes easier, more productive, more efficient, more likely, and so on. In other words, our actions can increase the probability that learning will happen. 'Teaching' at any level can surely be summarized as a purposeful attempt to cause learning to happen by those being taught.

Understanding

Knight and Yorke (2003) acknowledge that there is a problem with 'understanding', and also point out that the kinds of assessments learners meet in post-compulsory education have a significant effect upon the extent to which learners develop understanding.

> There is uncertainty about what counts as understanding. Side-stepping some important philosophical issues, we suggest that a student who understands something is able to apply it appropriately to a fresh situation (demonstration by far transfer) or to evaluate it (demonstration by analysis). Understanding cannot be judged, then, by evaluating the learner's retention of data or information; rather, assessment tasks would need to have the student *apply* data or information appropriately. This might not be popular in departments that provide students with a lot of scaffolding because their summative assessment tasks only involve near transfer, not far transfer. Where far transfer and evaluation are the hallmarks of understanding, assessment tasks will not be low-inference, right or wrong tasks, but high-inference ones, judged by more than one person with a good working knowledge of agreed grade indicators. (Knight and Yorke, 2003: 48, emphasis in original)

Perhaps we have a problem in the English language in that words such as learning, knowing and understanding overlap so much in their everyday usage. If we intend learners to become able to soft-boil an egg, it is normally enough that they become able to soft-boil an egg, and do so successfully most times they attempt the task. We could say then that they have learned to soft-boil an egg, and equally we could say that they then 'know how to soft-boil an egg'. But we wouldn't (I trust) say that they 'understand' about soft-boiling eggs until a lot more had happened in their brains, not least all of the chemistry of the colloidal processes varying with temperature within the egg, the physics of the differences in boiling temperature of water at different heights above sea level, the meteorology of the effects of the variation in air pressure under different climatic or weather conditions, not to mention the zoological considerations of the differences between different kinds of egg, and so on. But such knowledge is not necessary to boil an egg (fortunately), though for some people such knowledge may indeed enrich the thinking which might just accompany the routine process of making a soft-boiled egg.

A musical diversion

When the subject matter becomes more complex, the dangers in using words like 'know' or 'understand' inappropriately become more significant. Let's take as an example J.S. Bach's '48 preludes and fugues' written for keyboard instruments of his day, but frequently nowadays also played on various kinds of modern piano. 'Do you know Bach's 48?' is a question which might produce an affirmative answer from a fair number of people. Some of them might be saying 'yes' because they knew *of* Bach's 48, others might say 'yes' because they were able to play one or more of the 48 themselves, or had once been able to, or even had done so successfully only once. (We'll leave aside for the moment what 'successfully' might mean.) Students on a music module might, we think, be expected not just to perhaps become able to *play* one or more of the preludes and fugues, but also to know how the pieces of music themselves actually *work* – in other words, to analyse the notes and work out more about what the composer may actually have been achieving when he wrote the notes on manuscript paper – or when he experimented with playing the notes himself prior to writing down his final version of them on paper.

But what might we mean by '*understand* Bach's 48'? Has anyone other than Bach ever achieved this, and how would we know such understanding if we saw it – or, more precisely, *heard* it? Indeed, did Bach himself *understand* what he had achieved in this quite small but important facet of his large output? His intention in writing the first set was stated as 'for the profit and use of musical youth desirous of learning, and especially for the pastime of those already skilled in this study'. Now Bach himself would not be in a position to *understand* what changes this set of pieces were to make on the development of instrumental music and, indeed, on what we now call 'tonality' and 'counterpoint'.

So who has (so far) *understood* this tiny corner of the musical world best? Who gets the only first-class degree in the 48? Who gets the PhD or DMus in it? Certainly a likely condition might be that this someone should be able to play all of them successfully. This might be interpreted to mean 'note-perfect' – in other words, without hitting any wrong keys on the keyboard. But that is relatively simple to achieve – lots of people can play this music perfectly *accurately* and hit all the right notes at the right time in the right order. Many an unwilling and uninterested music student has achieved at least some of this at one time or another, without any real commitment or feeling. We can indeed program a computer to generate all of the notes in such a way, and it will do so in exactly the same way every time it is required to. So does the computer *understand* Bach's 48? No more, of course, than the person or persons responsible for capturing their own *understanding* of the music into the technology. There are important aspects of *interpretation* to consider – which notes should *stand out* at any given moment? At what *speeds* (tempi) should the different elements of the music be played? How loudly or softly are the notes meant to be heard? What sort of instrument is the best one to bring Bach's conception to realization?

Let's take one musician as an example – Glenn Gould. For much of his relatively short life he was associated with playing the music of Bach, not least the 48. We still have access to his recordings of this music, made over some years, and always since then available in catalogues of recordings. Anyone, however, who has been involved in making recordings of music (or indeed drama, documentaries or many other 'captured events') knows that the recording studio tends to work in 'takes' and 're-takes', and so on. Often, several attempts at getting a piece 'right' are made, and the best of these preserved or welded together. But those who saw and heard Glenn Gould making his legendary recordings agree with the performer himself that he never played the same piece in exactly the same way twice. All his attempts may indeed have been note-perfect, but the *interpretation* varied every time, as he continued to explore in his own mind the patterns, balances and dynamics of each tiny part of this large set of keyboard pieces. Even on just a single instrument – a piano – there remain infinite possibilities of *realizing* Bach's original composition. Bach himself would, we may speculate, have been the first to welcome this multiplicity of 'getting it right' regarding his music. But we could argue, perhaps, that Glenn Gould had developed a deeper *understanding* of this particular music than most people. But did Glenn Gould *feel* that he had developed a full understanding of this music after playing it for years? He probably would have been the first to say that his 'understanding' was continuously unfolding and developing.

But was Glenn Gould's *understanding* of Bach's 48 the best? And how wise was it to try to realize Bach's conception on a modern piano? Glenn Gould hardly ever touched the sustaining pedal on such an instrument. Different performers have played this music in countless different ways, all note-perfect. Shostakovich was no mean pianist, and no doubt played the 48 to at least some degree of accomplishment. Shostakovich, however, went on to compose 24 preludes and fugues himself, and there is little doubt that he was influenced – or perhaps a better word is *inspired* – by Bach's work. So should we say then that Shostakovich, too, *understood* the 48? And what of a present-day musician who is able to play both Shostakovich's 24 *and* Bach's 48 – is this a pathway to a greater *understanding* of either or both works?

Then there's another problem. Suppose Glenn Gould's *understanding* of the Bach 48 was in some way deemed to be 'the best', and was taken to be the benchmark for this particular achievement. Would all the critics *agree* with this decision? Surely not. And sooner or later this benchmark would be replaced, or go out of fashion, as different ways of thinking about the 48 came into prominence. So perhaps this boils down to understanding being ephemeral as a concept in any case?

Back to learning, and mapping it out for learners

One of the problems of formulating a curriculum is that in the English language people tend to use the word 'understand' much too loosely. Intended learning outcomes are too often badly phrased along the lines 'by the end of this course students will understand x, y and z'. Nor is it much use to soften the outcomes along the lines 'this course will help students to deepen their understanding of x, y and z'. Yes, the course may indeed help students to *deepen* their understanding, but do they know how much they are deepening it, and can we measure how much they have deepened it? In short, we can't measure what students *understand.* We can only measure the evidence that students produce to *demonstrate* their understanding. That evidence is all too easily limited by techniques of demonstrating understanding – their written communication skills perhaps. Or whether they are note-perfect in music. We can measure such things, and give students feedback about them, but we can't ever be sure that we're measuring what is present in learners' minds. In some religions, blessings are phrased along the lines 'the peace of mind which passes all understanding'. Perhaps in education we need to be aware of 'the piece of understanding which passes all attempts to measure it'! Or, when it comes to understanding, 'if we *can* measure it, it almost certainly isn't *it*'.

Similar problems surround the words 'know', 'knowing' and 'knowledge'. I've already quoted Einstein's 'Knowledge is experience – everything else is just information'. Think of a person you know. What do you *mean* by know? There are all sorts of levels of knowing someone. Even at the closest levels, people often find out (usually too late) that they never *really* knew whoever-it-was.

So where does this leave us with 'making learning happen'? Setting out on the journey towards developing learners' understanding may well be a useful direction to go in, but we need to be really careful to spell out exactly *how far* learners are intended to develop their understanding, and what *evidence* they need to be aiming to produce to prove that they have developed their understanding, and what *standards* this evidence must measure up to, to indicate that they have successfully developed their understanding sufficiently. We also need to think hard about which *processes* are best to help learners to develop their understanding, and to recognize that different processes and environments suit different learners best. We can use similar arguments about knowing and knowledge. We only measure what learners *know* as far as we can assess the evidence which learners produce. In other words, we can only measure what learners *show* of what they know. And what they show depends so much on what we *require* them to show in our various assessment contexts.

Slow learning, repetition and building on what learners already know

Perhaps when, in two or three decades, we look back at the development of post-compulsory education, in the UK in particular but often enough elsewhere as well, we may be surprised at the speed with which we rushed into modular provision in the 1990s. In many higher education institutions, this was coupled with semesterization, splitting the academic year into two main sections (rather than three terms), with what has often turned out to be an awkward and uncomfortable inter-semester break, towards the end of January. Many institutions are now moving back in some subject disciplines to the design of 'long thin modules' which last a full year.

Claxton (1998) referred to the idea of 'slow learning', suggesting that some learning takes weeks, months or even years to construct. This resonates well with work by Meyer and Land (2003) on 'threshold concepts' or 'troublesome knowledge'. Knight and Yorke (2003: 53) argue that 'complex learning is almost invariably slow learning, taking longer to grow than most modules last'. They also suggest that 'an advantage of monodisciplinary programmes is that, almost without the need for curriculum planning, some of the learning can take place over the full span of the programme' (2003: 140).

Another problem which can be exacerbated by too wide-ranging a mixture of available modules is that learners begin any element of study with widely differing amounts of existing knowledge. Ausubel (1968: 235) stated: 'If I had to reduce all of educational psychology to just one principle, I would say this: The most important single factor influencing learning is what the learner already knows. Ascertain this, and teach (him) accordingly.' This leads me in Chapter 3 on curriculum design to suggest the importance of 'learning incomes' alongside intended learning outcomes.

Knight and Yorke (2003) go further into the assessment implications of some learning being 'slow', and the problems this causes when the curriculum is too fragmented. Practising teachers in post-compulsory education can often cite aspects of their own subject which seem to be necessarily learned slowly. In my own former discipline, the Second Law of Thermodynamics is one such topic. It has to be 'lived with' for quite a while before it begins to make sense. It is an example of what many refer to as 'troublesome knowledge', or a 'threshold concept' (see Meyer and Land, 2003) which has to be passed. It is often quite some time after being able to *use* it successfully, and solve problems with it, that the meaning of it gradually dawns. This is not just because historically it tends to have been expressed in rather forbidding terminology, perhaps following on from the precedent of Newton's *Principia* (containing his Laws of Motion) in the 1690s, of making concepts intentionally difficult to understand, leading to his masterpiece being described as 'one of the most inaccessible books ever written'. Notwithstanding, Dennis Overbye (adapted by Bill Bryson, in *A Short History of Nearly Everything*, 2004) is not far from simplifying the truth when he sums up the three main laws of thermodynamics as (1) you can't win (that is, can't create energy from nothing), (2) you can't break even (that is, there is always some energy wasted) and (3) you can't get out of the game (that is, can't reduce the temperature to absolute zero).

For many years, when teaching thermodynamics to chemical engineers on Friday afternoons, I found that by saying 'You don't have to *understand* the Second Law; all you've got to become able to do is solve problems with it' the relief on their faces was very evident. When later the students came up to me after practising solving problems sufficiently, and proudly say 'I've got it now', I would congratulate them and reply, 'Great. I'm really glad. But of course I can only measure how you apply it.'

In our target-driven systems of post-compulsory education, there seems little room for *not-yet-successful* learning. Yet the more elusive ideas and concepts, which can only be learned relatively slowly, often need to be re-learned several times during that pathway where slow learning leads to successful achievement. It is in fact useful to encourage learners to celebrate *forgetting* things as part of the natural process of becoming less likely to forget them next time round. The most complex ideas probably need to be grasped then lost several times before they are gradually retained more permanently and safely. Learners, however, often feel frustrated and disappointed when they have mastered something one moment, and then find that it has slipped shortly afterwards. For example, the light may dawn during a lecture, then be found to have 'gone out again' when learners try to do the same things on their own as they seemed to be doing perfectly successfully during the lecture.

One way of helping learners take ownership of the benefits of slow learning, when appropriate, is to point out to them that repetition not only pays dividends in the permanence of learning, but can be a very efficient way of using time and energy as part of an intentional learning strategy. For example, if a particular concept takes one hour to get one's head round first time, but then slips away, it may only take 10 minutes to regain the ground a few days later. If it slips away again, it may only take five minutes to get it back a few more days later, and so on. By the twentieth time round it may only take a minute or less of re-learning and it will be safely recaptured. Encouraging learners that 'it's not how long you spend learning it, it's how *often* you've learned it and lost it and regained it that counts' is a way of allowing them to feel ownership of a successful strategy for approaching those things which are best learned slowly. It is also worth encouraging them *not* to spend too long on trying to learn anything the first time round, but to come back to it frequently until it begins to make sense. Meanwhile, rather than struggling to force the brain to make sense of a difficult concept, they can spend the time more productively between attempts, refreshing their learning on things already learned successfully and ensuring that these don't just slip away.

Trying to sort out the picture

I quoted Einstein earlier as advocating 'Everything should be made as simple as possible, but not *too* simple'. I argue that the plethora of terms and processes that have arisen in the models of learning widely available in the literature of pedagogy are not at all simple enough to describe adequately something as fundamental as how our species learns – but perversely that the 'going around in a circle' idea in a particular direction, as in a learning cycle, is much *too* simple. In other words, though all of the processes may have a part to play in successful learning, they are unlikely to follow on from each other in a neat cycle. In fact, they are much more likely to interact with each other, and affect each other and to occur concurrently rather than consecutively. How then can we simplify the picture, but at the same time enrich it? My belief is that the way ahead is to find out what factors are involved in all the main processes involved in learning – what is the underlying picture?

One of the most detailed critical reviews of models of learning in general, and learning styles approaches in particular, is the work of Coffield et al. (2004). The cover text on their report is as follows:

> Learning styles and pedagogy in post-16 learning – A systematic and critical review

> This report critically reviews the literature on learning styles and examines in detail 13 of the most influential models. The report concludes that it matters fundamentally which instrument is chosen. The implications for teaching and learning in post-16 learning are serious and should be of concern to learners, teachers and trainers, managers, researchers and inspectors.

In the conclusions they refer back to their original aim as follows:

> This report has sought to sift the wheat from the chaff among the leading models and inventories of learning styles and among their implications for pedagogy: we have based our conclusions on the evidence, on reasoned argument and on healthy scepticism. For 16 months, we immersed ourselves in the world of learning styles and learned to respect the enthusiasm and the dedication of those theorists, test developers and practitioners who are working to improve the quality of teaching and learning.

> We ourselves have been reminded yet again how complex and varied that simple-sounding task is and we have learned that we are still some considerable way from an overarching and agreed theory of pedagogy. In the meantime, we agree with Curry's summation (1990, 54) of the state of play of research into learning styles: 'researchers and users alike will continue groping like the five blind men in the fable about the elephant, each with a part of the whole but none with full understanding'. (Coffield et al., 2004: 157)

They continue by voicing various concerns, including:

> Fortunes are being made as instruments, manuals, videotapes, in-service packages, overhead transparencies, publications and workshops are all commercially advertised and promoted vigorously by *some* of the leading figures in the field. In short, the financial incentives are more likely to encourage further proliferation than sensible integration. It also needs to be said that there are other, distinguished contributors to research on learning styles who work in order to enhance the learning capabilities of individuals and firms and not in order to make money.

In the first edition of *Making Learning Happen*, I published a new questionnaire that aimed to put learners in the driving seat of the vehicle which is their own learning, by addressing directly the first five of the seven factors underpinning successful learning identified in Chapter 2. The 100 statements in the questionnaire were intended to be seen as learner-friendly language, rather than remote pedagogic terminology and to allow people to reflect on their own individual ways of learning, and their preferences and dislikes. This questionnaire continues to be available in the first edition, but I have withdrawn it from the present edition for three reasons:

1. There were so many new things I wished to add to the present book, and space is limited.

2. Extending the questionnaire to cover the additional two factors to be discussed in Chapter 2 would have limited the practical usefulness of the questionnaire for many learners, as these two factors relate to teaching and assessing, areas which most learners would not readily identify with.

3. I continue to worry about the validity of many questionnaires I see (not least in the UK the questions upon which the National Student Survey, administered since 2005, is based), and now do not wish to divert the main aim of this book – helping to make learning happen for learners.

Coffield et al. conclude their large-scale report as follows:

> Finally, we want to ask: why should politicians, policy-makers, senior managers and practitioners in post-16 learning concern themselves with learning styles, when the really big issues concern the large percentages of students within the sector who either drop out or end up without any qualifications? Should not the focus of our collective attention be on asking and answering the following questions?
>
> - Are the institutions in further, adult and community education in reality centres of learning for *all* their staff and students?
> - Do some institutions constitute in themselves barriers to learning for certain groups of staff and students? (Coffield et al., 2004: 157)

It is with these conclusions and questions resounding in my own mind that I set about the task of preparing this book about making learning happen in post-compulsory education.

Conclusions

In short, we have got to be really careful about the language we use to *describe* learning, and we must accept that we can never really measure *learning*, but only evidence of achievement as a result of learning. Evidence of achievement is our best proxy in attempts to quantify learning, understanding, knowing, and so on, so we need to become ever more skilled at describing intended evidence of achievement in terms which will provide learners with targets to aim towards (and aim to exceed). In some instances, it takes a great deal of adjustment to put into words what might at first sight appear to be a perfectly reasonable learning target. Such targets only work well when everyone who sees the words, and *hears* the words, knows exactly what those words are intended to mean. Different teachers teaching the same module need to be able to agree with each other about the standards and evidence descriptors that are associated with intended learning outcomes. Much more importantly, learners themselves need to be able to 'know' what the words mean. They more than anyone else need to be able to make realistic and accurate interpretations of the wording of our intended learning outcomes.

A small but vital part of 'making learning happen' is to get our wording right when we try to describe what we intend learners to become able to do. This is why learners find it so valuable to be shown examples of evidence of *successful* achievement – and equally evidence of *not-yet-successful* achievement – so that they become more aware of the directions in which they are intended to be moving and more aware of the nature of the intended destination of each element of their studies. All this, however, is more or less about pinning down *what* is to be learned. We need to ask *why* too. We need to think about *when* and *where*. And we need to address the '*so what*' of learning, so that learners can see the point of it all.

Most importantly, we need to think about the *processes* of learning, and avoid the danger of oversimplifying them. *How* does learning happen best? This leads nicely towards the purpose of Chapter 2 – to think about learning in straightforward language which we can share with our learners, so that all of us can co-operate and play our respective parts in making learning happen, but to avoid oversimplifying the processes an instrument as complex as the human brain uses when learning.

Seven Factors Underpinning Successful Learning

Background

In this chapter, I introduce you to investigations I have been doing for the last two decades, asking getting on for a 100,000 people about how they learned (and what went wrong in their learning). The responses prove to be very convergent. From very marked trends in their responses we can identify that there are seven factors which underpin successful learning. Moreover, it is really important to consider how these factors overlap with and interact with each other. The way of thinking about learning presented in this chapter has been developed from asking all these people four two-part questions about their learning, and two more questions about how they deepened that learning. The seven factors identified in this chapter form the basis of much of the rest of this book, as we link them in turn to assessment, feedback, large-group teaching, small-group learning, reflection, and various other aspects of higher education.

Who are all these people?

The respondents to my questions come from the following main groups:

- students I work with on developing their study skills approaches to further and higher education;

- lecturers and teachers in higher and further education, during courses and workshops on the design of teaching, learning and assessment;

- large groups of people from higher education, and various other professions, at conference interactive keynote sessions I run in the UK and beyond;

- trainers I work with on the design of training processes and resources.

I've often developed the discussion of these factors at conferences, as well as in training workshops and staff development programmes. I've recently asked similar questions to groups of school pupils, and have found that their thinking about learning is very close to that of adults (further increasing my concerns about 'andragogy' having a special nature!). The ages of respondents now spans 8 to 80, and I've worked through the analysis which follows widely around the UK and Ireland, but also in Australia, New Zealand, Denmark and, occasionally, in Singapore, Canada, Sweden and Switzerland. I therefore feel able to argue that the common ground which emerges is about fundamental processes underpinning successful learning by adults from several cultures, rather than pertaining only to a relatively focused cross-section of learners.

The main stage of this investigation involves me asking people four questions, each in two parts, and getting them to jot down their responses to the second part of each question, in no more than about half-a-dozen words for each response – in other words, headline responses. The first part of each question asks them to identify an element related to one instance of their own learning, whether formal or informal. I then ask them to jot down their answers to the second part of each question, and sample the responses if working with a large group, or take everyone's response when working with 20 or less people. Then I ask two further questions, and each time ask people to indicate by show of hands the extent to which they believe that their own learning was deepened by two more processes.

To enter into the spirit of this book, however, I prefer not to say anything more about these questions or the factors which emerge from people's answers to them, until you have had a go at answering them yourselves. (If, however, you've already noticed the factors which emerge from the Preface, please see whether you think that they link to the four questions in Table 2.1.) Please therefore jot down your own responses in Table 2.1.

Table 2.1   Questions about how you learned well – and less well

---

Questions about your own learning

Please use this table to focus on your own learning – past or present. The first part of each of the first four questions which follow is to get you thinking about particular instances in your own learning. The second part of each question asks you to put pen to paper to capture some of the processes which led to the success – or otherwise – of the respective instances of your learning.

1   Think of something you are good at – something which you know you do well. (This may be an academic subject, but equally could be a hobby or skill – in short, anything at all that you're good at.)
Next, jot down a few words about *how* you became good at this.

2   Think of something about yourself which you *feel* good about – something which you like about yourself. This could be anything about yourself which gives you a sense of pride.
Now jot down a few words about how you *know* that you can be proud of this – in other words, upon what evidence is this positive feeling based?

Table 2.1 *(Continued)*

3   Think of something which you don't do well! This could be the result of an unsuccessful learning experience, maybe long ago or maybe recently. If you've nothing in this category, you can miss out question 3. (I usually add that no one has admitted, so far, to have nothing in this category!).
    Now jot down a few words about each of the following: what went wrong, do you think, in your learning relating to this thing you do not do well? And who, if anyone, might have been to blame for this?

4   Think of something you can indeed do well, but that you didn't *want* to learn at the time you learned it. This could be something like 'driving', 'swimming', 'cooking' or, equally, it could relate to a particular area of academic study – perhaps 'statistics' or 'economics' and so on. Whatever it is, you're probably pleased *now* that you succeeded with it – it's likely to be useful to you now, or to have served its purpose some time ago.
    Jot down a few words about what kept you going, so that you did indeed succeed in this particular episode of learning.

    Next, proceed to questions 5 and 6 if your experience includes teaching other people, explaining things to others, coaching others, and measuring the work of others as an assessor or judge.

5   Think of something which you've taught for some time. This could include helping people to learn, coaching them, training them and so on. Think back particularly to the first time you taught it (or explained it, or coached people in it and so on).

    To what extent did you find that you 'had your own head around it' much better after teaching it for that first time? Tick one of the following options:

    • Very much better
    • Somewhat better
    • No better

6   Still thinking of the first time you taught (explained, coached, etc.) that particular topic, think back to the first time you measured your students' learning of the topic.

    To what extent did you find that after that first occasion of measuring or assessing their learning, you yourself had made sense of the topic even more deeply? Choose one of the three options which follow:

    • Very much better
    • Somewhat better
    • No better

Now that you've answered the questions above and noted down your own replies to the second parts of each of the first four questions, and your choices for questions 5 and 6 if you've taught and assessed the topic, look back over your answers and see if you can pick out what these answers can tell you about how you yourself learn best – and, indeed, what gets in the way of successful learning for you.

After pausing to reflect on your learning as illustrated by these facets of it, please continue to read my account of most people's responses to the same questions. You can then compare to what extent your answers are mirrored by those of other people.

Towards the factors underpinning successful learning

In the next section of this book, I summarize the responses I have had to these questions and draw from them the factors which underpin successful learning.

1 How most people become good at things

What people think of as something they do well ranges enormously – everything imaginable has been covered in the responses of those who have shared with me their replies to the first part of question 1. Most people's answers to the second part of question 1 are much more convergent, along the lines:

- practice (far and away the most common response)
- learning through getting it wrong at first
- experimenting
- trial and error
- repetition
- experience
- having a go

and so on. All of the above answers have one thing in common – they're about 'doing' of one kind or another.

There's nothing new about this of course. The ancient Greeks and Chinese knew a lot about the importance of learning by doing. Sophocles is reported to have said words to the effect that 'Though one thinks one can do something, one has no certainty until one tries to do it'. Indeed, many of the Ancients could have said this.

Ancient wisdom about learning is worth revisiting. *How* we learn has not changed much over the millennia. Even though there have been vast changes in *what* we learn, and indeed in the resources and tools we *use* to aid our learning, those essential processes of 'learning by doing' remain. Or, in other words, there may have been huge changes in our learning environments over the years, but the human brain evolves very slowly, and the processes underpinning successful learning are slow to evolve.

Included in learning by doing is trial and error – learning through mistakes. Niels Bohr, the nuclear physicist, is reported to have defined 'an expert' as follows: 'Someone who has made all of the mistakes which it is possible to make – in a very narrow field!' Sadly, at present we often seem to undervalue the potential of learning through mistakes. There's a tendency to take note of people's mistakes and use these against them in evidence. I now regularly encourage lecturers and trainers to help their students to *celebrate* learning by trial and error as a productive and efficient way of learning many things – so long as the environment in which the mistakes are made is productive, unthreatening, safe, and without the risk of humiliation or embarrassment.

Although most replies about how people became good at things relate to *doing* of various kinds, at least some relate to ways in which they were affected by other people. In particular, there are usually some responses about how other people caused or enabled practice or repetition, and even 'training' comes up occasionally – but quite rarely 'being taught'. 'Being inspired' comes up rather more often, along with 'being enthused'.

2 How people come to *feel* good about things

Question 2 yields very convergent replies to 'how you *know* that you can be proud of this – in other words, upon what evidence is this positive feeling based?' Typical answers include:

- feedback
- other people's reactions
- praise
- compliments
- people come to me for help
- seeing the effect on other people
- seeing the results.

All these can be summed up as 'feedback' of one kind or another. Feedback clearly plays a vital part in helping people to develop positive feelings about things they do, and things they are. The majority of such feedback arises from other people, including fellow learners, tutors, teachers, trainers, mentors, friends, just about everyone or anyone. Some feedback is also linked to self-assessment or self-evaluation, for example, the 'seeing the results' replies often refer to looking at the *evidence* arising from the learning – the visible side of the achievement (including drawings, paintings, musical compositions, sculptures, and many other artefacts which are products of the learning concerned).

While most people readily accept that feedback plays a vital role in helping them to learn, there are two key problems which can get in the way of feedback reaching its optimum value:

- The feedback needs to be provided very soon after the actions on which it is based.
- Feedback needs to be 'received' and not rejected or dismissed.

A further response often arises from question 2: this is 'my confidence increased'. This too, on probing, often links back to feedback from others, or confidence gained by seeing the results of the learning concerned.

In Chapter 5 I go into much more detail about how adjusting the timing of feedback can make a lot of difference to its value to learners, and about how a wide range of feedback processes can be analysed in terms of which are the most effective for learners in various contexts, and which are most efficient for teachers.

3 Learning going wrong!

Question 3 yields a rich harvest of causes of learning going wrong. People's replies to the questions 'what went wrong, do you think, in your learning relating to this thing you don't do well? And who, if anyone, might have been to blame for this?' show that a wide range of things can be the causes of unsuccessful learning – 'things people aren't good at' – and that though many people accept the 'blame' for this, even more blame other people. In fact, the blame is often directed at particular teachers and lecturers at virtually any stage of learning.

Many replies link back to the overlap between question 3 and the previous two questions. For example:

- didn't get enough practice
- I didn't work hard enough at it
- I got poor feedback
- poor communication between myself and teachers (or trainers, tutors, fellow-learners)
- I was made to feel small about it
- no one explained to me how to become better at it

and so on. But even more replies bring in some important further factors:

- I didn't want to learn it in the first place
- I couldn't see the point of it
- I couldn't see what I was supposed to be aiming to do with it
- I couldn't get my head round it
- I just didn't understand it
- the light wouldn't dawn
- I couldn't make sense of it.

A further, even more common factor is:

- poor teaching!

When running this exercise with learners themselves, they often write down the *names* of teachers here (more often than not Maths teachers, but teachers of French for some reason often share the blame attributed!).

A further dimension underpinning successful learning is clearly to do with 'getting one's head round it', or *'making sense'* of it. This is all about developing deeper understanding of what is being learned, but bearing in mind my reservations about the word *understanding*, as expressed in Chapter 1, I prefer to use 'making sense' as there is less risk of thinking that the process is necessarily 'complete' or 'final'. In addition, replies to question 3 often bring in aspects of motivation. In particular, when learners don't really *want* to learn something, we should not be surprised that they may be unsuccessful at learning it well. Conversely, when learners *really* want to learn something, little will stop them from succeeding. There are countless tales of learners who had a very strong *want* to succeed in learning difficult and complex things, who succeeded even when people around them did not think they would make it.

It can be useful to think of the *making sense* process as mentally *digesting* the experience of learning, and *digesting* the feedback being received. The everyday use of the word 'digesting' is about extracting what we need from what we eat and drink – taking what will sustain us for the next few hours or days. But just as important in normal 'digesting' is discarding what we don't need – 90-odd per cent of the total amount eaten and drunk no less.

We can think of *digesting* as being a parallel process where the human brain sorts out the floods of information sent to it by the various senses, and keeps just a little of this information in one form or another, discarding perhaps 99.9 per cent of it quite rapidly. We can therefore regard the process of *digesting* to be turning information into knowledge. The metaphor linking *making sense* to digesting food and drink can, of course, be extended much further. We can think of mental *indigestion* arising from various conditions and environments. We can think of some *ailments* which can be caused by exposure to adverse kinds of information or inappropriate amounts of information, or failure to *digest* caused by poor reception of feedback or even total lack of feedback. Too much of one kind of information may be bad for us. Low-quality information can't be good for us. Incomplete processing of important information decreases the amount of *making sense* we achieve.

4 What keeps learners going when the going is tough?

Just about everyone to whom I have posed question 4 has no difficulty in thinking of something they did learn successfully, but didn't actually *want* to learn at the time. Often they are now glad that they did succeed – whatever it was has proved worthwhile in the long run. The things people have learned in this way include just about everything imaginable, for example:

- swimming
- driving
- cooking
- ironing
- keyboard skills.

Moreover, all sorts of academic learning come into this category for many learners, not least:

- statistics (e.g. SPSS: the Statistical Package for the Social Sciences, first developed in 1968)

- calculus

- thermodynamics

- critical theory

- counterpoint

and so on.

But what then keeps learners going, when they don't really *want* to learn something? People's answers to the second part of the question reveal at least three factors.

- Some learners are kept going by strong support and encouragement. Such support often comes from teachers or tutors, but also from mentors, friends, family and just about anyone. In a large group, however, it is usually only about one in 10 people who attribute their 'being kept going' to strong support and encouragement. For these people, that support is indeed critical, and without such support they probably would not have succeeded – or would have taken much longer to succeed. This has implications for the feedback we give learners on their work. It is all too easy for carelessly phrased feedback to stop such learners in their tracks. Also, those learners who *need* strong support and encouragement could wilt without it.

- Rather more learners are kept going by something which at first sight seems rather negative – not wanting to be found lacking, or not wanting to be humiliated, or wanting to prove to other people that they can indeed do it – sometimes to people who may have implied that they did not expect them to succeed. Some learners need to prove to *themselves* that they can succeed – they take ownership of the challenge and put everything into meeting the challenge head on. The implications of feedback are more profound when learners don't want to be seen to fail, however. Any critical feedback can all too easily stop them in their tracks, and we need to be particularly careful with the wording of feedback when they have not yet accomplished something. In practice, this range of 'negative' drivers of learning is surprisingly common – about one in three learners seem to be kept going by not wanting to be seen to fail.

- The majority of learners (typically six out of 10), however, give different accounts of what kept them going when they didn't actually *want* to learn something, the common factor being 'need' or 'necessity'. People say 'I kept going because I needed to become able to do it' or 'It was a necessary step in the pathway I was heading along' or 'I needed this to open the door to what I really *wanted* to do', and so on. But it's not just about there being a 'need', it's usually about people accepting *ownership* of the need. This is all perfectly *rational* of course. Learners who take ownership of a particular *need* to learn are quite robust – they are not easily stopped, even by critical feedback when they get things wrong.

The first five of the factors underpinning successful learning

From people's answers to these four questions, the following five factors can be seen to be involved in successful learning.

1. *Wanting* to learn. We could call this 'intrinsic motivation' but no one has yet used these words in answer to any of my questions. Such language may *mean* the same, but remains cold, remote and academic-sounding. Everyone knows what a 'want' is, and that if the 'want' to learn is powerful enough, success is likely to follow.

2. *Needing* to learn – or, to put it more precisely, *taking ownership* of the need to learn. This could be called 'extrinsic motivation' but again learners (or their teachers and trainers) don't use this sort of language when describing what kept them going when the going was difficult.

3. *Learning by doing* – practice, experience, having a go, repetition, trial and error. This fits well with all that has been said about 'experiential learning', but includes both 'concrete experience' and 'active experimentation' which in practice overlap so much with each other that in my opinion it is not wise to think of them separately, and much more satisfactory to think of them all simply as learning by doing.

4. *Learning through feedback* – other people's reactions, confirmation, praise, compliments and simply seeing the results. Constructive critical feedback helps too, particularly in the context of learning by trial and error. Feedback, of course, is directly connected to everything under the 'learning by doing' banner. The quicker the feedback, the better it helps learning.

5. *Making sense of things* – 'getting one's head round it' or 'digesting'. This process is perhaps the most important in most learning situations. This is about 'the light dawning' or 'gaining understanding', and so on. But this is very firmly linked to each and all of the other factors in the list above. For example, *feedback* plays a vital part in helping most people make sense of the results of their *learning by doing*. If there was already a strong *want* to learn, it is not surprising that the *making sense* is catalysed dramatically. Even if there is only a distinct *need* to learn, *making sense* is aided. This factor is different from the first four, however, in that we can't *make sense* of things for our learners – only *they* can do it. So our job becomes to provide them with the best possible environment in which they can achieve the *making sense* parts of their learning.

Ripples on a pond

So how do these factors work together? I have already argued that they all affect each other. They don't just follow on from each other in a particular order, nor are they necessarily *different* stages of an ongoing process. My argument is that they all affect each other, and all occur more or less simultaneously and concurrently. One way of thinking about this is to imagine them as ripples on a pond, bouncing backwards and forwards and interacting with each other in the same way as ripples do when a pebble falls into a pond.

Imagine that initially the water on the surface of the pond is mirror-smooth. Then a 'pebble' falling into the pond starts the water rippling. The energy to start learning happening can arise from *wanting* to learn. It can also arise from *needing* to learn. Better still, both may be involved. When learners really want to – *and* need to – learn, it is very likely that some learning will take place. See Figure 2.1.

Figure 2.1　Wanting to learn and/or needing to learn starting the 'ripple'

But how often do we know that we *want* to do something – or indeed *need* to do something – but we don't actually get round to it? All too easily, if we do nothing more, the *want* or *need* just fades away. We could think of this as the pond smoothing itself out again as if nothing had happened. However strong the *want* or *need* to learn may be, nothing tangible happens unless some *learning by doing* happens next. This can take many forms – practice, trying something out, experimenting, trial and error, repetition, application, and so on. Figure 2.2 illustrates this.

However, just *doing* something is no guarantee that learning is happening. For example, I often talk to learners coming out of other people's classes, and ask them about what they feel has happened during the last hour or

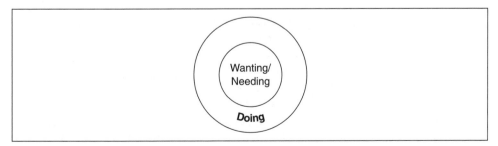

Figure 2.2　Learning continuing by doing – practice, repetition, trial and error

so. They often say that they have *enjoyed* the last hour, and feel inspired and empowered to go on learning whatever it was. But all too often when I ask them to tell me a little about what they learned during the session, their replies are along the following lines: 'Sorry, I haven't actually *read* it yet, I've just taken down the notes, or collected the handouts' and so on. In other words, they've got the *information* but they haven't yet really started on converting it into their own knowledge.

Put bluntly, they've been wasting their time during the session. They may have been *taking* notes, but often without even thinking about what they were writing down. They've been copying things down from the screen or board, and copying things down verbatim that the teacher or lecturer said, but without thinking about what the meaning was. There has been precious little *making sense* going on. Sometimes they have been far too busy trying to capture all the information and they have not even had time to try to make sense of what they have been writing. Now if they had been *making* notes rather than *taking* notes, things might have been much better and they would then be able to tell me a lot about what had been going on in their minds during the session.

So for effective learning to be taking place, *doing* needs to be accompanied by *making sense* or *getting one's head around it,* as illustrated in Figure 2.3. Learners need to be *processing* information and turning it into their own knowledge, not just capturing information.

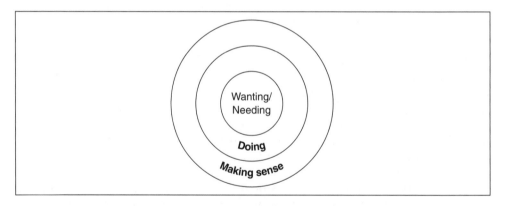

Figure 2.3   Learning continuing with making sense of what has been done

But how can learners know that they've *made sense* of the subject matter they have met? It's one thing to *feel* that they've made sense of it, but another thing to *know* that they've made sense of it. That's where *feedback* comes in. If they have been getting a lot of feedback on their thinking *during* a teaching session or while working through learning resource materials, they are in a much better position to know whether they've got their heads round the subject matter that has been the content of the session. Feedback from whom? The lecturer or teacher of course, but also from each other, and from comparing their own thinking with what's on handout materials and other learning resources associated with the session.

The feedback helps them to *make sense* of their own *learning by doing.* The feedback helps them to digest the information they have been processing, and turn it into a start towards building their own knowledge from it. The feedback also clarifies the *purpose* of the information – for example, by linking it to the frame of reference provided by the intended learning outcomes for the session. Feedback allows learners to see *why* an element of learning will be useful to them or relevant to them. It helps them to gain a sense of ownership of what they *need* to learn. If they already *wanted* to learn it, feedback may confirm that they have succeeded or help them find out what they still need to do to achieve the intended outcome. See Figure 2.4.

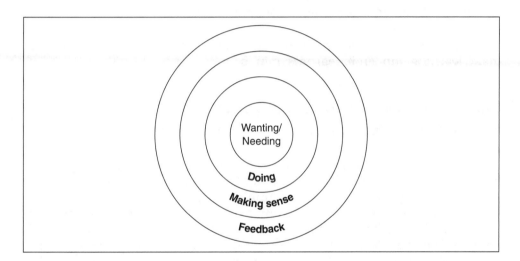

Figure 2.4   Feedback flowing in from the outside

In many ways, feedback is perhaps the most important of these factors underpinning successful learning. Thinking of ripples on a pond as a metaphor, we can imagine the feedback ripples bouncing back towards the middle of the learning ripple, strengthening the *making sense* process, causing more *doing* to occur, clarifying the *need* and, when constructive and helpful, enhancing the *want* to continue learning. Without feedback, much less *making sense* is likely to occur – perhaps none at all.

Making learning happen by addressing these factors

It is useful to think of these five factors as continuously affecting each other, not just in a particular sequence, but simultaneously and concurrently, just as ripples bounce backwards and forwards on a pond. More importantly, all five of these processes are tangible and easily understood by teachers and learners alike. However, perhaps the real breakthrough is that these five factors can be addressed and harnessed both by teachers and by learners themselves. As teachers, we can set out to:

- enhance or initiate the *want* to learn

- clarify the *need* to learn, and help learners to take ownership of this need

- cause learners to *learn by doing* – practice, trial and error, repetition and so on

- help learners to *make sense* of what they are learning, rather than just store information for later processing that may never happen

- cause learners to receive *feedback* on what they do, and on what they think about what they have done, and so on.

Several parts of this book refer in much more detail to what we can do to make learning happen in learners' minds.

But what can we do if there isn't a want and if learners are not even conscious of a need?

Partly as a result of policies to increase participation in post-compulsory education, many groups of learners nowadays contain at least some learners who don't really *want* to learn anything at a given moment in time, and who may also be quite oblivious of any real *need* to put in the effort to learn something. We can try to initiate a *want* but that can be an uphill struggle. We may, however, be able to convince at least some of the 'unwilling' learners that they have a *need*. One of the most useful ways of approaching this task is to remind ourselves that we may need to convince learners of the benefits which will accrue when they have put in some effort to achieve some learning.

When faced with an array of disinterested, bored-looking faces in a class, it can be worth asking ourselves 'What station am I broadcasting on just now?' I sometimes suggest to staff that the most appropriate one is 'WIIFM' – 'what's in it for me?' In other words, we need to try to help our students to take ownership of the *need* to learn, and spelling out the benefits they will derive from having learned something successfully can sometimes win them round. We can point ahead to:

- what they will be able to do when they have learned something successfully

- what doors this may open for them in their future lives and careers

- how learning this bit will make the next bit achievable

and so on. But even these tactics leave some learners unmotivated, especially if they are there against their will in the first place. So what else can we try?

Experience suggests that the best approach is to get them *doing* something. Choose something that:

- does not take long
- is interesting in its own right
- can be linked back at least in some way to a relevant intended learning outcome
- will stretch them a bit, but not intimidate them
- may win them over to the idea of doing something more very soon.

This is illustrated in Figure 2.5.

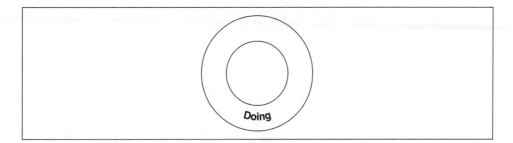

Figure 2.5 Starting the whole process with learning by doing

Then, as soon as possible, get them *making sense* of what they have been doing by getting them to compare with each other, argue, discuss, debate – in other words, deepen their learning through feedback and digesting, as shown in Figure 2.6.

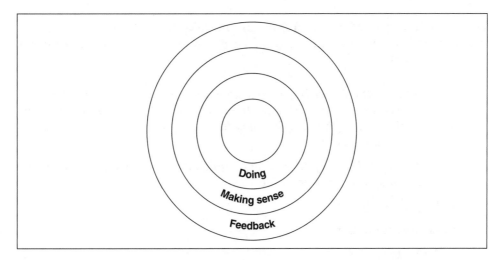

Figure 2.6 Following doing by feedback and making sense

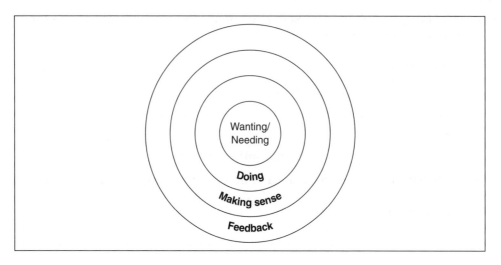

Figure 2.7 The 'want' and/or ownership of the 'need' now present

If they enjoyed the episode of learning by doing, found that making sense of it was interesting too and liked gaining and giving feedback about it, the ripple can 'bounce back' right to the centre and alert them to the *need* they have now addressed. In other words, we can help them to realize that the small increment of learning they have just done links to something worthwhile and relevant to them. The more they enjoyed it, the more likely they are to be willing to engage in the next element of learning by doing – in other words, they now have at least some degree of *wanting* to continue learning, as illustrated in Figure 2.7.

5 Learning through teaching, explaining, coaching

Let me remind you of question 5 again (as we've been thinking a lot about how the first five factors connect to each other, and there are two more factors to be identified).

5   *Think of something which you've taught for some time. This could include helping people to learn, coaching them, training them, and so on. Think back particularly to the first time you taught it (or explained it, or coached people in it, and so on).*

To what extent did you find that you 'had your head around it' much better after teaching it for that first time?

- *Very much better*

- *Somewhat better*

- *No better*

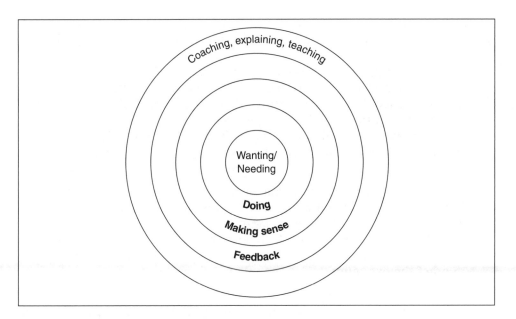

Figure 2.8   Deepening learning by explaining, coaching, teaching

The vast majority of my respondents choose 'very much better' for this one! People remember surprisingly well the very first time they attempted to teach something, or to explain it to others, or to coach others in it. They often remember that they didn't at that stage do it particularly well, but more important, they remember that they made sense of the topic a great deal more than they had done hitherto. They were learning fast as they tried to teach it or explain it or provide coaching in it. And they were learning 'deep'. We can think of any or all of these as a further ripple in the model discussed so far, as shown in Figure 2.8.

We can interpret this as evidence for the processes of *teaching* or *explaining* or *coaching* yielding a high learning pay-off for teachers. Good news for teachers, explainers, coaches! But we can of course turn this round, and get our students teaching, explaining and coaching. Why three words this time? In the first edition of this book, I pointed to *teaching* as a way of deepening learning. But not everyone who learns teaches. However, most people who learn have the opportunity to *explain* their learning to other people. Sometimes indeed, their learning will be assessed on the basis of how well they can explain things. And many people who learn *coach* other people in the subject they're learning. This is, in a way, different from teaching, and deeper than just explaining. Coaching can be regarded in many ways as the highest form of teaching, as it is such an interactive and intimate process, and the feedback between both parties has to be extremely good for it to work at its best.

The old cyclic models of learning did not lend themselves to demonstrating the full power of learning through teaching. Looking at it as a further ripple in the model in Figure 2.8, however, it can be seen *why* we learn so much when we teach – and particularly when we teach anything for the *first* time.

- We gain vast amounts of *feedback* as we teach. All the eyes in a class-room or lecture theatre are feedback to us. All the work our learners do give us feedback – everything they do successfully as a result of our teaching and their learning is feedback to us. Even more so, all the mistakes they make are further feedback to us. It is not surpris-ing that all this feedback helps us to deepen our own learning while we teach.

- We're *making sense of the topic* ourselves all the time that we teach. How often have you found yourself, while in the middle of explaining something to learners, *getting your head round it properly* for the very first time as you explain it? It is often halfway through the process of explaining things to other people that the real meaning dawns in the mind of the explainer.

- We're also *doing* when we teach. We're not only learning by doing things ourselves, but we're learning by getting other people doing things too. So teaching is full of experiential learning for us, let alone for our learners.

- We're addressing the *need* as we teach. We are trying to help learners to see the point of what they're learning. We're trying to help them to see what it's for, what it will do for them and where it fits in to the bigger picture. We're trying to convince them that the intended learning outcomes are for them, not just for us.

- And we're confronting the *want* all the time we teach. More acutely, often we're confronting the *lack of want* as we teach, and using all our skills to try to 'warm up' learners so that they take ownership of the need to learn *and* want to learn as well.

It therefore should not surprise us how much we learn as we teach. And particularly that *first* time we try to teach something, we're plotting our own course in uncharted territory regarding *how* we explain things to learners, *what* we get them to do, *how* we help them to get feedback, and so on.

If teaching is so good in terms of the learning pay-off for us, the obvious question is 'should we be getting our learners themselves to maximize their learning pay-off through teaching?' My answer is 'Definitely!' Imagine, for example, a maths lesson, where the teacher has explained a proof or deri-vation to the extent that a third of the learners in the room have seen the light. That is the time, I argue, for the teacher to stop, and get the learners into threes, each containing one who has seen the light and can now *do* it, and two who haven't yet seen the light and can't yet do it. Then get the one who can do it to talk the other two through until they too can do it. When one does this, the *explainers* remember it for ever! It's one of the deepest learning experiences there is, to see the light about something, then within minutes, talk a couple of fellow human beings through it until they too can do it. The explainers are benefiting from the high learning pay-off associated with teaching.

The 'explainees' are having a good deal too. They are *now* having it explained to them by someone who remembers how the light dawned. For us as teachers, all too often we've known things for so long that we've forgotten how the light dawned that vital first time round. Perhaps the moral is that we are better able to teach things that we can clearly remember *not* understanding? If it seems that we've always understood something, we probably are not the best person to try to teach it to others.

6 Learning through assessing – making informed judgements

We've now got six ripples – but I think there is one more vital ripple in learning anything really thoroughly – *assessing*. Let me remind you of question 6.

6   *Still thinking of the first time you taught (explained, coached, etc.) that particular topic, think back to the first time you measured your students' learning of the topic.*

To what extent did you find that after that first occasion of measuring or assessing their learning, you yourself had made sense of the topic even more deeply?

- *Very much better*

- *Somewhat better*

- *No better*

Thinking again back to that first time you taught a particular topic, did *you* understand it even better *after* marking the first pile of learners' work after that teaching element? Just about always when I ask this question to a large group of lecturers, the majority indicate that the making sense of it 'very much better' option applies. As we mark that first pile of work:

- we find out all the mistakes that we never imagined anyone would make

- we discover the different ways in which individual learners have made their own sense of whatever it was

- we gain a great deal of feedback about how to go about teaching the same thing next time round, to minimize the mistakes learners will make and maximize their learning pay-off.

We can think of the act of *assessing* as causing all the other ripples to resonate in our own learning of what we're assessing, as in Figure 2.9.

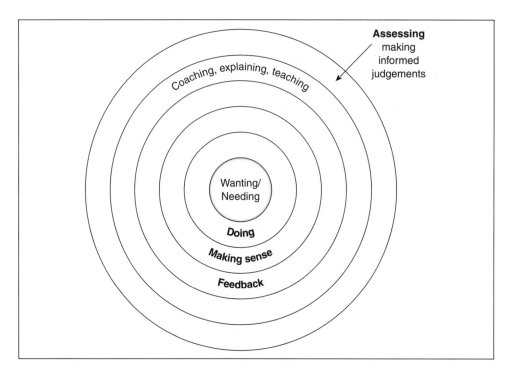

Figure 2.9 Learning being further deepened by assessing – making informed judgements

While we make assessment judgements,

- we're getting a great deal of feedback on how our learners' learning has gone
- we're finding out a lot about how our teaching has gone, and what to do to make it better next time
- we're continuing to make sense both of the topic and of other people's disasters and triumphs as they learn the topic
- we're learning by doing yet again – this time particularly by applying criteria and designing feedback for learners about their achievements and their problems
- we're continuing to learn by explaining and coaching, as we formulate feedback for learners and help them to improve their learning
- we're defining – and redefining – the standards of learners' evidence of achievements of the intended learning outcomes, clarifying in our own minds priorities and balances
- we're gaining yet more information about learners' *need* to learn and their *want* to learn.

In short, the process of assessing deepens our own learning every time we make informed judgements on learners' work, but particularly those first few times we engage in the process, where we find out a great deal very rapidly. In other words, learning through assessing has a very high learning pay-off indeed *for us.*

Once more, we can ask 'If the process of *assessing* yields such a high learning pay-off, should we be causing *learners* to assess rather than just assessing their work for them?' I believe that we should indeed do so. Causing learners to self-assess their own work leads to deepening their learning in ways which just don't happen if we do it all for them.

As long ago as 1989, the Australian guru on feedback and assessment, Royce Sadler, wrote:

> The indispensable conditions for improvement are that the student comes to hold a concept of quality roughly similar to that held by the teacher, is able to monitor continuously the quality of what is being improved during the act of production itself, and has a repertoire of alternative moves or strategies from which to draw at any given point. In other words, students have to be able to judge the quality of what they are producing and be able to regulate what they are doing during the doing of it. (Sadler, 1989: 121)

Furthermore, causing learners to peer-assess each other's work achieves even more:

- They may get a great deal more feedback from each other than we ourselves would have been able to give them.

- They may find it easier to take feedback from a fellow learner than from figures of authority such as teachers or tutors.

- They deepen their own learning by making informed judgements of fellow learners' work.

- They find out about things that other learners did better than they did themselves, and can emulate these things in their future work.

- They see mistakes that they themselves avoided making, and increase their awareness of what to avoid doing in future.

Once learners are convinced of the value of self-assessment and peer assessment, it can become one of our strongest teaching tactics to set this up and facilitate it. However, there are always some learners who will argue that 'This is *your* job, not mine' or 'You're paid to do this, not me!' We therefore have to work hard sometimes to convince learners that the act of assessing is one of the best ways to deepen their own learning, and a useful pathway towards their own success and achievement.

I would now go so far as to argue that learning is only 'complete' when it has been deepened both by some form of teaching/explaining/coaching *and* assessing. In earlier versions of my 'ripples on a pond' model of learning I focused on the central five factors, but now believe that the outer two are indispensable. It could be argued that these two are not as 'distinguishable' as the central five factors, but serve to make those five resonate so that learning is deepened. But if, without them, learning has not yet happened completely, I think that is reason enough to include them in their own right as essential elements of the whole model.

The time factor

We've been thinking about these seven factors, and the way they all affect each other, and 'bounce backwards and forwards' to impact on each other. One thing, however, that I'm keen to remind you is that this does not mean they always happen in a linear fashion when it comes to timing. In particular, the *making sense* part of the process happens a bit at a time in several iterations. For example, we can start to make sense of something in the act of *learning by doing*, but this is unlikely to be 'complete' making sense if the topic is complex. We proceed to make *more* sense of it when we gather and analyse feedback on our learning by doing. But even then, we may not have made complete sense of it. We continue to increase the extent to which we've made sense of it by explaining it to others, or coaching other people in it, or teaching it. Even then, as many teachers agree, we may still not have made complete sense of it in our own minds. We can, however, go even further towards making sense of it by making informed judgements, for example in assessing students' work relating to the topic, or facilitating their self-assessment or peer assessment of it. So the *making sense* stage is part of the picture which is accomplished little by little, in a series of iterations backwards and forwards across the various factors underpinning successful learning. Moreover, we've probably *never* made complete sense of it! More than once, a very skilled and experienced teacher has asked me 'What can I do when I realize that the thing I'm about to teach yet again is something I now know I don't completely understand?' This can be regarded as yet another positive stage in learning it. We're more knowledgeable about it when we realize we don't fully understand it than when we thought we did! This is another way of arguing that the idea of *understanding* something is fragile, and that it is better to think of learning as gradually making more and more sense of it but without imagining that there is an end to this journey. Even very accomplished teachers admit that their *making sense* journey continues for the foreseeable future. Admitting this to learners is very reassuring to them. 'Don't worry too much about trying to understand it', a good teacher might say, 'You'll gradually make more and more sense of it the more often you revisit it, especially if you try explaining it to others, and extend this to trying to make informed judgements about your own learning of it, and about other people's learning of it'. So in a way, we could argue that it's the number of times the seven processes have resonated backwards and forwards that governs the extent of that vital process – *making sense* of what is being learned. It's not just about the time taken!

In at the deep end: teaching and assessing?

We explored earlier how *doing* can start off the whole process, when there isn't a *want* or a *need*. What about *teaching* and *assessing*? Every teacher has tales to tell of how quickly they learned things they had previously never encountered when they were plunged in at the deep end and given a new topic to teach at short notice. This can be very frightening, but it often works surprisingly well. We can easily examine the situation and draw out that there is indeed a great deal of *learning by doing and trial and error* in teaching a new subject, and a great deal of *feedback* gathered in action. This in turn causes a lot of *making sense* and so on.

Similar arguments can be applied to *assessing*. Suppose you were appointed as an examiner for a major examining body and your first big pile of exam scripts included one or two topics that were quite new to you – a scary prospect. However, many examiners report that this has happened to them quite often, though they would have been wary of admitting this to a Chief Examiner at the time! Nevertheless, the act of applying assessment criteria to other people's evidence of *doing* (even when that 'doing' is just writing things down in exam halls) causes accelerated *making sense* to occur. Those unfamiliar elements of the syllabus may take considerably more time and energy to mark, but where is all that extra energy going? – into *making sense* of the new topic.

This flexibility is perhaps the most significant aspect of a way of thinking about learning which allows the process to begin at quite different starting points. That said, I would hesitate to suggest that as teachers or trainers our main approach to making learning happen should be intentionally to drop learners into the deep end of the pond! However, we would do no harm in alerting them to the fact that they can indeed survive and prosper when they unexpectedly find themselves in these deeper waters.

So where may 'understanding' come in?

In Chapter 1 I suggested that the word 'understand' is not a particularly useful one for various reasons – especially that it's unsuitable as a key word when we express intended learning outcomes. However, perhaps it's the next ripple? Please see Figure 2.10.

It can be argued that one never really *understands* something until one has learned it, then taught it, then assessed it. In other words, *understanding* something can perhaps be regarded as the cumulative effect of:

- taking ownership of the need to learn, and clarifying the evidence of achievement which will match successful attainment of the intended learning outcome

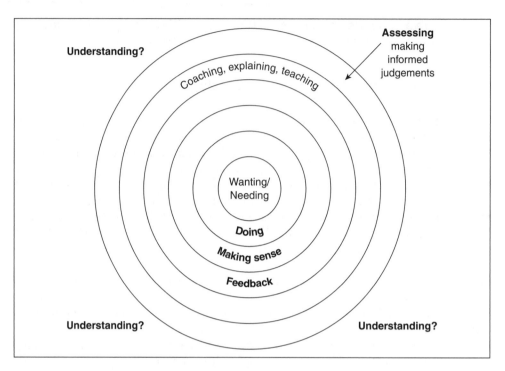

Figure 2.10 'Understanding' at last?

- wanting to achieve the learning outcome and to continuously make informed judgements on the learning as it is happening

- purposefully learning by doing – not just during practice, trial and error, repetition, but also in teaching, explaining, coaching, and making informed judgements during self-assessing and peer-assessing

- building on feedback gained about evidence of achievement, and feedback arising from making informed judgements on other learners' evidence

- maximizing the learning pay-off arising from all the *making sense* which accompanies learning in the first place, and continues in the acts of explaining, teaching, coaching and assessing.

Noel Entwistle (2009) provides perhaps the most in-depth account of 'understanding' in the context of university education to emerge in recent years, distinguishing between the idea of 'personal understanding', as developed by students, and 'target understanding', as perceived by their tutors. Entwistle comments that:

> Relying too much on the teacher's understanding may leave the student without a fully functional personal understanding, being able to pass exams by mimicking the lecturer's understanding, but not able to use it in other situations. (Entwistle, 2009: 50)

Also discussed is difference between 'fixed understanding' and 'flexible understanding' – a continuous restructuring and reframing of facts and knowledge. Fascinating as this discussion is, my concern remains with what do we actually measure with our various assessment processes and instruments, and I remain unconvinced that we measure anything more than echoes of understanding in most contexts.

The value of 'time out'

But *understanding* does not usually just 'stop'. As we continue to teach something over the years, continue to assess learners' work on it and continue to refine our teaching through all the feedback we get in these processes, it is not surprising that our own understanding continues to deepen. However, even this is not as straightforward as it seems. For example, if we just continue teaching and assessing, we get to a certain level in our own understanding. But if we move on to different things for a year or two and *then* revisit the original topic in our teaching and assessing, we are often surprised at how much *more* we feel that we now understand it. We could think of this as 'different' ripples in our own learning adding to 'previous' ones – or the whole pond becoming more agitated. Many an experienced teacher has admitted to me how scary it was when teaching something again after many times doing so, they suddenly realized 'I don't quite understand this now!' This goes to show that the 'understanding' stage has perhaps endless depths, and at any one moment we've only reached a particular level of this – greater understanding may follow. It is not surprising that industrious teachers sometimes feel that they are learning so much that it's almost like becoming seasick – a good excuse to laze on a beach somewhere to recharge our batteries now and then!

'Look – no *teacher!*'

Learners, too, can be involved in taking charge of how these seven factors work for them. In my work with learners developing study skills, I encourage them to:

- explore their own motivation, seeking good reasons which will fuel their *want* to learn – in other words, building their own rationale for *why* they are learning and what they want to *become* as a result of their learning

- clarify exactly what they *need* to learn – in other words, identify exactly what they need to become able to do as a result of their learning, taking ownership of the real purpose of the intended learning outcomes involved

- recognize that *learning by doing* is how it all happens in practice, encouraging them to put their energy into practice, repetition, trial and error, and so on

- accept that *making sense* of what is being learned is important, and is something that only *they* can do, and that we can't do it for them. Encourage them to try hard to *digest* information, selecting from it the really useful parts, rather than just collecting and attempting to store as much information as possible

- make the most of *feedback* on their learning from all possible sources – from each other, from teachers or trainers, from books and articles, and from anyone else who can give them feedback on their actions, their evidence, their *making sense*, and so on

- take every opportunity to explain things to other people, for example to teach others, coach fellow students, to maximize the learning pay-off which accompanies putting ideas into words, showing others how to do things, and so on

- make opportunities to make informed judgements about their own learning, to self-assess their evidence of achievement of the learning outcomes, and even better to peer-assess others' evidence, to gain the vast amount of making sense which accompanies the act of assessing, and work towards being able to continuously monitor their own learning as suggested by Sadler (1989).

Learners find it perfectly acceptable that the actions listed above all affect and enhance each other, and that any combination or, indeed, all of the actions can be happening at any instant during their learning.

Since learners themselves can take control of all these factors and develop them for themselves, it is not surprising just how much learning takes place without any teaching, training, instructing or tutoring processes. The phrase 'self-taught' has always been in widespread use, often in contexts where particular people have reached outstanding levels of achievement without teaching interventions. It could often be said that the people concerned have simply found their own ways of mastering how they learn, and have developed their own ways to address the factors described above.

Imagine you yourself needed to learn something new, and there was no one to help you to learn it. Imagine you found yourself in a library, surrounded by books, articles, videos, web access and so on – in other words, adrift in a sea of information about the topic. This taxes our imagination rather weakly because most people have been exactly there! What do we do about it? What works is to start *processing* all that information – finding out what the important parts really are, finding out what they mean and rearranging the information in ways where we can handle it. We learn by doing – practice, repetition, trial and error. We reduce the vast sea of information down to manageable proportions – summarizing it. We try to get feedback on how our learning is going. We gradually digest and make sense of the information. We test our learning out by communicating it – explaining things to others, having a go at teaching it.

And of course, we're looking ahead towards our own evidence of achievement being assessed. We look for detail about the sorts of judgements which will be made on our learning. We look for past assessment criteria and apply them to our own learning. Even better, we try to get others to make some judgements on our learning, or have a go at getting into the assessor's mind by making judgements on other people's learning.

Perhaps, therefore, in our bid to make learning happen in post-compulsory education, we need to be spending much more time helping learners to see how learning really happens. I firmly believe, of course, that we should be starting to help people to be in control of their own learning long before they reach post-compulsory education. Developing learners' control of their learning is already happening under a variety of labels – key skills, transferable skills, and so on – but, possibly because we so often use the word 'skills' for such things, people don't yet quite realize that these are exactly the 'skills' which underpin even the most sophisticated levels of knowledge or understanding. And perhaps the most important outcome of any element of learning is that of becoming a better *learner* bit by bit. This chapter ends with some suggestions for learners themselves regarding how they can address the factors we've been exploring.

Helping learners to make learning happen

There are numerous sources of study skills advice for learners, many suggesting tried-and-tested approaches to learning. My own latest contribution to the genre (Race, 2007) is built around helping learners to get their heads inside the processes of assessment so that they optimize their performance when their achievement is being measured formally. I have chosen to end this chapter on learning with a set of two dozen key suggestions written directly to learners, which you may find useful to copy for your learners or, better still, adapt for them, tuning the suggestions into the particular contexts of their own studies in your own discipline.

1. *Want to succeed.* Don't just *hope* to be successful. Be determined to get your result and to do everything you need to do to make it happen. Think positive. Keep reminding yourself of 'What's in it for you?'. Think ahead to how much better your life will be *having* succeeded. More choices available in your career. A better developed brain.

2. *Make good use of the intended learning outcomes.* These tell you a lot about what you need to become able to do to actually get to your target. These help you to sort out what to learn from what not to learn. These help you to find out about what is fair game as an exam question and what is not. These help you to work out what your assessors are looking for in assignments.

3. *Don't bury your head in the sand.* Getting your learning to work for you is a big job, but like any big job is done a little bit at a time. Keep doing little bits of the job all the time rather than hiding from the enormity of the whole task. You get your result for doing all the *little* jobs, not just for tackling the whole task.

4. *Confront your work avoidance tactics.* It's all too easy to put off the evil moment of starting a task. Meanwhile, you could have got the task well under way. Don't waste time feeling miserable about all the back-log of work you've got – just do one thing from the backlog and you'll immediately feel better. Then do another thing, and you'll feel ahead of the game.

5. *Don't mix up 'important' with 'urgent'.* The danger is that if you're too busy doing things that seem urgent, you'll miss out on things that are really important. Do one short important thing *before* you do the urgent thing you've got to do that day. That's one less thing that will become urgent. Revising last week's lecture for 10 minutes is often more important than the first 10 minutes you will spend writing up this week's assignment.

6. *Don't confuse being busy with working effectively.* It's all too easy to be busy working at something which will only contribute a mark or two towards your overall result, when you could have spent the same time on something that would count for a lot more. Being busy can actually become an advanced work-avoidance tactic. Keep your eye on the big picture, not the small detail.

7. *Don't spend too long on any one thing.* Don't get so involved in writing a particular essay or report that you miss out on spending time getting your head round the important concepts and ideas from the last couple of weeks' lectures. An extra two hours might just get you one more mark on that essay. Two hours spent consolidating the last two weeks' stuff might pave the way to earning you 20 marks in a forthcoming exam.

8. *Take charge of your workload.* Don't just respond to the pressures around you. Be your own manager. Do what's expected of you, and what's required of you, but also do things that no one has told you to do – for example, going back over things you've already learned, making sure they're not just slipping away again.

9. *Think questions.* Any important fact or concept is just the answer to a question or two. If you know all the questions, you're well on your way to being able to answer any question that will come your way. Write your own questions down all the time – in lectures, when you're reading, when you're thinking, when you wake up, any time.

10. *Find out the answers to important questions.* Look them up. Ask fellow students. Ask lecturers when necessary. Don't just guess the

answers – check whether your guess is good enough. Life is too short to learn 'wrong' stuff.

11. *Learning happens by doing.* Don't just read things or listen to lectures or browse websites or books, handouts and articles. *Do* things all the time. Make your own headline notes. Practise solving problems. Practise answering questions. Do it again – repetition deepens learning. Find out about those things you need to do *six* times before you get your head round them – these will usually be more important than something you only have to do once.

12. *Find out how you're doing – all the time.* Get as much feedback as you can – from lecturers, from fellow students and by comparing your own work with what's in books, articles, websites, everything. Don't just wait for feedback to come to you – go looking for it. Don't be defensive when the feedback is critical – learn from it. Don't be glib when the feedback is complimentary, build on it consciously.

13. *Keep records of all the feedback you get.* Written feedback from tutors is easy to return to, and re-learn from, but make sure you also keep short notes of advice received in face-to-face feedback too – it's easy to forget important points otherwise.

14. *Use your friends.* Show your draft assignments to anyone who will read them – fellow students, friends, family members, anyone who can read. Even people who don't know anything about your subject can give you at least some useful feedback – even if only on spelling or punctuation.

15. *Don't think that studying is something you have to do alone.* It's much more sociable studying with like-minded fellow learners. The only time it's really important to do things on your own is writing up the final versions of assessed coursework – you don't want to risk being accused of copying then.

16. *Practise communicating what you've learned.* In due course, it's what you communicate that gets you your qualification, not just what's inside your head. Use every opportunity to explain things to other people. Do this with fellow learners, family, friends, everyone. Even explaining things to a dog helps you become better at making sense of what you've learned (and dogs love being talked to about anything!).

17. *Self-assess all the time.* Don't just wait for someone to assess your work. Apply the assessment criteria to your own work before you hand it in for tutor assessment. Cross-reference your work to the intended learning outcomes, and work out which of these you've achieved and which you have not yet achieved. The more *you* know about the standard of your own work, the better you'll fare when others judge your work.

18. *Make the most of peer assessment too.* Get fellow students to give you feedback about your work. Take every opportunity to apply assessment criteria to their work. Making informed judgements about their work helps you become better at continuously monitoring your own work as you do it, and thereby produce work of better quality, gaining higher marks.

19. *Practice makes perfect.* Exams measure how good you are at answering exam questions under exam conditions. Practise answering questions as your main revision strategy. The more *often* you've jotted down the answer to a tricky question, the *faster* you can do it correctly one more time in the exam itself. Don't just hope it will be all right on the day in the exam – *make* it all right by practising all the way up to the day itself.

20. *Have a life.* Getting your result isn't *all* hard slog. You need time out for your brain to be refreshed. But build this time out *into* your overall strategy, rather than feeling guilty about it. There's no better way to enjoy some time out than to take it at the point of just having achieved a useful chunk of learning. So earn your time out, then enjoy it.

21. *Be cue-conscious.* All the time, your lecturers are giving you cues about what's really important and what's less important. The intended learning outcomes give you cues too. You'll get lots of cues from past exam questions. You'll get even more cues by talking to fellow students and finding out what *they* think is important. But don't let all these cues evaporate away – jot them down, preferably in the form of questions you need to become able to answer or things you need to become able to do. When you know where you're heading, you're much more likely to become able to get there.

22. *Take setbacks in your stride.* A low mark for an assignment is a useful learning experience – find out what to avoid doing again so that you don't lose the same sorts of marks next time. Don't just grumble that you deserved better marks. Learn what you can from each setback, then let it go and don't brood over it.

23. *Take pride in your achievements.* Don't just worry about all the things you haven't yet done – learn from things you've done well and build on that learning. There's no way you can ever feel that you're doing *everything* possible towards getting where you're heading so be reasonable with yourself.

24. *Keep becoming better at studying.* At the end of the day, your learning is a measure of how well you've developed your study techniques, not just how much information you've crammed into your brain. Become ever more conscious about *how* you learn best. Explore all the possibilities. Find out the techniques which really work for you, and develop them.

Conclusions

The seven main factors underpinning successful learning, as developed in this chapter, form an agenda for much of the rest of this book. They are just as useful for learners as for tutors. Their strength lies in their simplicity – at least in terms of the language we can use to describe them, and is easily shared by teachers and learners alike. But the strength of this way of thinking about learning also lies in its complexity – the way the factors all interact with each other and don't need to occur in a set order or pattern. And perhaps the most significant factor is that any or all of these processes can be going on at any instant in our learning – and we can choose to address any or all of them quite intentionally at any moment in our teaching.

Designing the Curriculum for Learning

Towards learning outcomes which work for learners

Whenever the topic of 'curriculum design' comes up, we tend to think of learning outcomes – whether we like them or not. In this chapter, I'd like to help you to get to learning outcomes which will be really useful for your learners. After all, learning outcomes are for students. It's their learning we're talking about. They need to know what they're supposed to become able to do, so they can set their sights on some definite targets and work purposefully towards being able to show that they've achieved these. That said, wisely chosen and well-developed learning outcomes are extremely useful to us as teachers. They help us to map the curriculum, so that we can plan the routes we use to navigate our learners through their learning.

'Constructive alignment' – a 'slice' of the pond?

In the previous chapter we looked at the seven factors underpinning successful learning, including in particular how teaching and assessing can increase learning pay-off. But what about the documentation – the paperwork associated with some of these processes? Important parts of this documentation are of course the learning outcomes, and the assessment criteria we apply to learners' evidence of achievement of the outcomes. All this can be thought of as a 'slice' of the central parts of the pond discussed in Chapter 2, as shown in Figure 3.1.

We can think of intended learning outcomes as right at the centre of the picture. These should define the *need* to learn. Better still, if the outcomes can be designed in such a way that learners find them attractive, we may

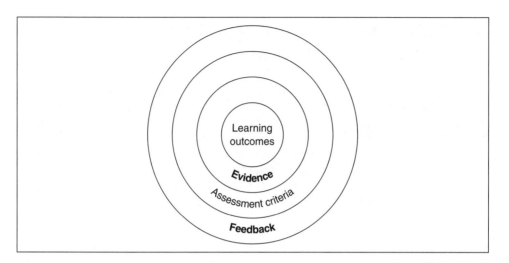

Figure 3.1 A cross-section of the pond?

even manage to link them more strongly to their *want* to learn, especially if we can build the 'What's in it for me?' dimension into the outcomes.

Learning by doing: this becomes *evidence.* This evidence of achievement can take many forms:

- written assignments done by learners – essays, reports, problem sheets, and so on

- practical work – laboratories, studios, fieldwork, work-based learning, and so on

- written test and exam answers

- performances, interviews, presentations, discussions, debates, and so on.

Regarding the *making sense* part of learning, this evidence of achievement needs to link to our assessment criteria, defining the expected *standards* of achievement of the intended learning outcomes we are aiming our learners towards.

Feedback: this should enable us to help learners to see to what extent their *evidence* in all its different forms has demonstrated their achievement of the *intended learning outcomes* to the standards specified by the *assessment criteria.* This can be regarded as one way of visualizing what Biggs (2003) means by 'constructive alignment' of the curriculum, further clarified in Biggs and Tang (2007).

Designing curriculum to achieve constructive alignment

I believe that it's best *not* to start drafting learning outcomes as the first step in designing an element of curriculum. It is much more productive to start our thinking in terms of *evidence* of achievement. It's really helpful to students to know what success *looks* like. Then, in a nutshell, work backwards towards the intended outcomes for which this evidence is valid, and choose how best to measure reliably students' achievement, and work out the criteria which will set the standards for this achievement. Then go backwards and forwards until the whole lot are in harmony. It's an iterative business. We should not just start with some outcomes, then work out some criteria whereby we measure whether students have achieved them or not. The evidence of achievement is what it's all about – the learning outcomes are merely a means of setting the scene for the arena in which students will head towards furnishing this evidence.

In most of this chapter, we will explore how to link learning outcomes to the seven factors we've explored in Chapter 2, and how to work backwards from evidence of achievement so that we end up with learning outcomes which align really well to assessment and everything else!

Then we can give students feedback about the extent to which their evidence shows that they have achieved the learning outcomes to the level of the assessment criteria. That's what John Biggs' 'constructive alignment' means to me. But continue to think that all of these iterate – they all affect each other. Feedback helps tease out the evidence of achievement, and helps us to fine-tune the learning outcomes and the assessment criteria until they all resonate. 'Ripples on a pond' continues to be the analogy which I suggest.

Learning outcomes should be heard as well as seen!

You can't *hear* a module handbook page, or even a web screen (well, you can in fact be enabled, using appropriate technology, to hear the latter, but not with the various subtleties which teachers can add to the words in person, as below). Learners need the additional communication of what the learning outcomes actually mean, as given through:

- tone of voice

- emphasis on particular words

- speed of speech

- repetition, when something is important enough to hear again and again.

And when possible:

- eye contact
- facial expression
- body language
- gesture.

All of these dimensions of communication add enormously to the power of printed words, helping learners to work out exactly what the intended learning outcomes mean for them. All these additional dimensions can indeed be achieved in our use of learning outcomes – if we provide them – in each lecture, tutorial, or practical briefing we give.

Stepping back from this, it's very useful for *us* to hear our learning outcomes read out to us, as we go through the process of putting a curriculum element together. If we get someone else to read out one of our draft learning outcomes to us, we can almost always improve it, for example as follows:

- If the reader has difficulty reading out the outcome, it is probably too long or too clumsy; if breath has to be taken in mid-sentence, the 'thought' is probably too long as expressed in the present draft to be comfortable to a learner meeting the idea for the first time.

- While listening, we often think to ourselves 'Ah, that's not quite what I meant here' and have the chance to change key words to make the real meaning clearer.

- If it *sounds* boring, it will no doubt be read as boring by learners!

Linking learning outcomes to the seven factors underpinning successful learning

In Chapter 2, we explored how successful learning is underpinned by the seven factors, which all affect each other and interact with each other rather like 'ripples on a pond'. So how exactly should a set of intended learning outcomes address these seven factors?

1. *Wanting* to learn: the learning outcomes need to arouse curiosity, and be attractive and interesting. At best, the learning outcomes should trigger the 'wow' factor. At worst, they should at least manage to address the 'so what?' as well as the 'why should I bother to learn this?', and 'what's the point of me paying attention to these learning outcomes?'

2. Regarding ownership of the *need* to learn: the learning outcomes should *define* the need, helping students to see exactly what they need to work

towards becoming able to achieve. Learners may simply wish to know 'What exactly do I need to do?' Some will go much further, and look carefully at the learning outcomes to find out 'What do I need to do to get a really good qualification?'. Others will take a more strategic view, asking of the outcomes 'What's the minimum I must do just to pass?'

3. *Doing*: this relates most directly to the production of evidence of achievement. 'What exactly should I be expecting to be required to do as I learn this topic?' This also needs to include clear answers to the questions: 'When and where will I need to do these things on my way to achieving the learning outcomes, and providing evidence of my achievement for the various assessment contexts I will meet?' Learners may also be asking 'What's the difference in "doing" between a first-class degree and a pass?' Learning outcomes need to be designed to help students to see exactly what they should be practising, what they should be learning from trial and error and from experimenting, and should indicate where repetition is going to be useful.

4. *Feedback*: learners are likely to look at a set of learning outcomes with the following questions in their minds: 'How will I know I'm on the right track while learning this material? How will I know that my evidence of achievement is pitched at the right level? What can I do to get back on track if I've slipped?' Learners need feedback on their achievement of the learning outcomes – not just at the end, but all the way along the route. Learners don't just need feedback on what they've done, but also feedback on where they are in their journey towards evidencing their achievement of the learning outcomes.

5. *Making sense*: 'How will I know that I've really achieved the outcomes? How will I know that I've reached the standard that's being looked for? How will I know my evidence isn't just a fluke and that I've really got there?' Learning outcomes need to help students to see what's supposed to be going on in their heads at the end of the journey, and at points along the route. Of all the seven factors discussed in Chapter 2, 'making sense' is the process we can't do for our learners. We can, however, illustrate what it looks like to have 'made sense' of something, and we can show evidence specifications so that learners can test out for themselves the extent to which they have made sense of things along the learning journey.

6. *Teaching, explaining, coaching*: these all relate to communicating the achievement resulting from successful learning. Learning outcomes need to clarify as well as we can what we want learners to become able to show for their learning, and very often that boils down to becoming able to explain things fluently. Many an exam question includes 'explain' as a key word. We want learners to make sense of what they're learning so well that learners can coach fellow-learners, or teach someone starting to learn the topic concerned. It is useful if learners can see from the

way we design the curriculum for them that we intend them not just to sit in solemn silence filling their heads with information to communicate back to us, but to practise communicating their knowledge to fellow human beings on the journey towards demonstrating their evidence of achievement to us in formal settings such as exams or assignments.

7. *Assessing – making informed judgements*: we need to encourage learners, through every available means, to optimize the deepening of their learning by applying assessment criteria to the evidence they produce of achievement of their learning. We can partly achieve this by making sure that learning outcomes show that we're not merely requiring learners to reproduce information for us as evidence of their learning. Where possible, we need to illustrate by the wording of learning outcomes that we're looking for high-level critical analysis as evidence of achievement, encouraging learners to practise producing this kind of evidence using self-assessment and peer assessment to raise the standard of that evidence.

It is no mean feat to produce a set of learning outcomes which links well, as proposed above, to these seven factors underpinning successful learning. As I suggested at the beginning of this chapter, the best way of arriving at this destination is *not* to start with the learning outcomes, but to work backwards from evidence of achievement, and iterate the process until everything fits fluently in the big picture. In the next section, we'll look in more detail at how we can go about this design process.

Curriculum design from scratch

In the following discussion, I would like to share how I work with staff who are planning a new curriculum element. In practice, of course, it's quite rare that we have the luxury of starting from scratch. We've usually got some existing learning outcomes to start with – and they're not always good ones! We've often got pre-specified evidence of achievement to think about, and existing ways of assessing learners' achievement. Nevertheless, the ideas in this section can be used even when we're not starting from scratch, so long as we are willing to make adjustments to what we're already starting with. What follows is a description of a set of processes that I use with participants at curriculum design workshops, and I invite you to adapt the various stages to meet your own needs.

I Start with evidence of achievement

As mentioned above, I suggest that they start by working out *evidence of achievement* first, even before thinking of draft learning outcomes. By half-way

Intended learning outcome	Assignment task briefing	Marking scheme	Notes
Evidence of achievement of the learning outcome...	Rationale for choosing the particular assessment process to link the evidence to the intended outcome...		
1			

Figure 3.2   Start by thinking about evidence of achievement

through a day's workshop on curriculum design, I have participants in groups, each group with a flipchart marked out as shown in Figure 3.2.

The aim is to populate the various boxes on the chart. However, rather than write on to the charts, I get participants to stick post-its on to them, as the post-its can be edited and improved as discussion goes on during the workshop, starting with the box numbered '1' in Figure 3.2. In practice, participants end up with layers of post-its in each box, showing the successive improvements and adjustments made to each area of the chart as the links are strenghtened between the various elements.

2 From evidence of achievement to assignment briefing

Next, I ask groups of participants to work out how they are going to 'get at' the evidence of achievement, so that it can be measured and duly accredited. I ask them to come up with (on post-its) draft examples of any or all of the following:

- test or exam questions
- draft briefs for written assignments
- practical exercises
- briefings for reports

and so on, each measuring in its own way a facet of the evidence of achievement identified in the box labelled '1', and to stick their post-its on box '2' in Figure 3.3.

I ask groups to fine-tune '1' and '2' so that the assignment briefings and evidence of achievement match each other more and more closely. For example, if something does not lend itself to some kind of measurement, it may need to disappear from box '1', or better, ways need to be thought of to set some kind of task which does measure it. Equally, if something important which was not already in box '1' is being measured in box '2', it may need to be duly added to the evidence in box '1'.

Intended learning outcome	Assignment task briefing	Marking scheme	Notes
	2		
Evidence of achievement of the learning outcome...	Rationale for choosing the particular assessment process to link the evidence to the intended outcome...		
1			

Figure 3.3   Now design assessment to link to evidence of achievement

3 Rationale – learning by explaining

It's now time to tackle the rationale for choosing particular assessment processes to link evidence of achievement, in due course, to the intended learning outcome. See Figure 3.4.

Intended learning outcome	Assignment task briefing	Marking scheme	Notes
	2		
Evidence of achievement of the learning outcome...	Rationale for choosing the particular assessment process to link the evidence to the intended outcome...		
1	3		

Figure 3.4   Work out rationale linking assessment to evidence of achievement

I ask groups to sketch out on post-its justifications for why particular assessments or assignments in box '2' are indeed fit for purpose to get at the 'evidence of achievement' specifications in box '1'.

Then I ask groups to exchange membership, so that each group retains one or two of its original members, but has one or more members from *other* groups present. I then ask the 'resident' members of each group to explain the rationale in box '3' to the newcomers. This leads to quite a lot of opportunity to further improve the links between boxes '1' and '2', and the post-its in all three boxes can be amended as necessary to make these links ever more transparent and direct.

I then ask the groups to return to their original formation and bring what has been learned from the 'explaining' (and listening to others' explanations) to bear on further improving the contents of boxes '1' to '3'. Invariably, groups significantly improve the contents of all three boxes by the end of these processes, learning a great deal from each others' attempts to put the rationale into words.

4 First-draft intended learning outcomes

Now it's time for each group to think of how the *evidence of achievement* is going to be expressed to learners in the form of learning outcomes, ensuring that these too will link to the rationale already established for the assessment processes. See Figure 3.5.

Intended learning outcome	Assignment task briefing	Marking scheme	Notes
4	2		
Evidence of achievement of the learning outcome...	Rationale for choosing the particular assessment process to link the evidence to the intended outcome...		
1	3		

Figure 3.5   Next make first draft of intended learning outcome

Groups now draft (on post-its) intended learning outcomes and stick them in box '4'. I have found that the best way forward is to ask each group to work up some learning outcomes as well as they can, copy them on further post-its, and then, returning to plenary formation, I ask participants to swap post-its so no one knows who has their post-it. I then ask participants individually to read out the draft learning outcomes as written on these post-its, usually reading them out more than once, while we all join together in any suggestions for clarifying, editing or refining the wording of the outcomes. When participants return to their groups, they usually have a range of ideas to bring to improving the learning outcome drafts in box '4' on their charts.

5 Sharpening the alignment by thinking about marking

By this stage, each group has drafted parts of the curriculum, aligning learning outcomes to assessment, informed by the rationale for choosing particular assessment formats to measure appropriate facets of the desired evidence of achievement. As you will know from your own assessment work, nothing sharpens up assessment better than actually getting down to marking students' work. Therefore, the next stage is to ask each group to draft out marking schemes (including draft assessment criteria) for each of the assessment elements they have devised in box '2', and attach details (as post-its or, more usually, as small post-its linking to separate numbered sheets) in box '5'. See Figure 3.6.

Intended learning outcome	Assignment task briefing	Marking scheme	Notes
4	2	5	
Evidence of achievement of the learning outcome...	Rationale for choosing the particular assessment process to link the evidence to the intended outcome...		
1	3		

Figure 3.6 Design marking scheme

Designing a marking scheme almost always leads to adjustments in assignment or assessment briefings, and groups are encouraged to make these and amend the post-its in box '2' as necessary. This in turn impacts on exactly what parts of the evidence specifications in box '1' are in fact addressed by the assessment elements, and to the rationale in box '3'. Naturally, to maintain the alignment between assessment and evidence of achievement, it is now necessary to make further adjustments to the intended learning outcomes in box '4'. See Figure 3.7.

Intended learning outcome	Assignment task briefing	Marking scheme	Notes
4a	2a	5	
Evidence of achievement of the learning outcome...	Rationale for choosing the particular assessment process to link the evidence to the intended outcome...		
1a	3a		

Figure 3.7 Make adjustments to all previous drafts

6 Designing how exactly students will get feedback

The next consideration is feedback. This of course depends a lot on which of the assessment elements in box '2' are formative and which are summative (and not so suitable for feedback). I suggest to groups that in box '6' they draft out the feedback processes (e.g. written, face-to-face, and so on) which best lend themselves to giving students feedback on their achievement as measured by successive assessment tasks, choosing which process is likely to be most effective depending on the nature of the evidence of achievement being measured, and the extent to which feed-forward can usefully be provided to help learners to optimize their performance of oncoming tasks. It is clearly important that students get formative feed-back on their evidence of achievement of the learning outcomes to as great an extent as can reasonably be achieved without increasing the burden of assessment unduly. So it is now time to have another iteration right round the boxes in the chart, as assessment elements, marking schemes (including assessment criteria) and the intended learning outcomes them-selves are fine-tuned to take into account the matter of optimizing feed-back to students on the evidence of achievement which they produce. This is demonstrated in Figure 3.8.

Intended learning outcome	Assignment task briefing	Marking scheme	Notes
4b	2b	5b	
Evidence of achievement of the learning outcome...	Rationale for choosing the particular assessment process to link the evidence to the intended outcome...	How learners will get feedback on their achievement	
1b	3b	6	

Figure 3.8   Think about feedback, and make further adjustment to all previous drafts

I have now indicated the further adjustments as '5b', and so on, in Figure 3.8.

7 Improving curriculum design after teaching it and assessing it for the first time

We all know that after teaching a new chunk of curriculum for the very first time, we gain all sorts of ideas on how to do it better next time. And we normally go on to do just that! Moreover, after we've run the various assess-ment elements for the first time, done the marking and given feedback to students, *and* found out how best that feedback can be further adjusted on a future occasion to help students even more, we have a further great deal of information about how best to express the curriculum concerned. The sad thing is that too often the curriculum documentation does not get upgraded, and languishes in its initial state in filing cabinets and module handbooks alike. I suggest next the best way to capitalize on the experience gained through teaching a curriculum element.

   At the curriculum review stage, preferably very closely after completing the first run of teaching and assessing, it is useful to get staff back together to adjust all of the elements in the chart we've been thinking about, on the basis of replies to various questions, including the ones I've now added to the right-hand column of the chart (see Figure 3.9). Successive versions of

Intended learning outcome	Assignment task briefing	Marking scheme	Adjustments after teaching it the first time...
4c	2c	5c	How well did the assessment elements work?
Evidence of achievement of the learning outcome...	Rationale for choosing the particular assessment process to link the evidence to the intended outcome...	How learners will get feedback on their achievement	How well did the marking schemes work? What adjustments were made to the assignment then?
1c	3c	6c	What parts of evidence were actually measured? What changes were made to the outcome at each stage? ...

Figure 3.9 Make further adjustments after the first teaching run

learning outcomes, assessment elements, etc., are now labelled '4c', '2c', and so on.

The list of questions I've put into the right-hand column is only meant to be a start here. Further questions could include:

- What worked best about this curriculum element, and why was this?
- What didn't work so well, and how could this be adjusted?
- What *else* might it have been useful to include in evidence of achievement?
- How *else* might that evidence of achievement have been assessed?
- How *else* might feedback have been given to learners?

A consequence of this kind of developmental review of curriculum is that the specification should never be more than a year old! This is, of course, contrary to existing practice, where all too often curriculum design can be set in stone for five years or more, or until some sort of external review (or change of staffing) causes us to revisit the design of teaching, learning and assessment.

How well do learners know how to use the intended learning outcomes?

I've included a self-assessment checklist which you can give to learners (or better still, fine-tune and adapt for your own learners) to help them get a sense of how well they're using your intended learning outcomes. In practice, the reflection that such a checklist can start off may alert learners to the fact that they *can* actually make good use of the outcomes.

Putting learning outcomes to work

Please tick one or more of the columns for each row, as appropriate.	This is what I do.	I would like to do this, but do not manage to.	I don't think this is necessary.	This just is not possible for me.	I'll try to do this in future.
1 I locate the intended learning outcomes in my course documentation.					
2 I already use the intended learning outcomes as a frame of reference for my studying.					
3 I find it easy to work out exactly what the intended learning outcomes mean in practice.					
4 I carefully work out exactly what I'm supposed to become able to *do* to show my achievement of each learning outcome.					
5 I keep the intended learning outcomes to hand, so I can see how each study element relates to them.					
6 I know how to link learning outcomes to assessment, and to what I need to be able to do in assignments and exam questions to show I've achieved them.					
7 I find it useful when tutors give me feedback about the extent to which I've demonstrated my achievement of each learning outcome involved in an assignment.					
8 I ask for clarification when I'm not sure about the standards I need to meet in the context of an intended learning outcome.					

9	I discuss the meaning of intended outcomes with fellow students, helping me to get a better idea about which are the really important outcomes.					
10	I've made sure that the intended learning outcomes for each lecture are included in or with my notes.					
11	I've checked how well I reckon I've already achieved each of the intended learning outcomes, and marked these decisions against the outcomes for future reference.					
12	When I can't find out exactly what the intended learning outcomes are, I design some myself and check with tutors and fellow students whether I've made a good attempt at this.					

Beyond learning outcomes

In this chapter on curriculum development, we've explored how intended learning outcomes need to be developed and adjusted iteratively, so that they fit naturally into the bigger picture of syllabus content, assessment, feedback and teaching. But intended learning outcomes can be thought of as part of an even bigger picture, which also includes *learning incomes*, *emergent learning outcomes* and *intended learning outgoings*. Having sprung on you three things you won't find mentioned yet in the literature about curriculum design, let me explain and illustrate what I mean by these terms, and how we might usefully address them in curriculum design.

Learning incomes

These may be different for each different learner. By learning *incomes*, I mean all the things learners are bringing to the learning situation. These include:

- what they already know about the subject

- what they can already do, related to the subject

- other things in their experience which they can link to the new subject.

As long ago as 1968, Ausubel wrote:

> If I had to reduce all of educational psychology to just one principle, I would say this: the most important single factor influencing learning is what the learner already knows. Ascertain this, and teach him accordingly. (Ausubel, 1968)

So how can we find out, before we start teaching them, what our learners already know? Ask them! For example, when about to start a new topic with a large group of learners, it can be useful to give each of them two post-its of different colours (e.g. pink and yellow). On the yellow one, ask everyone to jot down their response to 'The most important thing I already know about "x" is...'. And on the pink one, 'One question I really want to know the answer to about "x" is...'. Then get learners to show their post-its to each other and discuss. Next, arrange that they stick all the post-its up on charts or walls. The most important step is then for us to collect all these post-its, and sift through what they already know and what they want to find out. This helps us to:

- avoid spending too much time telling the class all sorts of things they already know. We still may need to cover some of these things for the sake of the learners who don't yet know them, but we can minimize the tedium for those who already do know them.

- give learners the chance to explain things they already know to each other – the explainers learn a great deal and we avoid boring them with our own explanations.

- spot misconceptions that some of our learners may have about things we're going to build on. We can then put them right on these as we introduce topics.

- build on what members of the class *want* to find out. This helps learners to feel an increased degree of ownership of what we tell them – in effect, we're structuring the curriculum around *their* questions.

Emergent learning outcomes

Let's think about the *emergent* learning outcomes, which learners achieve at the same time as they achieve the *intended* ones. In just about everything we do as human beings, there are emergent outcomes as well as intended ones. Sometimes the emergent ones turn out to be even more important than the intended ones. As teachers, every time we explain things to learners, and assess their learning, as discussed in Chapter 2, *we* gain a lot in terms of our own learning. We can think of this as our own emergent learning outcomes. But think again about *students'* learning. When they work through an element of curriculum, much more happens to them than merely achieving our intended learning outcomes. What *else* might they have learned? They learn all sorts of additional things, which might include:

- things they learned about the subject concerned above and beyond what we intended them to learn

- things they learned about the links between *our* subject and other subjects they are learning

- things they learned by getting things wrong on their journey towards achieving the intended learning outcomes

- things they learned *about themselves* as learners – for example, techniques they developed while learning this particular bit of curriculum which will be useful to continue to apply to other learning contexts

- things they learned from each other, and skills they gained in working with each other.

We can find out from students a lot about emergent learning outcomes. I have often issued post-its to a large class and asked everyone to jot on a post-it responses to the question 'What *else* did you learn?' I've then asked students to stick these on a chart on their way out of the teaching session. More often than not there are many *emergent* learning outcomes which prove to be just as relevant and important as any of the *intended* outcomes, and are well worth adding into the intended outcomes next time round.

So what about *assessment* of the emergent learning outcomes? We can't really do this! This would be unfair. These are not part of the overt targets – even when they are important and desirable. And besides, the emergent learning outcomes are going to be different for different learners. But we can still give learners *feedback* on their *evidence* of achievement of their own emergent learning outcomes, alongside giving them feedback on the extent to which their evidence demonstrates their achievement of the *intended* learning outcomes. It would be tragic to refrain from congratulating learners on particular aspects of their achievement just because these aspects weren't part of the picture as defined by our curriculum.

Intended learning outgoings?

How often have you told learners 'This will be really useful to you later in your career...', and so on. In vocational teaching, we're often preparing learners for the world of work, and aiming to equip them with skills and knowledge which they will need in years to come. Very often, these things are above and beyond what we're actually going to be able to get learners to *show* for their learning while they're with us. In other words, some of these things can't be included in the evidence of achievement upon which we base our assessment, and therefore can't be included formally in the intended learning outcomes as discussed in this chapter. But we can refer to them as intended learning *outgoings*, to help learners to see where they fit in to the bigger picture of the curriculum, and indeed to link the intended learning outcomes to the wider world of future learning and employment.

One way of achieving this is to present the intended learning *outgoings* alongside the intended learning incomes so that learners can see what is on the immediate agenda, compared to the bigger picture of their ongoing learning and development. This can help them to gain increased ownership of the curriculum, addressing their 'What's in it for me?' question more fully.

Conclusions

This chapter on 'Curriculum design for learning' has focused strongly on making the curriculum flexible and learner-centred, and avoiding the curriculum becoming dominated merely by the detail of the subject content itself. We've looked at the importance of thinking about *evidence of achievement* as the first stage in working towards our documentation describing the curriculum. We've explored how to arrive at specifications of intended learning outcomes as a result of considering assessment and feedback before, rather than after, reaching the wording of the outcomes. By adding in thinking about learning *incomes* and researching with learners their *emergent* learning outcomes in practice, and by including in the picture the intended learning *outgoings* which learners will need later in their lives and careers, I believe we can make curriculum design address the full picture of student learning, assessment and feedback, working towards making it fit for purpose as part of our bid to encourage lifelong learning, rather than just the short-term achievement of particular targets.

4

Assessment Driving Learning

This chapter is one of the most important in the book, and it has grown in this edition. To make it easier to navigate, it is now divided into three main parts:

4.1 **Assessment is broken in higher education!** This section ranges widely, exploring what's wrong with assessment, examining some links between assessment and learning, and discussing validity, reliability, transparency and authenticity, as well as pointing forwards about how we can work our way out of the problems which are endemic today.

4.2 **Analysis of particular assessment processes.** This is a critical discussion of the cases of time-constrained, unseen written exams, links between these and the factors underpinning successful learning, with short notes about some of the better alternatives that exist. Next follows a similar discussion of that other most-common assessment format – the essay. It is worth noting straightaway that most people who graduate from higher education don't sit an exam or write an essay ever again thereafter.

4.3 **Towards assessment *as* learning.** This section consists of a tool to enable you to interrogate any assessment instrument or process of your choice against factors such as validity, reliability and so on, and also against the seven factors underpinning successful learning. This section ends with some recommendations for improving assessment in post-compulsory education.

4.1 Assessment is broken in higher education!

Several indicators tell us this, including:

- Students' perceptions (for example, as gathered from final-year students annually in the National Student Survey in the UK since 2005) tell us that assessment and feedback continue to be the least satisfactory elements of the higher education experience, that the assessment criteria are not clear, and that students do not believe that marking and grading are fair.

- Academic staff responding to the starter 'Teaching would be much better for me if only I...' mention 'had more time' more frequently than any other factor, and when further questioned usually cite the time it takes to mark students' work as the main oppressing factor.

How has assessment become broken in higher education?

What are the factors which make it harder and harder to make assessment work well for students, and keep the processes of marking and giving feedback to students manageable for staff? The factors which have caused our present problems include:

1. Student numbers have grown: we can't use the same processes and instruments for a system where nearly 50 per cent of the 18–21 year-old population study at university level, compared to 5 per cent a couple of decades ago.

2. The world has opened up, so that our assessment processes and practices need to be more compatible with those in vastly different cultures and traditions.

3. It is widely accepted now that assessment is the major driver for student learning, and if assessment is not working as a *good* driver for learning, the effectiveness of our entire higher education provision is jeopardized.

4. We now know much more about the standards we should strive towards in assessing students' work, in particular the need to improve assessment to make it more valid, more reliable, more transparent to students, more authentic for students, and more inclusive so that assessment does not disadvantage students with identified special needs, and enables them to demonstrate their learning in ways where they can show their optimum achievement.

5. We need to continue to diversify the assessment processes and instruments we use, so that no students are repeatedly disadvantaged by the predominance of particular assessment formats.

In short, we need a richer mix of high-quality assessment formats, and we also need to *reduce* the overall burden of assessment for ourselves and for our students. We need to measure less, but measure it better. We need to measure a wider spectrum of students' evidence of achievement, with a broader more versatile set of tools. Presently, we spend far too much of our (and students') time on things they write, at the expense of other ways they can show they have achieved the learning outcomes. But to repeat myself, we still need to *reduce* the burden of assessment: more assessments, but much shorter ones.

Fortunately, help is at hand. There now exists a rich literature about assessment, containing a great deal of authoritative wisdom to bring to bear on assessment design, helping us to address the factors listed above, and work towards making student perceptions of assessment more satisfactory, at the same time as allowing us to make it a more reasonable and realistic proportion of our jobs as academics in post-compulsory education.

What students think

In the National Student Survey, administered to all final-year students every year in the UK since 2005, in the section on 'assessment and feedback', statements 5 and 6 link directly to students' experience of assessment. The design of this particular survey if far from ideal, but its use right across the higher education sector in the UK makes it an important indicator of at least some of students' feelings about their higher education experience. Students are asked to make judgements as follows:

- definitely agree
- mostly agree
- neither agree nor disagree
- mostly disagree
- definitely disagree
- not applicable

on the following two statements (numbers 5 and 6 out of the 22 in the survey):

5 The criteria used in marking have been clear in advance.

6 Assessment arrangements and marking have been fair.

Widely across the sector, institutions have been dismayed at students' negative responses to these statements, compared to most of the rest of the survey, and this trend has continued throughout the five years of the Survey as implemented so far. Many factors can account for student dissatisfaction with assessment, including:

- For students, assessment is of course the sharp end of their overall experience in higher education – it's what determines their qualifications.

- Even when the criteria have been clearly formulated in module handbooks or on course websites, students may not have *heard* the criteria sufficiently in face-to-face contexts, allowing them to know better exactly what they mean in terms of evidence of achievement of the intended learning outcomes.

- Even when assessment and marking *are* fair, students often do not know the lengths institutions go to to achieve this. Students may know little of the detail of assessment questions being moderated and improved by external examiners, for example.

- Overall, students do not have sufficient opportunity to get their heads inside the assessment culture of higher education – it is sometimes a 'black box' to them, where they do their best and hope it will all work out well in the end.

- Students have not sufficient opportunity to familiarize themselves with the assessment culture in which they are competing, for example by *making informed judgements* themselves on their own and each other's work.

- Sometimes, of course, students are right! Assessment criteria are not always made clear to them in advance, and sometimes assessment and marking are far from fair!

However, going back to the design of the survey, both of the statements involved in this section are in fact 'bipolar'. In other words, is it 'clear' or 'in advance' (or both) which triggers the student's choice of options for statement '5', and is it 'assessment arrangements' or 'marking' (or both) being 'fair' which triggers students' choices for statement '6'? I regard it as unfortunate that such a widely used instrument incorporates (and repeats annually!) such clumsiness! Nevertheless, the discussion in this chapter aims to address all of the reasons why students are dissatisfied with the assessment culture they meet in higher education.

Why assessment counts

This book is about making *intentional* learning – or *purposeful* learning – happen. Perhaps the most significant difference is that learning in post-compulsory education ends up being *assessed* in various ways. Some of this assessment usually relates to *completion* of stages of learning. Not all learners in post-compulsory education complete their learning programmes.

Yorke (2002) has analysed 'leaving early' in higher education (i.e. non-completion) and finds that:

> Roughly two-thirds of premature departures take place in, or at the end of, the first year of full-time study in the UK. Anecdotal evidence from a number of institutions indicates that early poor performance can be a powerful disincentive to continuation, with students feeling that perhaps they were not cut out for higher education after all – although the main problems are acculturation and acclimatisation to studying. Having recognised that deleterious consequences of early summative assessment and that the first year of full-time study is typically only a kind of qualifying year for an honours degree, some institutions are removing from their assessment regulations the requirement that students pass summative assessments at the end of the first semester. This should allow students more of an opportunity to build confidence and to come to terms with academic study, and ought to allow more of the vital formative assessment to take place. (Yorke, 2002: 37)

People lose interest in learning for a range of reasons and become at risk of dropping out. How and when assessment takes place is one of the more important critical factors which can influence people's decisions to drop out. As we will see in the next chapter, the timeliness, quality and nature of formative feedback is perhaps the most critical of the factors under our control in post-compulsory education, especially when such feedback 'goes wrong' for various reasons.

But getting assessment right should be seen as an opportunity, not a threat. Sally Brown (2009) in the closing keynote of a conference on the first-year experience used the following words:

> Concentrating on giving students detailed and developmental formative feedback is the single most useful thing we can do for our students, particularly those who have had a struggle to achieve entry to higher education. Assessment and feedback are two of the best tools available to us, to support student achievement, progression and retention. Getting assessment and feedback right from the beginning of the first year makes a real difference.

There are also economics to consider. Making learning happen in post-compulsory education costs money – a great deal of money. So it is natural that accountability is necessary, not least in times of recession, such as at the time of preparing the second edition of this book. It is now more important than ever that we are efficient and effective in post-compulsory education. We can only measure what students produce as evidence of their learning. That's where assessment – and, indeed, completion – come in. 'Making learning happen' is not just about causing learning to happen; it's about 'making learning *being seen* to have happened'. It's about results. These affect funding. We're not paid just to make learning happen; we're paid on the basis that we can *show* that learning has happened and that we've played a part in making it happen. We've got to take care with making sure that what we measure is indeed learners' *achievement* of these outcomes, as directly as possible, and not (for example) just a measure of how well learners can communicate with a pen in exam rooms, how well they may have achieved those bits of the outcomes which are amenable to showing on written scripts. That would be only an echo of the achievement we are seeking to measure – perhaps only a ghost of the learning. We need to be very careful that our attempts to measure the achievement of intended learning outcomes are not skewed or muffled by filters such as exam technique, which may have little to do with the intended outcomes.

Gibbs and Simpson (2002) share concerns about assessment practices and policies driving learning in the opposite direction to improving learning, as follows:

> When teaching in higher education hits the headlines it is nearly always about assessment: about examples of supposedly falling standards, about plagiarism, about unreliable marking or rogue external examiners, about errors in exam papers, and so on. ... Where institutional learning and teaching strategies focus on assessment they are nearly always about aligning learning outcomes with assessment and about specifying assessment criteria. All of this focus, of the media, of quality assurance and of institutions, is on assessment as measurement. ... The most reliable, rigorous and cheat-proof assessment systems are often accompanied by dull and lifeless learning that has short lasting outcomes – indeed they often directly lead to such learning. ... Standards will be raised by improving student learning rather than by better measurement of limited learning. (Gibbs and Simpson, 2002)

This is the main reason that assessment is the principal driving force for learning for so many learners in post-compulsory education. Their exam grades, certificates, degrees, and even higher degrees, depend on them being able to prove that they have met standards, demonstrated achievement and communicated their learning. Learners are rewarded for what they *show*, not just for what they know. Indeed, we can even argue that *showing* is actually *more* important than knowing. In some assessment contexts learners can gain credit by becoming competent at writing *as if* they had mastered something, even when they have not!

Assessment and deep, surface and strategic learners

Deep learning gets a good press in the scholarly literature. Deep learning is, we might argue, closer to developing real *understanding*. But we've already seen that this is difficult or even impossible to measure. So deep learning may be the wrong approach to wean our learners towards when our assessment may only be measuring something rather less than deep learning. Deep learning may, of course, be much more appropriate for those learners going on to higher levels, and is doubtless the kind of learning which leads to the most productive and inspired research. Perhaps that is why deep learning is regarded so favourably by educational researchers on the whole. However, 'Save your deep learning for your postgraduate years. For now, your priority is to make sure that you get to *having* some postgraduate years' could be wise advice to give undergraduates!

Surface learning gets a bad press in the literature. However, probably most of the learning done by most people in post-compulsory education is actually only surface learning. Learners learn things 'sufficient to the day' – the exam day or the assessment week or whatever. When it has been learned successfully enough to serve its purpose – pass the module, gain the certificate, whatever – it's ditched. It's not entirely wasted, however. Something that's been surface learned is a better starting point for re-learning, or for learning more deeply, than something which has not been learned at all. But learners can all tell us tales of the countless things they have learned only well enough to give back when required to demonstrate their achievements, which have been quite deliberately 'eased out' of their minds as they moved on to the next stage of their learning journey. 'You are what you learn' may be a noble sentiment, but it can be argued that our assessment processes and instruments cause learners to learn far too many things which aren't important, diluting the quality of learning that is afforded to those things that *are* important.

Despite the criticisms of surface learning approaches, sometimes it is a fit-for-purpose choice. Where a limited amount of factual information needs to be available at will in a particular scenario, but will not be needed after that scenario is completed, surface learning can be a wise enough choice. There are things that just are not important enough to warrant a lot of time and energy being invested in learning them deeply. An example could be the statistics relating to stopping distances in wet and dry conditions, which need to be learned to pass parts of the driving test in the UK. Few experienced drivers can quote these facts and figures correctly a few years after passing their driving tests, but probably are perfectly capable of judging stopping distances well enough simply based on experience. This aspect of the learning for the test seems to be almost entirely a surface learning business.

What's wrong with *strategic* learning?

Strategic learning has perhaps had the worst press of all. It's not just *accidental* surface learning. It is perhaps sometimes *deliberate* surface learning, consciously engaged in at the expense of deeper learning. Strategic learning is regarded as 'learning for the exam'. It's associated with 'seeking out the marks or credit' quite consciously in essays, reports, dissertations and theses, and extends readily to preparing strategically for job interviews, promotion boards, and so on. Moreover, it can be argued that strategic learners may make informed judgements about *what* to learn deeply and what to learn *just* at a surface level.

Strategic learners tend to be successful, or at least moderately successful. Deep learners may well *deserve* success, but quite often shoot themselves in one foot or the other by mastering *some* parts of the curriculum very very well while leaving other parts of the curriculum underdeveloped, and not getting the overall credit that they might have achieved had they spread their efforts more evenly across the curriculum. Surface learners can also fare well enough if and when all that is really being measured in our assessment systems is surface learning. Strategic learning is often thought of in terms of doing the *minimum* to get by. But there are various 'minima'. In the present degree classification system in the UK, perhaps there's the minimum to get by and get a degree at all, the (different) minimum to get by and get a 2.1, the (different again) minimum to get by and get a first-class degree, and perhaps the minimum to get by and get a first-class degree with a margin for safety?

So what *is* strategic learning? We could regard it as making informed choices about when to be a deep learner and when to be a surface learner. It could be viewed as investing more in what is important to learn and less in what is less important to learn. It could be regarded as setting out towards a chosen level of achievement and working systematically to become able to demonstrate that level of achievement in each contributing assessment element.

There is growing recognition that the curriculum in post-compulsory education is content-bound. There is just so much subject matter around in every discipline. Any award-bearing programme of study necessarily involves making informed decisions about what to include in the curriculum and what to leave out. But is not this the very same thing that strategic learners do? Isn't being an *effective* strategic learner to do with making wise and informed choices about where to invest time and energy, and where not? It can be argued that strategic learning, when done well, is a demonstration of a useful kind of *intelligence* – that of handling quite vast amounts of information, narrowing the information down to a smaller proportion and then processing only that smaller proportion into knowledge. It can also be argued that those learners who go far are the strategic ones, rather than the deep ones. It can be argued that they know *when* to adopt a deep approach and when it is sufficient to adopt a surface approach.

In the UK, for example, every year there is an annual clamour about the A level results. This year (2009) some 97.5 per cent of A level candidates passed, with about 27 per cent of candidates attaining three 'A' grades. The clamour echoes the usual protests that standards have not fallen, that there has been no 'dumbing down'. Could it not be that A level candidates are becoming better prepared to achieve at A level? Could it not be that they know more about what is being looked for in good exam answers? Could it not be that they are more aware about what is required for good grades in associated coursework? Could it not, indeed, be that they are now better versed in the virtues of strategic learning? And is this really a 'bad thing'?

Sadler (2009a: 823–4) brings his long experience of assessment in higher education to the issue of grade inflation, and argues that we have repeatedly buried our heads in the sand regarding tackling the problem systematically. He offers suggestions regarding what needs to be done to make the problem amenable to systematic research.

'I'm sorry, but I haven't got a cue!'

As long ago as 1974, Miller and Parlett discussed what can now be thought of as one way of thinking about strategic learning: 'cue-consciousness'. They proposed three approaches which learners can use in the ways that they structure their learning in systems where assessment is a significant driving force – an assessment regime which then in the UK was mainly comprised of written exams. They wrote of:

- cue-seeking learners: more likely to get first-class degrees
- cue-conscious learners: more likely to get upper second-class degrees
- cue-deaf learners: less likely to succeed.

Gibbs and Simpson (2002) expand on, and quote from, Miller and Parlett's work as follows:

> Miller and Parlett focussed on the extent to which students were oriented to cues about what was rewarded in the assessment system. They described different kinds of students: the cue seekers, who went out of their way to get out of the lecturer what was going to come up in the exam and what their personal preferences were; the cue conscious, who heard and paid attention to tips given out by their lecturers about what was important, and the 'cue deaf', for whom any such guidance passed straight over their heads. This 'cue seeking' student describes exam question-spotting: '*I am positive there is an examination game. You don't learn certain facts, for instance, you don't take the whole course, you go and look at the examination papers and you say "looks as though there have been four questions on a certain theme this year, last year the professor said that the examination would be much the same as before", so you excise a good bit of the course immediately…*'. (Miller and Parlett, 1974: 60)
>
> In contrast these students were described as 'cue-deaf': '*I don't choose questions for revision – I don't feel confident if I only restrict myself to certain topics.' 'I will try to revise everything…*'. (Miller and Parlett, 1974: 63)
>
> Miller and Parlett were able to predict with great accuracy which students would get good degree results…. '*people who were cue conscious tended to get upper seconds and those who were cue deaf got lower seconds*'. (Miller and Parlett, 1974: 55)

Things have not really changed much in three decades. I am, however, readily persuaded by Sally Brown's suggestion that the phrase 'cue-deaf' is unfortunate, and indeed unacceptable. 'Cue-blind' is equally problematic. 'Cue-oblivious' is a better way of thinking about those learners who just don't take any notice of cues about how assessment is going to work, or about how useful the intended learning outcomes may be as a framework upon which they can prepare for assessment, or about how valuable formative feedback on assessed coursework can be to help them improve their techniques for future assessments.

Knight and Yorke (2003) put the matter of cue-consciousness in perspective as follows:

Learned dependence is present when the student relies on the teacher to say what has to be done and does not seek to go beyond the boundaries that they believe to be circumscribing the task. The construction of curricula around explicit learning outcomes risks the inadvertent building-in of circumscriptions or, for the 'strategic' student seeking to balance study and part-time employment, a welcome 'limitation' to what they have to do. Formal and informal feedback can be interrogated for what it can tell about what is expected, and can become part of a vicious spiralling-in towards 'playing it safe', basing action on perceptions of the implicit – as well as the explicit – expectations. It is a paradox that active 'cue-seekers' (Miller and Parlett, 1974) can exhibit a form of learned dependence, through 'playing it clever' (at least, superficially) by hunting for hints that will help them to maximise the grade received for their investment of effort. Over-reliance on the teacher can thus give achievements a meretricious ring: these may look worthier than they actually are. (Knight and Yorke, 2003: 134)

It is interesting to think a little more about cue-seekers, cue-conscious learners and cue-oblivious learners, and to analyse how the seven factors underpinning successful learning may be at work in their respective cases as they tune in to their differing ways of looking forward to assessment in their choices of learning approaches.

Cue-seeking learners

These could be regarded as strategic learners, who are setting out to find out how assessment works so that they can produce their optimum performances in each assessed situation. They are likely to be much more receptive to *feedback*, using critical constructive feedback to fine-tune their learning, and to work out what gets them good marks and what doesn't. They are likely to probe quite deeply into feedback – both positive and critical – to find out as clearly as they can where they are meeting assessment expectations and where their shortfalls presently lie. They are likely to be particularly skilled regarding taking ownership of the *needing to learn* dimension, paying close attention to the cues they can draw from published intended learning outcomes, evidence descriptors and assessment criteria. Likewise, they may consciously seek explanation and interpretation of the real meaning of criteria and standards, so that they know more about just how to optimize evidence of their own achievement.

The *wanting to learn* dimension may still be strong, but is steered in the direction of investing time and energy in what they *need* to learn, as above. The *learning by doing* dimension is likely to be governed by their thinking about what is really *worth* doing and what is not. They may indeed invest in practice and trial and error where they see that there are likely to be dividends at the end of the road for them, and may deliberately *not* do things which they see as not paying such dividends in due course.

The *making sense* dimension is perhaps the most profoundly affected, with cue-seekers making strategic decisions about what they *try* to make sense of, and about what they will be perfectly content to use surface approaches to learn. Cue-seeking learners are likely to make the most of opportunities to find out how assessment works by making informed judgements on their own work, and each other's work. They are also amenable to encouragement that explaining things to each other is a good rehearsal for formal assessment.

Cue-seeking can therefore be thought of as a rich approach to learning, linking directly to each of the seven factors underpinning successful learning explored in this book. It is therefore not surprising that cue-seekers are usually identified as the learners most likely to succeed.

Cue-conscious learners

This group of learners may include at least some 'deep' learners, but who are balancing their intrinsic *want* to learn with more strategic approaches to ensure that they do indeed achieve what they believe they *need to learn* as well. They are likely to be almost as receptive to *learning through feedback* as their cue-seeking counterparts, but are not likely to go the extra mile to *seek* additional feedback or to ask for clarification of aspects of feedback they are not sure about. They may remain conscious of cues in structuring their *learning by doing*, but may be less likely to be as analytical as their cue-seeking counterparts in deciding how much time and energy to invest in each element of their studying.

Cue-conscious learners are likely to use cues to help them to *make sense* of what they are learning, but perhaps gain more from the cues they derive from teaching sessions and learning materials, and are likely to be less aware of cues in assessment contexts than their cue-seeking counterparts. That said, cue-conscious learners may benefit considerably from the process of *making informed judgements* in self-assessment and peer-assessment opportunities, bringing home to them some of the more important cues which will help them in formal assessment contexts. They are perhaps less likely to regard time and energy spent in *explaining, coaching* or *teaching* as really relevant to developing their own learning more deeply.

Cue-conscious approaches can therefore be seen as relating directly to at least some of the processes underpinning successful learning. There are some parallels with strategic learning approaches, but the strategy can be regarded as underdeveloped. However, the difference between cue-seeking and cue-consciousness may too often end up as a difference in achievement between the most successful and the adequately successful learners.

Cue-oblivious learners

Whatever else, these are probably *not* to be regarded as strategic learners. Sometimes, they can be more like deep learners or, alternatively, surface learners.

Some of these may be learners whose *want* to learn is very high but who perhaps do not make sufficient use of establishing a real sense of ownership of the *need* to learn. They are less likely to draw on published intended learning outcomes, evidence specifications or assessment criteria to structure their learning. Their motivation may, however, be so strong that they learn some parts of the curriculum really deeply, but thereby increase the risk that they fail to achieve on those parts of the curriculum which interest them less strongly. They may derive much less value from *feedback* than their cue-seeking or cue-conscious counterparts and, indeed, may become demotivated by critical feedback, which otherwise they could have used to their advantage.

Their *learning by doing* may be more haphazard, following their interests rather than attending to the parts of the curriculum in which they may need to invest some practice. They may *make sense* very well of those parts of the curriculum which interest them, and do so much less well where they lack such interest.

Cue-oblivious learners are less likely to internalize the benefits of learning by *making informed judgements* in self- or peer-assessment processes, and while they may still engage in explaining things to each other, this can happen at a somewhat superficial level, without them really optimizing the *making sense* which accompanies such actions for cue-seekers or cue-conscious learners.

Among the constituency of cue-oblivious learners, however, may be those learners who have not got much *want* to learn at all, and who are likely to end up as the casualties of assessment in due course. They, too, are unlikely to take ownership of the *need* to learn, as might have been indicated had they been aware of the cues connected with learning outcomes and assessment criteria.

All in all, it is not surprising that cue-oblivious learners are not nearly so successful as their cue-seeking or cue-conscious counterparts, as they miss out on the contribution which making use of cues can make to all seven of the factors underpinning successful learning.

Validity, reliability, transparency and authenticity

We've already seen that it is widely accepted that for most learners assessment drives learning to a quite profound extent. This is particularly the case for cue-seeking learners and strategic learners, and unsurprisingly they fare best in most common assessment processes and procedures. But is this state of things satisfactory? Institutional policies on teaching, learning and assessment make much of the design of assessment processes and instruments being adjusted to address the following four qualities:

- validity
- reliability
- transparency
- authenticity.

So assessment should be valid, reliable, transparent and authentic. Anyone who cares about the quality of the assessment they design for learners will say how they strive to make it so. We are also *required* in the UK, for example, to make assessment valid, reliable, transparent and authentic by the Quality and Curriculum Development Agency in secondary and further education, and by the Quality Assurance Agency in higher education.

Most institutional teaching and learning strategies embrace these four qualities in the aspirations of colleges and universities. But hang on – why have we all got 'teaching and learning' strategies in our institutions? Why have most institutions got 'teaching and learning' committees? (Or, indeed, 'learning and teaching' committees – small difference?) Why haven't we got 'teaching, learning and assessment' strategies – or, indeed, 'assessment, learning and teaching' committees, which would be the way round I would name them? Because assessment is the weakest link, I suggest. It's much easier (and safer) to fiddle around with the quality of teaching or learning than to tackle the big one: assessment. It's actually quite hard to *prove* that some teaching has been unsatisfactory, but only too easy to demonstrate when something has gone wrong with assessment. But, as shown below, there are significant shortfalls in the extent to which many of the most common assessment practices measure up to bringing these qualities to bear on assessment.

Validity?

Valid assessment is about measuring that which we should be trying to measure. But still too often, we don't succeed in this intention. We measure what we can. We measure echoes of what we're trying to measure. We measure ghosts of the manifestation of the achievement of learning outcomes by learners. Whenever we're just ending up measuring what they *write* about what they *remember* about what they once *thought* (or what we once *said* to them in our classes), we're measuring ghosts. Now, if we were measuring what they could now *do* with what they'd *processed* from what they thought, it would be better.

'But we *do* measure this!' Ask learners, they know better than anyone else in the picture exactly what we end up measuring. For a start, let's remind ourselves that we're very hung up on measuring what learners *write*. We don't say in our learning outcomes 'When you've studied this module you'll be able to write neatly, quickly and eloquently about it so as to demonstrate to us your understanding of it'. And what do we actually measure? We measure, to at least some extent, the neatness, speed and eloquence of learners' writing. What about those who aren't good at writing? Or to be more critical, what about those learners who have at least some measure of *disability* when it comes to writing?

In the UK, the writing is on the wall for us regarding any tendency for our assessment instruments and processes to discriminate against learners with disabilities. Since 2002, the Special Educational Needs and Disabilities Act (SENDA) and subsequent amendments to disability legislation have caused us to make far-reaching changes to our assessment just to keep it within the law. We are required to make 'reasonable adjustments' so that no learner should be unfairly discriminated against by our education provision, not least the assessment-related aspects of this provision. Legislation also requires these reasonable adjustments to be made in an *anticipatory* manner. In other words, they should not just deal with instances of discrimination when they are found to have happened. This is a tricky situation, as in one sense the purpose of assessment *is* to *discriminate* between learners, and to find which learners have mastered the syllabus best, and least, and so on. If we're honestly discriminating in terms of ability, that might be lawful. But if we're discriminating in terms of disability, it won't be lawful. But aren't they the same thing? Where does ability stop and disability begin?

For a long time already, there have been those of us strongly arguing the case for diversifying assessment, so that the same learners aren't discriminated against *repeatedly* because they don't happen to be skilled at those forms of assessment that we over-use (such as, in some disciplines, tutor-marked, time-constrained, unseen, written examinations, tutor-marked coursework essays and tutor-marked practical reports).

We're entering an era where *inclusive* assessment will be much more firmly on the agenda than it has ever been to date. We now know much more about the manifestations of dyslexia in assessment, and are beginning to work out the effects of dyscalcula, dysgraphia, dyspraxia, and so on. Many of us are beginning to realize for the first time that, even in that packed lecture theatre, we do have learners with disabilities, not just the occasional learner visibly in a wheelchair, but perhaps a quarter or a third of our learners who are affected at some times in their learning by factors which we don't know about and which many of them don't even know about themselves. So is it ever going to be possible for us, in our assessment practices, to be satisfied with the levels of validity to which we aspire?

So we're not really in a position to be self-satisfied regarding the validity of even our most used, and most practised, assessment instruments and processes. But the situation isn't new – we've used these devices for ever it seems. That doesn't make them more valid, but we are experienced in using them. Admittedly, that makes us better able to make the best of a bad job with them. But should we not be making a better job with something else?

Reliability?

For many, this word is synonymous with 'fairness' and 'consistency'. Reliability is easier than validity to put to the test. If several assessors mark the same piece of work and all agree (within reasonable error limits) about the grade or mark, we can claim we're being reliable. This is not just moderation, of course. Reliability can only be tested by blind multiple marking. Double marking is about as far as we usually manage to get. And, of course, we agree often enough, don't we? No we don't, in many disciplines.

There are some honourable exceptions. 'Hard' subjects, such as areas of maths and science, lend themselves better to measures of agreement regarding reliability than 'softer' subjects, such as literature, history, philosophy, psychology, you name it. By 'hard' and 'soft' I don't mean 'difficult' and 'easy' – far from it. Not surprisingly, staff are resistant to the suggestion that they may need to undertake yet more marking. 'But multiple marking just causes regression to the mean' can be the reply. 'And after all, the purpose of assessment is to sort learners out – to discriminate between them – so it's no use everyone just ending up with a middle mark.' 'And besides, we spend quite long enough at the assessment grindstone; we just haven't room in our lives for more marking.'

Sadler (2009a) suggests four propositions which have a bearing on the difficulties we face in ensuring that assessment is reliable. He proposes:

(1) Students deserve to have their work graded strictly according to its quality, without their responses to the same or similar tasks being compared with those of other students in their group, and without regard to the students' individual histories of previous achievement.

(2) Students deserve to know the basis on which judgements are made about the quality of their work. There should be few if any surprises.

(3) Students deserve their grades to have comparable value across courses in the academic program in which they enrol, and across the institution. Courses should not exhibit characteristically tough or lenient grading.

(4) Students deserve grades that are broadly comparable across institutions and maintain value over time, so that the standing of their educational qualifications is protected not only by the college or university in which they study, but also in higher education as a social institution. (Sadler, 2009a: 809)

Sadler's propositions here show that there is much more to be achieved, in the context of reliability, than simply reliability within the marking of a set of assignments.

So why else is reliability so important? Not least, because assessing learners' work is the single most important thing we ever do for them. Many staff in education regard themselves as teachers, with assessment as an additional chore (not to mention those who regard themselves as *researchers*, with teaching and assessing as additional chores). Perhaps if we were all to be called *assessors* rather than teachers it would help? And perhaps better still, if we all regarded ourselves as researchers into assessment, alongside anything else we were researching into, it would help more? 'Students can escape bad teaching, but they can't escape bad assessment' says David Boud (1995).

In countries with a degree classification system, our assessments can end up with learners getting first-class degrees or thirds. This affects the rest of their lives. Now if our assessment were really fair (reliable), we could sleep easily about who got firsts or thirds. The learners who worked hardest would get better degrees and the learners who lazed around wouldn't. This indeed is often the case, but most of us can think of exceptions, where learners got good degrees but didn't really deserve them, or where learners who seemed worthy of good degrees didn't come up with the goods in the assessed components of their courses, so we couldn't award these to them. So perhaps it's not just that our assessment isn't too reliable, it's our discrimination that's sometimes faulty too. In the UK, at last, the question is now being asked: 'Is our degree classification system actually fit for purpose?'

When the Burgess Report (Burgess, 2004) was published, Rebecca Smithers, education editor of the *Guardian*, wrote in November 2004:

> The 200-year-old system of awarding students degrees classified as firsts, upper seconds and so on could be scrapped under recommendations published by a government-appointed review today. The body set up by the government to evaluate existing ways of measuring students' achievement has concluded that the system fails to provide adequate differentiation of performance and give employers the information they need. (Smithers, 2004)

However, the Burgess Committee was asked to think further about the classification system, and in the Burgess Group final report (Burgess, 2007), while retaining many of the former reservations about the system, the report proposed:

> Replacing the current honours degree classification system represents a major upheaval for the sector and other stakeholders and the Steering Group insisted that there must be clear, and clearly understood, benefits at the root of any change it proposed. The Group consulted the sector on the possibility of using either a shortened or a lengthened scale of degree classification. Neither stakeholders generally, nor the sector itself, coalesced around a particular approach. On the whole, respondents tended to suggest changes within the current system rather than considering a new system. This reinforced the Group's resolve to ensure that its proposals should build on existing practice that the sector could develop. (Burgess, 2007: 8)

Transparency?

One way of describing 'transparency' is the extent to which learners know where the goalposts are. The goalposts, we may argue, are laid down by the intended learning outcomes, matched nicely to the assessment criteria which specify the standards to which these intended outcomes are to be demonstrated by learners, and also specify the forms in which learners will present evidence of their achievement of the outcomes. There's a nice sense of closure matching up assessment criteria to intended learning outcomes. But how well do learners themselves appreciate these links? How well, indeed, do assessors themselves consciously exercise their assessment-decision judgements to consolidate these links? Learners often admit that one of their main problems is that they still don't really know where the goalposts lie, even despite our best efforts to spell out syllabus content in terms of intended learning outcomes in course handbooks and to illustrate to learners during our teaching the exact nature of the associated assessment criteria – and sometimes even our attempts to clarify the evidence indicators associated with achievement of the learning outcomes are not clear enough to learners. In other words, learners often find it hard to get their heads inside our assessment culture – the very culture which will determine the level of their awards.

The learners who have least problems with this are often the ones who do well in assessment. Or is it that they do well in assessment *because* they have got their minds into our assessment culture? Is it that we're discriminating positively in the case of those learners who manage this? Is this the ultimate assessment criterion? In systems with degree classification, is it *this* difference which is the basis of deciding between a first and a third? And is this the *real* learning outcome, the achievement of which we're measuring? If so, is this stated transparently in the course handbook?

Therefore, we're not too hot on achieving transparency either. In fact, the arguments above can be taken as indicating that we rather often fail ourselves on all three – validity, reliability and transparency – when considered separately. What, then, is our probability of getting all three right at the same time? Indeed, is it even *possible* to get all three right at the same time?

Authenticity?

This one seems straightforward. It's about (on one level, at least) knowing that we're assessing the work of the candidate, not other people's work. In traditional, time-constrained, unseen written exams, we can be fairly sure that we are indeed assessing the work of each candidate, provided we ensure that unfair practices, such as cheating or copying, are prevented. But what about coursework? In the age of the internet, word processing and electronic communication, learners can purchase and download ready-made essays and incorporate elements from these into their own work. Some such practices can be detected electronically, but the most skilful plagiarists can remain one step ahead of us and make sufficient adjustments to the work they have found or bought to prevent us from seeing that it is not their own work.

Plagiarism is becoming one of the most significant problems which coursework assessors find themselves facing. Indeed, the difficulties associated with plagiarism are so severe that there is considerable pressure to retreat into the relative safety of traditional, unseen written exams once again, and we are coming round full circle to resorting to assessment processes and instruments which can guarantee authenticity but at the expense of validity.

However, probably too much of the energy which is being put into tackling plagiarism is devoted to *detecting* the symptoms and punishing those found guilty of unfairly passing off other people's work as their own. After all, where are the moral and ethical borderlines? In many parts of the world, to quote back a teacher's words in an exam answer or coursework assignment is culturally accepted as 'honouring the teacher'. When learners from these cultures, who happen to be continuing their studies in the UK, find themselves accused of plagiarism, they are surprised at our attitude. Prevention is better than the cure. We need to be much more careful to explain exactly what is acceptable and what is not. While some learners may deliberately engage in plagiarism, many others find themselves in trouble because they were not fully aware of how they are expected to treat other people's work. Sometimes they simply do not fully understand how they are expected to cite others' work in their own discussions, or how to follow the appropriate referencing conventions.

It is also worth facing up to the difficulty of the question 'Where are the borderlines between originality and authenticity?' In a sense, true originality is extremely rare. In most disciplines, it is seldom possible to write anything without having already been influenced by what has been done before, what has been read, what has been heard, and so on.

In this discussion of authenticity, I have so far only taken up the matter of *ownership* of assessed work. There is, however, another aspect of authenticity – the extent to which the work being assessed relates to the real world beyond post-compulsory education. In this respect, authenticity is about making assessed tasks as close as possible to the performances that learners will need to develop in their lives and careers in the real world.

Why is now the time to move towards fixing assessment?

By now, you may be convinced that assessment is broken in higher education. OK, there's a problem, but we've just not got enough time to fix it? *Why* haven't we got time to fix it? Because we're so busy doing, to the best of our ability and with integrity and professionalism, the work which spins off from our existing patterns of assessment, so busy indeed that we haven't left ourselves time to face up to the weaknesses of what we're doing? Or we simply *dare not* face up to the possibility that we may be making such a mess of such an important area of our work? It can help to pause and reflect on just how we got into this mess in the first place.

A couple of decades ago, the proportion of the 18–21 year-old population of the UK participating in higher education was in single figures; now it's well on the way to 50 per cent. When it was only 5 per cent, it could be argued that the average ability of those learners who participated in higher education was higher, and they were better able to fend for themselves in the various assessment formats they experienced. Indeed, they usually got into higher education in the first place because they'd already shown to some extent that they'd got at least a vestigial mastery of the assessment culture (from the tips of their pens at least). Now, there are far more learners who haven't yet made it in getting their heads around our assessment culture, let alone gearing themselves up to demonstrate their achievement within it.

At the same time, when we were busy assessing just a few per cent of the population, we had time to try to do it well, using the time-honoured traditional assessment devices at our disposal. Trying to do the same for five or ten times as many learners is just not on. We can't do it. We can't do it well enough. We're assessing far too much to do it reliably, for a start.

And what about the learners? Their lives are dominated by assessment. The intelligent response to this (thank goodness our learners remain intelligent) is to become strategic. In other words, if there aren't any marks associated with some learning, strategic learners will skip that bit of learning. If it counts, they'll do it. It's easy to go with the flow, and make everything important 'count' so that learners will try to do all of it. But in the end this just leads to surface learning, quickly forgotten as the next instalment of assessment looms up. We're in danger of using assessment to *stop* learning instead of to start learning. It's no use us bemoaning the increased extent to which learners have become strategic when our assessment is the cause of this.

Who *owns* the problem of fixing assessment in post-compulsory education?

We can only ever really *solve* problems which we own. But the assessment problem is so widely owned. It's dangerously easy to feel there's just nothing that any one constituency among 'the owners of the problem' can do about it. It's easy enough to identify scapegoats, including:

- professional bodies, in whose name we feel we need to stick to the status quo

- pre-university education systems, which cast the die and train pupils into particular expectations of learning and assessment

- institutional, faculty and departmental assessment regulations, which limit our room for manoeuvre

- teaching and learning strategies, which are so detailed and all-encompassing that we can't suspend belief and start afresh again

- heads of department or school, who are often seen (sometimes wrongly) to be content with the status quo

- external examiners, who would have to be convinced when radical changes may need to be made (despite the fact that the best of these would welcome us making these changes)

- learners themselves who could or would complain about rapid changes to the level of the playing field or the position of the goalposts (even if the whole field is enveloped in thick fog at present)

- the world outside academe, where there's a view about what a graduate should be, and so on (sometimes held deeply by those who prospered under the older order of things)

- journalists, broadcasters and editors, who would give us a hard time if anything were to be found wrong in the way we did the job we are paid to do

- politicians and policy-makers, who got to where they are by succeeding in the system of assessment we already have, and dare not admit that it might have been flawed

- parents, employers, taxpayers and others, who foot the bill for education.

However, if we're perfectly frank about it, each assessment judgement is almost always initially made in the mind of one assessor in the first instance. True, it may well then be tempered by comparisons with judgements made in other people's minds, but to a large extent assessment remains dominated by single acts of decision-making in single minds, just as the evidence which is assessed is usually that arising from the product of a single learner's mind at a given time within a given brief. Living on a crowded planet may be a collaborative game, but we tend to play the assessment game in predominantly singular circumstances, and competitive ones at that.

The fact of the matter is that to fix assessment in post-compulsory education will require individuals to change what they do, but that won't be enough to change the culture. Teams of individuals with a shared realization of the problem will need to be the first step.

How can we fix assessment?

We need to work out a strategy. But any strategy has to be made up of a suitably chosen array of tactics. Sometimes it's easier to start thinking of the tactics first. What could be a shopping list of tactics to play with for starters in the mission to get assessment right in post-compulsory education? They include:

- getting learners into our assessment culture, by using peer assessment and self-assessment more, so that learners are better tuned into our assessment culture when *we* assess them

- reducing the quantity of assessment (say by a factor of three) so that *we* have time to do it well, and learners have time for their learning not to be completely driven by assessment

- increasing the quality of assessment, so that it is fit for purpose and more valid, more reliable, more authentic and more transparent

- increasing the diversity of assessment instruments and processes, so that learner casualties (where particular learners are discriminated against repeatedly by the same old assessment formats) are not so frequent

- training (yes, training, not just educating) our learners to be better able to play the game of working out where the goalposts are, and practising how to demonstrate their achievement of our intended learning outcomes

- training (not leaving it to the chance of them becoming educated) our assessors to tackle head-on the problems we know about, and make assessment fit for purpose.

To sum up the problems with assessment, therefore, there are two principal weaknesses in assessment in post-compulsory education at present:

- Assessment often drives learning away from what we might agree would be *good* learning.

- Despite the importance of assessment, we're not very good at getting it right!

So what can *you* do to fix assessment?

Turning tactics into a strategy is a big job, and beyond the scope of a single chapter in a book such as this. I have, however, added a new interrogation tool – 'Towards assessment *as* learning' – to this chapter to help you to analyse particular examples of assessment, as a start towards making them better. Meanwhile, that big job won't even get started unless people are convinced that it needs to be done, and that has been the purpose of this chapter so far. My intention in this chapter has been to employ challenging language to convince you that you've got a problem regarding changing assessment so that it makes learning happen in post-compulsory education.

What are *you* going to do about it? I suggest that we can improve things by interrogating our various assessment processes and practices, putting them under the spotlight and looking hard at what exactly they measure. But, perhaps more importantly, we can analyse how they relate to how learners learn in post-compulsory education. This is the way forward to adjusting our assessment to contribute positively to making learning happen, rather than to continue to allow surface or reproductive learning to be the outcome of post-compulsory education. With this in mind, I would like you to consider how the assessment processes and instruments which you use contribute to making learning happen for your learners.

4.2 Analysis of particular assessment processes

In the analysis which follows, I am selecting two of the most common assessment processes, traditional exams and essays, and suggesting how they may impact on the seven factors underpinning successful learning. Although I am only interrogating two of the available assessment processes and instruments, they presently represent a large proportion of the assessment in post-compulsory education in the UK, for example, and I hope that this may help you to look in a similar way at other assessment processes you employ, and think through the implications in parallel to my analysis below. The analysis which follows is based not just on my work helping teaching staff in post-compulsory education to develop assessment processes and instruments, but even more on my parallel work over three decades in helping learners to develop the skills they need to demonstrate their optimum performance in a range of different assessment conditions and environments.

Traditional exams

In particular, let's take the example of time-constrained, unseen written examinations. In other words, candidates don't know the questions until they see them in the exam room. They work against the clock, on their own, with pen and paper. Assessment systems in the UK are quite dominated by this kind of assessment, usually at the end point of increments of learning. The assessment can therefore be described as summative.

As an assessment process, exams can be *reliable* – if there is a well-constructed marking scheme, each candidate can be reasonably confident that the marking will be fair and consistent.

The main problem with many traditional exams is that they don't rate highly on *validity*. In other words, too often they measure what the candidate can *write* about what they have learned, in the relatively artificial conditions of solemn silence, against the clock. Where, however, exams are based on problem-solving, case study analysis, and so on, validity can be much higher.

Exams can be improved in terms of *transparency* where candidates have been involved in applying assessment criteria to their own or other people's exam answers, and have found out all they need to know about how the examiner's mind works.

One of the major advantages of exams is that we are reasonably certain (with due precautions) that the work of the learner is being marked – in other words, that side of *authenticity* is assured. The other side of authenticity, however – the extent to which the assessed performance relates to the normal conditions in which the learning is intended to be applied – is less assured, and in some traditional exams the conditions under which achievement are measured are quite alien.

1 Traditional exams and wanting to learn

For many exam candidates, the 'want' to learn is damaged by the mere thought of looming exams. Many learners, if given the choice, go for learning modules that are continuously assessed rather than assessed by examination because of their fear – and even dread – of exams. Few assessment processes induce such high emotions.

This is not the case for everyone, however. Some candidates love exams – and are very good at preparing for them and doing them. Not surprisingly, the cue-seekers mentioned earlier in this chapter are among those who are good at traditional exams. Their cue-seeking approach is thus rewarded by this pervasive assessment format.

2 Traditional exams and needing to learn

This is where the intended learning outcomes should come into their own. Ideally, if learners have systematically prepared to demonstrate their achievement of these outcomes, and practised doing so sufficiently, they should automatically remain able to demonstrate the same achievements under time-constrained, written exam conditions. However, there is often a gulf between the intended learning outcomes as published and what is *actually* measured by traditional exams. Due attention to achieving constructive alignment can overcome this problem.

But there is another side to needing to learn. Candidates who prepare successfully for exams by mastering the intended learning outcomes so that they can demonstrate their achievement in answering likely exam questions often concentrate very firmly on what they perceive they need to learn, and don't invest time or energy in things they decide can't (or won't) come up in the exams. We are therefore favouring strategic learners by the use of exams (and, of course, cue-seeking strategic learners do best).

3 Traditional exams and learning by doing

There is plenty of learning by doing *before* traditional exams. But not much further learning by doing happens *during* traditional exams. It can, however, be claimed that a looming exam is as good a way as any of causing learners to get their heads down and do some learning. We could argue, however, that preparing for an oral exam (viva) would have just as much effect on learning by doing.

4 Traditional exams and learning through feedback

This is where traditional exams do really badly. As far as feedback is concerned, they are mostly lost opportunities. By the time the scripts are marked, learners have often moved on to the next part of their learning and are no longer really interested in which questions they answered well and why, or (more importantly) in where they lost marks. Many learners were *very* interested in these matters immediately *after* the exam, and spent some hours in post-mortem mode trying to work out how their answers measured up to what was being looked for by their examiners.

All the feedback that most learners receive – after some time – is their score, or their grade, or simply whether they passed or failed. It is feedback of a sort, but hardly formative feedback. We can, of course, argue that exams are intended to be summative measures, but they still seem to represent lost feedback opportunities. Where feedback *is* provided very quickly after an exam (for example, in computer-marked multiple-choice exams, where a feedback print-out can be handed to each candidate on leaving the exam room), feedback can, indeed, play a much more powerful role even in summative testing.

5 Traditional exams and making sense of what is being learned

This, too, links badly to traditional exams. As with learning by doing, a great deal of making sense of the subject matter occurs *before* an exam and, indeed, could be argued to be happening *because of* the exam. But few exam candidates report later that the moment when the light dawned was *during* the exam. More often, they report that they only found out that the light *had not* dawned during the exam.

And then we need to ask whether traditional exams are measuring the extent to which learners have made sense of what they learned. Too often, exams seem to measure what learners can *reproduce* rather than what they can *do*. Many learners can tell us about the frequent occasions where surface learning was all that they needed to engage in to address the task of answering a particular exam question.

6 Traditional exams and learning through teaching, coaching, explaining

In Chapter 2, we explored the significant benefits to learners resulting from them explaining things to each other, coaching each other, and so on. One of my worries about traditional exams is that learners tend to go into competitive mode, and hide their learning achievements from each other rather than celebrating such achievements. We can, of course, try to counter this tendency, and encourage learners to work together in their preparation for exams, quizzing each other, explaining things to each other, and so on, providing good rehearsal for doing similar things on their own in the exam room.

7 Traditional exams and learning through assessing – making informed judgements

We could argue that in the context of traditional exams, most of this kind of learning occurs in the minds of examiners, not learners! Too often, *exactly how* the informed judgements are made by examiners is hidden from learners; examiners seem to fear the consequences of sharing with learners details of how marking schemes work in practice, possibly dreading future appeals by learners against 'academic judgement'. We can indeed encourage learners to self-assess practice exam performance, and to peer-assess each other's practice as they head towards exams, but the competitive ethos of exams militates against them doing either of these wholeheartedly. Moreover, there is fear involved – fear of finding out that the performance is not going to be up to the standards desired – and this can lead to self-fulfilling prophecy and lower attainment in exams.

Perhaps the main problem regarding learning through making informed judgements in the context of traditional exams is that such assessments are often the 'mystery black box' in nature, where learners do the best they can, hoping it will be found to be satisfactory or better. Other assessment formats tend to be more open to learners regarding exactly how they work (though this is not always the case).

Traditional exams: summary

The picture painted above of the links between traditional exams and the factors underpinning successful learning is very bleak. It does not *have to be* so bleak, however. With care, for example, exams can be designed which are much better at measuring 'making sense' than suggested above. Problem-solving exams and case study exams are much better at *not* rewarding reproductive learning. But the concerns remain about the damage that can be inflicted on many candidates' *want* to learn, the artificial way that exams can skew the *need* to learn and the fact that so much work may be done by examiners making sure that the exams have been fair and reliable, yet very little feedback usually reaches learners. In some ways, it seems that traditional exams are diametrically opposed to all of the central factors underpinning successful learning! Couple this to the problems of achieving validity, reliability and transparency, and it is surprising that in some assessment cultures (including much post-compulsory education provision in the UK) traditional exams continue to hold sway to the extent that they do.

Other kinds of exams

The discussion above focused on the most common kind of exams – against-the-clock, written exams, and with candidates not seeing the questions until they sit at their exam desks. There are, however, many other kinds of exam, which overcome some of the problems about reliability, validity, transparency and authenticity in suitable contexts and discipline areas. These alternatives can also be thought of in terms of the seven factors underpinning successful learning, and some 'food for thought' implications are summarized below for just two of the alternatives.

Computer-marked multiple-choice exams

If candidates are aware that it is their decision-making that will be measured rather than their ability to put their knowledge into words in writing, then *wanting* to learn will not be threatened as much as it is by traditional exams. Ownership of the relevant *need* to learn can also be improved, so long as learners become practised and rehearsed regarding *which aspects* of their achievement of the intended learning outcomes can indeed be measured by this sort of exam. *Learning by doing* in such exams is primarily of the decision-making variety, but with skilful attention to the design of questions and option choices, decision-making can cumulatively be used to yield a good measure of the extent to which learners have *made sense* of what they have learned. At least we can be assured that the *learning by doing* that is measured by computer-assisted assessment is not skewed by such mundane factors as the speed of handwriting or its legibility. Perhaps the most significant link between computer-assisted assessment and making learning happen is *feedback*. There are many possibilities. Learners can be provided with on-screen feedback as they go through a computer-based exam, allowing them to avoid the possibility of carrying forward errors of thinking into their answers to the next questions they meet. Or they can be given feedback on-screen or in print-outs at the end of each exam, when at least the feedback is quick enough for them to still remember what their thinking – and their decisions – were as they answered the questions. The availability of speedy and specific feedback can help learners to *make sense* of the subject matter they have been working with, admittedly too late for the computer-based exam they have just undertaken, but better late than not at all. Learning by *making informed judgements* is of course involved in multiple-choice exams, especially when there is plenty of this kind of practice in advance of the actual test. Learning by *explaining* can be involved if much of this practice is done in small groups of students, discussing the reasoning for choosing particular options.

OSCEs

Objective structured clinical examinations (OSCEs) are widely used in medical education and health care studies, and lend themselves to many other disciplines where practical *doing* is important in the intended learning outcomes. Essentially, OSCEs are exams where each candidate *does* something at each of a number of assessment stations located around the exam room. In medicine, for example, candidates may visit successive stations and perform a series of assessed tasks, such as:

- interpreting some X-rays
- looking through a set of notes on a patient and approaching a diagnosis

- prescribing medication for a given condition in a given context

- briefing a ward sister about the pre-operative preparation of a patient

- talking to a patient to diagnose a condition (though in practice the 'patient' is an actor, as it is hard to get real patients to tell the same story to successive doctors).

The key claim made for OSCEs is that the assessment is valid, in that candidates are assessed on exactly the sorts of things they have been intended to become able to *do* in practice and not just on what they may have written in traditional exams about hypothetical cases.

Clearly, OSCEs link closely to learning by doing – practice, repetition and trial and error. Furthermore, the more feedback candidates get on their practice before such an exam, the more they can improve their performance. OSCEs also link strongly to well-defined *needing to learn* agendas, and as practitioners can see the relevance of developing their skills and knowledge to cope with such situations, the *want* to learn is enhanced. The variety of tasks which can be built into an OSCE add to the depth of *making sense* of what is being learned and assessed, as triangulation is possible, approaching key tasks from different angles. While it can take a considerable amount of time to design a good OSCE, when candidate numbers are large, this is time well spent, and the time spent *marking* an OSCE can be much less than a corresponding written exam, not least because most of the assessment decisions can be made at the assessment stations while the exam is in progress. In practice, it is wise to get groups of learners to design OSCE scenarios – they will often design better ones than we can! This also maximizes the learning pay-off they gain from discussing and arguing with each other, and making informed judgements about the material involved and the assessment criteria being addressed.

Essays

In some subject areas (notable exceptions include maths, science and technology-based disciplines), essays are key elements of both coursework and exams. We can again pose questions about how successfully essays relate to validity, reliability, transparency and authenticity. Essays do not do very well as an assessment method on such interrogation.

There are particular problems with *reliability* where subjectivity in marking is all too easily present and inter-marker reliability is a problem (different markers giving the same essay different marks), as also is intra-marker reliability (the same marker giving the same essay different marks on different occasions – for example, among the first half-dozen marked or the last half-dozen marked).

Validity is perhaps the weakest link for essays as an assessment device. If we look hard at 'what are we *really* measuring?', it is often essay-writing *skills* rather than mastery of the subject matter concerned. Academics often defend the importance of essay-writing skills, but in practice for most learners, these tend to be skills that they are unlikely to need when they leave post-compulsory education, unless they too are heading towards becoming academics! Moreover, writing scholarly contributions to the literature involves much more than essay-writing skills – not least addressing fully the intended target audience of the writing. Writing for the examiner is just a special case of this wider picture.

Transparency can be improved a lot by involving learners in self-assessing and peer-assessing essays so that they become much more aware of how marks are earned and lost, and how the assessment criteria work in practice – and, indeed, how the assessment links to the associated intended learning outcomes.

Authenticity is more problematic. At least in exam-based essays we can be reasonably certain whose work is being marked, but in coursework essays we can't. However, in time-constrained essay-type exams we are perhaps penalizing the slower learners – perhaps by measuring speed of writing rather than quality of thought. The other side of authenticity – the link between essays and the context in which learning may be intended to be applied – is also problematic. There are many learners in post-compulsory education who will never again put pen to paper (or fingers to keyboard) to compose an essay after leaving education.

Meanwhile, let's continue with our analysis of how essays may relate to the seven factors underpinning successful learning. I should point out at once that there are *very* significant differences here between coursework essays (with feedback in due course) and exam-based essays. As many factors relating to the latter overlap with what I've already said about traditional exams, the discussion which follows is mostly about the coursework essays.

1 Essays and wanting to learn

The effects here are widely variable. Some learners really enjoy 'sorting out their minds' by putting pen to paper to construct essays, particularly when they then get detailed and helpful feedback on their learning. Such feedback is unlikely to be forthcoming for exam-based essays. For other learners, actually getting round to putting pen to paper (or fingers to keyboard) is a major challenge. Ask a group of learners 'What was your best work-avoidance tactic that you used to delay starting to put together that essay?' and you will soon see how, for some learners, the task of getting started was the daunting part.

2 Essays and needing to learn

On one level, essays help learners to take ownership of the need to learn, by giving them something to do to cause them to get their heads into the books and resources relating to the task. However, the agenda of taking ownership of the intended learning outcomes is less successfully addressed, as all too often the links between these outcomes and a particular essay-writing task are not spelled out clearly enough in the briefings learners receive.

3 Essays and learning by doing

Essays certainly involve learning by doing. There are several kinds of *doing* in play, including information retrieval and sorting, planning, communicating in writing, comparing and contrasting ideas, making decisions and judgements, and summarizing. So this aspect of learning can be regarded as being satisfactorily addressed by the use of essays. Similarly, during the processes of drafting and redrafting an essay, a great deal of reflection and deepening of ideas can take place, and the act of writing the essay becomes much more than simply learning by doing.

However, it is worth asking how many of the same aspects of learning by doing are involved in constructing *essay plans* rather than fully-fledged essays. Such plans may miss out on some of the finer points of communicating in writing and on the reflective dimension, but making essay plans can involve many of the other important aspects of learning by doing. And if, let us suppose, 10 essay plans can be produced in the same time as it takes to write one fully-fledged essay, the learning pay-off associated with writing essay plans becomes all the more attractive.

Where, however, essays are primarily being used to train learners in the arts of marshalling their ideas, presenting them coherently and logically, and coming to a well-thought out conclusion or summary, and these are the primary intended learning outcomes, writing full essays will meet these aims to a much greater extent than simply preparing essay plans.

4 Essays and learning through feedback

Coursework essays can be very valuable in the context of making feedback available to learners. Feedback in general is discussed in more detail in the next chapter of this book. Meanwhile, it is worth bearing in mind that the timing and nature of the feedback on formative essays need to be managed well for optimum learning through feedback. It can be well worth considering ensuring that at least some of the feedback can be intentionally developmental. For example, if an essay is 'marked' three times, once where feedback is given on an essay plan, again when a rough draft is submitted and, finally, when the last version of the essay is completed, feedback on the first two stages can lead to much higher quality in the final products. This clearly takes extra assessor time, but the two earlier feedback stages do not need to be quantitatively 'marked', and can be required simply as conditions to be satisfied before the final essay version is submitted.

5 Essays and making sense of what is being learned

Coursework essays coupled with formative feedback can be very valuable in helping learners to get their heads around ideas and concepts, and also in helping them make sense of other people's ideas from the literature. It is often the act of trying to communicate an idea which causes the human brain to clarify it and put it into perspective. This is equally true of oral responses, but writing out ideas and progressively making them more coherent is probably one of the best ways of causing reflection and deepening learning. 'I don't know what I think until I've written about it' is said by many authors, who recognize the value of putting ideas down on paper as a way of helping the brain to make sense of them. Coursework essays can also cause learners to find and retrieve information from the literature and from other sources, and then to sift it and analyse it, and distil from the source materials their own conclusions or thinking about a topic, issue or question.

6 Essays and learning by explaining, coaching, teaching

Though coursework essays do indeed involve the development of skills of *written* explaining, essay-writing tends to be a somewhat solitary activity, and learners are rather unlikely to spontaneously involve themselves in explaining things to each other or coaching each other, especially if the competitive nature of assessment-by-essays is in the forefront of their consciousness. We can, of course, encourage learners to think that their final essays are likely to be much better if they have spent a fair amount of time and energy working together at least before nearing their final drafts, but both learners and assessors have justified worries that at least some plagiarism may happen.

7 Essays and learning through assessing – making informed judgements

More often than not, it's the assessors who gain all of this learning – not the learners. This can be counteracted by well-planned use of peer assessment, allowing learners to benefit from seeing work that is better than their own and worse than their own. Furthermore, learners can be encouraged to undertake self-assessment of their coursework essays, using the same criteria as will be used by their assessors. This practice can also help them to become more self-assessing when they come to write essays in exams.

Essays: summary

As can be seen from the above analysis, essays used formatively in a coursework context (rather than summatively in exam contexts) can involve many of the seven factors underpinning successful learning. Perhaps partly because they are time-consuming to plan, draft and polish, they are perhaps better than many assessment-related artefacts in enabling reflection and consolidation (important aspects of 'making sense'). They are, however, often solitary learning journeys, at least until the points where feedback is received. Peer-review, peer-assessment and peer-editing processes can be used profitably to enable learners to benefit from feedback along the way.

Beyond exams and essays

What other assessment choices can we think about? Brown and Knight (1994) identified over 80 alternatives to exams and essays. I will only list a few alternatives here, with just the briefest of indications about how these may link more successfully to some or all of the factors underpinning successful learning.

Question banks

Question banks are where learners compile a list of a specified number (for example, 300) of short, sharp questions about a topic or subject, and make a parallel list of answers to the questions or clues leading towards the answers. My own experience shows that this increases learners' *want* to learn, as it helps them break down the daunting task of getting to grips with a topic area into the more manageable steps of working out what questions they need to become able to answer, and linking the questions to the answers. Those learners who do not revel in trying to write in sophisticated language like the fact that the questions are intended to be short and direct, and the quality of a question bank depends on the relevance of the questions rather than the use of language.

Question banks also give learners a high sense of ownership of the *need* to learn, as they translate the meaning of the intended learning outcomes into a practical tool which they can use to develop their ability to achieve the outcomes. *Learning by doing* is involved in making a question bank in the first place. Then it lends itself to practice, repetition and trial and error as learners put it to use. What is more, they have control and ownership of all stages of the learning by doing. Learners get immediate feedback as they use their question banks, especially when they use them with fellow learners quizzing them with the questions and checking whether their answers are satisfactory. All this practice and repetition does a great deal to help learners to *make sense* of the subject matter covered by the questions and answers, at least to the extent of equipping them to be better able to answer questions in traditional exam contexts.

Using a question bank instead of a conventional coursework assignment can get learners to build themselves useful learning tools, where high learning pay-off results both from making the tools in the first place and then practising with them from there onwards.

Annotated bibliographies

Learners can be asked, for example, to select what they consider to be the best 20 sources on a topic, and write just a few lines relating to what they think is most useful (or most important) in each source in turn. This then equips them with a useful learning tool and gives them valuable practice at referencing sources accurately. The task of making an annotated bibliography involves a lot of learning by doing – for example, finding the sources, making decisions about which are the most appropriate sources, then working out what is special to each source.

This in turn causes learners to *make sense of* the subject matter, as they compare and contrast the different viewpoints or emphases of the various sources. As with question banks, there can be much more thinking per hundred words in making an annotated bibliography than just writing an essay or an exam answer. In other words, the learning pay-off can be much higher. Annotated bibliographies can be an excellent way of breaking down a lot of information into useful summaries, and can serve as useful learning tools, aiding revision and preparation for traditional exams.

Presentations

These are often part of an assessment mix. Learners can be asked to prepare a presentation with supporting materials (handouts, slides, sometimes posters) and then give the presentation to an audience of their peers (including tutors). Usually presentations are followed by a question-and-answer session with the audience. When the presentations are peer-assessed, and especially when the learners themselves have been involved in designing the assessment criteria and establishing their respective weighting, they learn not only from preparing and giving their own presentations, but also from applying the criteria to each other's presentations.

Learners often take presentations very seriously, and to some extent preparing and giving their first presentation might damage their *want* to learn, at least temporarily. When learners have ownership of the criteria, however, they feel more positive about the *need* to try to achieve them. There are several aspects of *learning by doing* involved, not least researching the content, preparing the support materials, rehearsing the presentation itself and preparing to be able to answer questions after giving the presentation.

Perhaps the most significant link between presentations and learning is the *making sense* which occurs as a result of their preparation and delivery. Learners are usually able to answer questions on the topic involved long after the event, and their learning about the subject matter can be said to be much deeper than if they had just written an essay or assignment on the topic.

Learners can also gain a great deal of *feedback* during the various processes, not least from fellow learners during rehearsal and during the presentation itself. Further feedback can be provided by tutors or other assessors. The skills which learners develop as a result of preparing and giving presentations, and answering questions about the topic concerned, link strongly to employability. In particular, oral communication skills can be developed and practised alongside the subject-matter learning going on.

4.3 Towards assessment *as* learning

It is widely accepted that in higher education internationally, assessment drives students' learning. As a consequence, students become ever more strategic, and only put energy into things that count towards their overall assessment. The section which follows offers you a practical way of setting about reflecting on the assessment processes and instruments you use. Many institutions have now adopted 'assessment for learning' approaches, to make better links between assessment and learning. I argue here that we can go even further and work towards 'assessment *as* learning', where all of our elements of assessment are designed with learning at the centre of our thinking.

This section provides you with a scoring grid, using which you can interrogate your own assessment elements and determine how well they measure up to a combination of 'assessment for learning' and 'assessment as learning'.

Assessment design: six key terms to address

In this chapter we've already explored four key terms: *validity*, *reliability*, *transparency* and *authenticity*. Now I'd like you to extend this thinking by adding two more factors (which have, of course, already entered into the discussion of assessment presented in this chapter):

- *manageability* – both for us assessors and for learners themselves

- *inclusiveness* – ensuring that no particular categories of learners are disadvantaged significantly by each particular assessment format being used.

Too often, terms like these six are explained in language which does not make addressing them any easier. Also, addressing them all at once is rarely possible, and is at the very least a highly complex balancing act. Later in this section, I will provide straightforward briefings to help you to interrogate your own assessment elements in terms of how well each of these variables is successfully addressed.

Linking assessment to the seven processes underpinning successful learning

We need to set out to address, in our assessment design, the seven factors underpinning successful learning:

1. *Wanting* to learn.

2. Taking ownership of the *need* to learn.

3. *Learning by doing*: practice, trial and error, experimenting, experience, repetition when appropriate.

4. Learning from *feedback*: praise, criticism, seeing the results of learning.

5. *Making sense* of what is being learned: 'getting one's head round it', 'light dawning'.

6. *Explaining* to others, *coaching* others, and *teaching* what has been learned.

7. *Making informed judgements* on one's own work, other people's work, self-assessment and peer assessment.

Within the grid which follows (see page 94), there are 20 decisions to be made for each assessment element of a course or module. The grid contains space to interrogate four separate assessment elements, but it is suggested that you start with a single element (Element A), and work through the discussion in which follows first, using this element (as rehearsal) before returning to further elements of assessment. In this discussion 'element of assessment' simply means any assessed task or activity which counts towards the overall award being studied for, and has marks or grades associated with the level of performance students show in it. Typical examples include those shown below, but any other assessment elements can be considered.

Written exam	Drawing	Oral exam
Presentation	Sculpture	Interview
MCQ exam	Dance	Short-answer exam
Essay	OSCE	Written reflection
Practical test	In-tray exam	Report

For each of the 20 lines of the grid, a decision is to be made on a 1–5 scale. '5' is where the design of the assessment element fits very well indeed with 'assessment as learning' as a goal, or is of very high quality in the context of the variables of 'validity', 'reliability', and so on. In each case, the discussion which follows provides guidance on how decisions may be made on this 1–5 scale.

Why '1–5' rather than '0–5'?

Simply so that an assessment element which is very poor at addressing the assessment variables, and has very little to do with 'assessment as learning', can still have a score – the minimum total score of 20, which can be said to describe an assessment element which has little to do with anything other than assessment *of* learning, and was also poor regarding validity, reliability, and so on.

Why are all the 20 lines interrogated on the same scale of 1–5?

Simply as a first approximation towards balancing the 20 factors considered towards an overall judgement of how well the assessment element approaches the goal of 'assessment as learning'. It is likely that adjustments to this 'equal rating' position will be desirable in future. This grid is simply meant as a starting point towards addressing interrogating assessment on a complex and interrelated set of variables, in a relatively straightforward manner.

Why not just fill in the grid straightaway, without reading further to find out how?

You may, in fact, wish to do this for a chosen element of assessment, and then revisit each item in turn on the basis of the discussion which follows for each line of the grid, to self-assess how well your instinct about your assessment element lines up with the thinking behind the scoring suggestions made in the discussion which follows. However, the meanings of such terms as 'validity', 'reliability', and so on may need to be further clarified in the context of this exercise to allow you to make informed judgements as you interrogate your own assessment elements, and for your scores to be compared to others' scores for their assessment elements, and so on. Furthermore, you would be wise to consult your students to help you make a scoring decision for several of the items in the grid.

   Another reason not to fill the grid in straightaway is that relatively familiar variables, such as validity and reliability, are interspersed with factors relating to the quality of learning associated with the assessment, and the final three lines of the grid refer to the place of this particular assessment element in the overall assessment pattern for the course or module. So the discussion which follows takes you through the agenda in a manner that is intentionally non-linear.

Guidance on making your 1–5 scoring decisions for each item

1 Students love it (wanting to learn)

If the assessment element is one which students dread (possibly a traditional exam) this might warrant a score of '1' – the minimum. If it's the sort of assessment which students really look forward to, and enjoy doing while they are performing it, that would be nearer a '5'. Of course, different students will have different views about how much they enjoy any particular form of assessment, so you may like to ask 20 or more students and average their views to help you to make your 1–5 decision here.

Towards assessment as learning: the 'interrogation' grid

Assessment element	A	B	C	D
Your name:				
Course or module:				
Assessment element A:				
Assessment element B:				
Assessment element C:				
Assessment element D:				
Assessment element	A	B	C	D
Factors relating to the particular assessment element in isolation				
1. Students love it (wanting to learn)				
2. Students learn by doing preparing for it				
3. Students make sense of their learning preparing for it				
4. Students coach each other preparing for it				
5. Students practise making informed judgements				
6. Students design the criteria				
7. Students own the weighting of the criteria				
8. Validity				
9. Reliability				
10. Transparency				
11. Self-authenticity				
12. Real-world authenticity				
13. Manageability – efficiency for students				
14. Manageability – efficiency for you				
15. Inclusiveness				
16. Students get *and use* feedback as a result of it				
17. Alignment: how well it links visibly to learning outcomes				
Factors relating to the particular assessment element in the overall context				
18. Students use several ways of communicating and explaining				
19. Diversity: overall range of assessment types				
20. The 'wow' factor, as gained from student feedback				
Total/100				

2 Students learn by doing preparing for it

This line is about the kind of learning students perform leading up to the assessment (and to some extent also any learning they achieve while actually doing the assessment). The minimum score of '1' would be warranted by any assessment where students merely 'filled their heads up with information' ready to regurgitate it during the assessment itself. This might apply to some traditional written exams in some disciplines, and equally to some kinds of essay or report where the learning by doing is quickly forgotten after the task is completed. Higher scores may be associated with useful practice, problem-solving, explaining things to each other (or to anyone else who would listen), learning by getting things wrong and finding out exactly why, and so on. Decide as honestly as you can the extent to which students' learning is active while preparing for this particular assessment element on the usual scale: 1–5. If you can, ask students themselves.

3 Students make sense of their learning preparing for it

This is linked to but is sufficiently different from '2' above to warrant a separate line on the grid. This is more about *how permanently* students 'get their heads round things' in the way that this assessment causes them to prepare for it. A low score might be warranted if students simply prepare themselves in a way where they are 'OK on the day' and then let their learning slip, perhaps quite intentionally, as they prepare for the next assessment on their schedule. A high score for this item would be where you know that most students prepare for this assessment in a way which really consolidates their learning (and not merely that you *intend* them to prepare in such a way!). You may indeed wish to check this out with a sample of students.

4 Students coach each other preparing for it

This time, the student activity represented by this line is quite explicit. If students are involved in coaching or teaching each other as they work towards this assessment, the score could be as high as '5'. If they prepare entirely on their own, in solemn isolation, it could be '1'. If they're involved in discussing, explaining to each other, and so on, the score could be nearer '5'. Remember, it's what students actually do that governs the score for this, and not necessarily what you *hope* they do. Ask them.

5 Students practise making informed judgements

If students' preparation for this assessment centres mainly around self-assessing their own learning and peer-assessing the products of fellow-students' learning, this would score a '5'. If this assessment does not involve students making informed judgements in such ways, it's more likely to be a '1'. If students do at least some self-assessment or peer assessment, the score might be somewhere between '1' and '5'. Making informed judgements on material from the literature is, of course, still useful (perhaps warranting a score or '2' or '3'), but almost certainly less intense an experience as self-assessing their own work, or peer-assessing each other's work, where their judgements need to be able to be supported by feedback to each other.

6 Students design the criteria

This relates particularly to the extent to which students 'take ownership of the need to learn'. When they have worked together to establish the criteria, the assessment is much more 'owned' by them. When they are using self-assessment and peer assessment, using criteria whose design they have shaped, the ownership is at its best, and a '5' might be warranted for this line. If students have merely been given 'the official criteria', the score might only be '2' or so, and if students have no idea of the exact nature of the criteria, the minimum of '1' might be appropriate here.

7 Students own the weighting of the criteria

While this might at first sight seem to overlap with '6' above, the process of students sorting out what is important and what isn't, in their design of the criteria, has so much to do with their 'making sense' of the topic that this criterion deserves a line of its own. If students have collectively worked out the marking scheme, a '5' may be warranted for this line, especially if this was done in the context of something they self-assessed or peer-assessed.

8 Validity

The crux here is the answer to the question 'Is this assessment really measuring what it is intended to measure?' rather than 'simply measuring what happens to be easily measurable'. For example, a traditional unseen written exam might score a '1' here, if it is just measuring what students can do on their own, in a quiet room, with what comes out of their heads and gets through in handwriting onto their answer scripts legibly enough to score them marks. That said, a written maths exam measures quite well whether students can do maths, and a problem-solving kind of exam does measure whether students can solve some kinds of problems, and the scores could be higher for this line.

However, higher scores may be more readily warranted on the grounds of validity for assessments such as an OSCE (objective structured clinical exam), as used by medical students, where what is measured is essentially what practitioners are intended to be able to do, such as interpreting a set of X-rays, scanning a patient's case notes to arrive at a prescription, talking to a patient (an actor in practice) to work out what is wrong, and so on. Similarly, a presentation may have high validity as an assessment format, if students need not only to master some learning but also to present it authoritatively and clearly to others. An oral exam (viva) may also score highly on validity, if it is felt that this is the most effective way of determining the extent of students' learning. Furthermore, an exam of the 'in-tray' variety may also score highly, as this depends on students making a series of informed decisions based on information supplied to them over the time of the exam.

9 Reliability

This would attract the minimum score of '1' for an assessment element where there are known to be problems regarding two or more people agreeing on the mark or grade for students' work (not least, essays!), but also in forms of assessment which may be more valid than essays, notably portfolios, but where different assessors can often come to quite different judgements. Even dissertations fare quite badly regarding reliability, as different assessors often look for different things while assessing them, and their overall marks can be influenced disproportionately by the presence or lack of particular things. A high score for this line might be associated with (for example) a multiple-choice test or exam, where the scoring is no longer likely to be influenced by human frailty (though the question design may still be!).

10 Transparency

This is about the extent to which students know how the assessment works, and how exactly it is marked, and how scores or grades are reached. If, as far as the students are concerned, it is a 'black box' assessment – they do their best, then find out if that was good enough – the assessment element probably merits the minimum score of '1' here. If it's something where students have had practice at marking examples you've given them, or better still their own or each other's work, the score may be a '5', if they feel they know exactly how the assessment works. It is important to distinguish between 'transparency' and 'familiarity'. For example, students can be quite familiar with traditional exams, while still not knowing exactly how they are marked. The same often goes for essays, dissertations and reports. 'Transparency' here is about how well students have a grasp of what will be going on in the minds of their assessors as they come to assessment judgements about their work.

11 Self-authenticity

This is in part about how well the assessment avoids plagiarism. Here, a traditional exam might score a '5', if precautions are sufficient to ensure that no one can substitute for candidates. Similarly, a solo presentation or an oral exam (viva) may score '5' as an assessment element. Assessment formats where plagiarism is possible score much lower on this line, including essays, reports, dissertations, and other written work, where it is possible for students to copy other people's work, buy or download work from the internet, and so on. In rating your assessment element on 'self-authenticity', it is perhaps wisest to step back from any feelings of 'I'm sure none of my students would do this', or 'The anti-plagiarism software makes this highly unlikely', as the most skilled plagiarists are never caught! For this item, it is best to consider the *possibility* rather than the *probability* of plagiarism occurring when deciding your 1–5 score.

12 Real-world authenticity

This is about how well the assessment element links to the real-world professions students may be qualifying to enter. For example, doctors, lawyers, accountants and managers hardly spend their working lives *writing* about medicine, law, accountancy or management – they *do* it, not write about it. So essays are likely to score a '1' in disciplines such as these, and in several others.

At the other end of the scale, OSCEs (objective structured clinical exams) in medical education are likely to deserve a '5' here, if they are designed to be what doctors need to be able to show that they can do, not just write about. The practical part of a driving test would be high on real-world authenticity, whereas the 'theory' part which accompanies such a test in some countries is more of a memory test and less well-linked to authenticity. (Do you still remember the stopping distance at 50 miles per hour on a wet road?)

13 Manageability – efficiency for students

This is essentially about the value of the time spent by students preparing for the assessment. You may need to ask a sample of your students about your particular assessment element to help you towards your 1–5 rating for this item. How much time do they know they *waste* in their preparations for this assessment? How do they see their time-efficiency relating to this item of assessment in the overall context of the bigger picture of their total assess-ment menu? Both of their answers to these questions need to be informed by how much this assessment element *counts* overall. The score for this item could be as low as '1' if students feel it takes them for ever to prepare for this assessment element, compared to other elements contributing to their overall assessment.

14 Manageability – efficiency for you

Whereas in many of the other items on the grid you may need to consult stu-dents to help you decide how assessment links to their experience of learn-ing, this time you will know only too well how much time and energy the assessment element takes from you. Perhaps one factor to help you decide your 1–5 score for this item is how well you think the time you spend mark-ing this element is well spent, considering the contribution of the element to students' overall award. For example, if the element involves you in marking a large pile of essays or reports, but only contributes 5 per cent or less to the overall award for students, the score will probably need to be a '1'! If it's a computer-based multiple-choice exam for a large cohort of students, even if the design time was very significant, but the marking is automated, the score may be nearer a '5'.

15 Inclusiveness

This is a very complex issue. Its significance may depend a great deal on the composition of the student group, and to some extent on the size. Factors which may need to be considered here include:

- How well the assessment provides a level playing field for students learning in a second language.

- The extent to which the assessment may disadvantage students with particular needs, such as dyslexia, visual impairments, hearing impairments, and so on.

- Whether some particular students, for whatever reason, are less successful than their optimum in this particular kind of assessment.

For this item, therefore, you will need to bear all manner of factors in mind when deciding your rating for 'inclusiveness' on the 1–5 scale. Sometimes you will have a very clear idea of how well the assessment concerned provides a level playing field for the particular student cohort, and at other times you may need to make judgements as best you can on the basis of what you know about the students.

16 Students get *and use* feedback as a result of it

The key words here are 'and use' feedback; we all know how common it is for students to get feedback and fail to use it. For summative assessment elements, students often get little feedback (perhaps just a pass/fail award, or a score or a grade), and for this item the score may only be '1'. Then there are the cases where students get quite a lot of feedback, but the feedback comes too late for them to put it to any real use – that too may warrant a '1' score. Or there may be cases where students don't seem to take any notice of the feedback, or don't even pick up their marked work containing feedback – that too could warrant a score of '1'. Some forms of assessment are much richer in feedback than others (including student peer assessment and student presentations to an audience), and you will need to take this into account when working out the score for this item.

Of course all students are different, and some may be making good use of the feedback they get, while others make much less use of it, so for the assessment element concerned you may need to consider an averaged score for this item.

17 Alignment: how well it links visibly to learning outcomes

This links both to the perceived quality of the design of the assessment and also to how well students have information about the targets they are meant to attain, as can be expressed through well-used, intended learning outcomes. When curriculum is validated or reviewed, either internally or externally (for example, by professional bodies), the alignment to learning outcomes is often required to be made more explicit. This also links to the extent to which students have developed ownership of the need to learn.

If students are not aware of the intended learning outcomes, or don't realize that such outcomes reflect their attainment targets, the score for this item is likely to be '1'. If students are fully aware of the links, the score could be more towards '5'. The score you decide could be regarded as a measure of the 'constructive alignment' of the assessment element in the context of students' learning, and the design of the curriculum as a whole.

18 Students use several ways of communicating and explaining

This item (along with 19 and 20 below) refers to the overall picture of assessment elements A to D (or more), so when you make your decision for assessment element 'A', you need to think about the nature of 'B', 'C' and 'D' as well. A single assessment may well focus on just one method of students communicating their learning, for example in writing or orally or in group contexts or online, and so on. And even 'in writing' can take many forms, for example unseen written exams, coursework essays and reports, written reviews, written reflections, and so on. If all of the assessment elements use very similar ways of students communicating their learning, the score for this item might be as low as '1' for each of the elements involved. If overall there is a rich mix in how students communicate their learning, the score could be '5'.

19 Diversity: overall range of assessment types

This item also refers to the overall picture of the complete set of assessment elements for the course or module. Every assessment format disadvantages some students. Therefore, the more different forms of assessment making up the overall picture, the less likely that the same students are likely to be repeatedly disadvantaged by any one format. The score for this item needs also to be considered in terms of the extent to which any particular assessment format dominates the overall picture. For example, if a written exam counts for 80 per cent or more of the overall award, the score for diversity should be as low as '1'. If there is a mix of four quite different forms of assessment, each counting for 25 per cent overall, a score of '5' may be justified. Note that there is a danger in attempts to achieve diversity of assessment ending up in *too much* assessment (affecting the two 'manageability' lines addressed earlier). It is best to work towards diversity by appropriately reducing the size of assessment elements as the range is broadened.

20 The 'wow' factor as gained from student feedback

This too refers to the overall picture of the assessment of the course or module, but this time in terms of students' *feelings* about the assessment element concerned. Of all the 'measures' in this grid, this is necessarily the most subjective one! However, it is linked to the value of the assessment as a positive driving force for students' learning, and links in its own way to the enhancement of their 'want' to learn the subject matter linked to the assessment element, but even more to the actual learning pay-off they derive while preparing for, and then undertaking, the assessment element. It is likely that only the occasional assessment element will, in practice, attract a 'wow' factor score from students, but when it does, it is important to recognize it.

Interpretation of scores for this exercise

Linking assessment firmly to learning can be regarded as one of the most complex of our tasks in higher education. At a series of workshops in 2009, I talked participants through each item of the grid in turn (and in different orders), and then invited them to add up their scores for the assessment element they chose to interrogate. Quite often, traditional forms of assessment have scored considerably lower (for example, scores in the 30s) than more innovative forms, which have sometimes scored as high as the mid 80s. Putting the grid to work with staff in higher education is showing that this attempt to interrogate assessment design can be a valuable prelude to working systematically towards 'assessment *as* learning' as it causes staff to reflect very deeply on the design of their assessment elements. I hope that this exercise helps you to think critically and developmentally in ways which will assist your own assessment design, not only to make learning happen better for your students, but also to place your assessments well in stakes such as validity, reliability, and so on.

It is hoped that this step-by-step process of trying to analyse 20 separate aspects of assessment design may contribute towards making assessment a more efficient and effective driver leading to better student learning.

Towards assessment becoming a *better* driver for learning

Let me end this chapter by returning to some tactics which can play their part in helping to bring assessment closer to our intention to make learning happen.

1. *Diversify assessment more and move away from overuse of just two or three assessment formats.* In particular, we need to ensure that our assessment systems do not end up just measuring how skilled (or unskilled) our learners are in a limited range of assessment contexts, such as *just* a mixture of time-constrained, unseen written exams, tutor-marked essays and reports.

2. *Make assessment fit for purpose so that we measure what we really should be measuring – not just ghosts of learners' learning.* We need to

revisit the validity of each and every form of assessment we employ, and choose those which are good at measuring what students have really learned.

3. *Make assessment a high-learning pay-off experience for learners by making the most of feedback to students.* We need to think ahead to how we will give feedback to students after each element of assessment, and to how useful that feedback can be, even when the main purposes of assessment are summative rather than formative.

4. *Reduce the burden of assessment for learners and for ourselves.* We have got our education systems into a state where assessment all too often militates against deep learning and takes much of the enjoyment out of learning. Reducing the amount quite dramatically – by a factor of three or four perhaps – can be part of the pathway towards increasing the quality of assessment and the usefulness of associated feedback to learners.

5. *Assess evidence of what learners have learned, not just what we have tried to teach them.* It may be instinctive to try to find out what students have learned as a direct result of what we have tried to teach, but there should be more to assessment than just this. We need to be able to credit learners for their achievements in learning they have done for themselves and with each other.

6. *Assess students' evidence of their learning more reliably.* Most assessors are aware that assessment is rarely an exact science, yet with so much depending on the marks and grades we award learners, we need to be constantly striving to make each assessment element as reliable as we can, so we can make learners feel more assured that they are being assessed fairly – and so that employers and others can have more trust in the results of our assessments.

7. *Focus learning outcomes on 'need-to-know' rather than 'nice-to-know' material – and stop measuring things which are 'nuts to know'!* Too often, it is possible to look at what is *really* being measured by an exam question or assignment and find ourselves asking 'why on earth are we causing learners to learn this bit?' Sometimes, our reply to ourselves – if we're honest – is as banal as 'Well, at least this lends itself to being measured!' Not a good enough reason. What is measured by assessment should be easily recognized as being important, not just interesting.

8. *Measure 'know-how' and 'know-why' much more and 'know-what' much less.* In other words, move learning away from information recall and regurgitation, and strive to use assessment to encourage learners to make sense of what they have learned, and towards being able to explain it and apply it rather than merely describe it.

9. *Involve learners in assessing their own and each other's work to deepen their learning, and help them to get their heads around how we conduct assessment.* The more learners know about how assessment really works, the better they can do themselves justice in preparing for it and demonstrating their learning back to us. There is no better way than helping them to develop self-assessment and peer-assessment skills, to deepen their learning and acclimatize them to the assessment culture they are part of.

10. *Get our wording right in our outcomes, briefings, tasks and criteria – write them all in English, not in 'academese'.* Too often, whether in exams or other assessment contexts, learners who are skilled at working out exactly what our assessment tasks actually *mean* achieve better results than equally deserving learners who are not so skilled. Teaching is about effective communication, not playing word games.

Learning Through Feedback

Already in this book, feedback has been identified as one of the seven principal factors underpinning successful learning. Feedback should interact with the other factors continuously, as follows:

- Feedback should help learners to *make sense* of what they have done.

- Feedback should help learners to clarify and take ownership of the *need* to learn as defined by the evidence of achievement of the intended learning outcomes defining their studies.

- Feedback ideally should enhance learners' *want* to learn by increasing their self-esteem and confidence whenever possible, and by helping them to believe that they can indeed achieve the intended learning outcomes *and* demonstrate this in ways where they will be duly credited for this achievement.

- Feedback should motivate learners to move forward into their next episodes of *learning by doing* and focus their efforts more sharply towards bringing the experience from their past work to bear on making their next work better.

- Feedback gained while *explaining, coaching* and even *teaching* fellow-learners can add enormously to learners' mastery of what they have learned, and increase their confidence as they work towards communicating their knowledge in formal assessments.

- Involving learners in *assessing – making informed judgements* can open up to them a great deal of further feedback on how their learning is progressing, and how well they are becoming able to provide evidence of their achievement in each of the forms which will make up their overall assessment.

Feedback or feed-forward?

Some writers already use the term 'feed-forward' to describe those aspects of feedback which particularly point towards what to do next, rather than merely looking backwards at what has (or has not) already been achieved by learners. Feed-forward can offer help along the following lines:

1. Details of what would have been necessary to achieve better marks or grades, expressed in ways where learners can seek to improve their future assignments or answers.

2. Praise relating to things which learners have done really well, so that they don't simply shrug off their success, but take on board what to *continue* to do well in future assignments and assessment contexts.

3. Direct suggestions for learners to try out in their next piece of work to overcome problems or weaknesses arising in their last assignment.

4. Suggestions about sources to explore, illustrating chosen aspects of what they themselves are being encouraged to do in their own future work.

Feed-forward can be regarded as *formative* – in other words, pointing towards improving and developing future work. This contrasts with *summative* feedback, referring back principally to what was – and what was not – achieved in past work. Ideally, feedback needs to achieve both purposes, but the danger is that it sometimes is not sufficiently formative and is too dominated by summative comments.

Is feedback broken too?

In Chapter 4, it was argued that assessment is broken in higher education. The same arguments extend to feedback too, as very often it is linked to assessment. For example, in the National Student Survey, administered to all final-year students every year in the UK since 2005, in the section on 'assessment and feedback', statements 7, 8 and 9 link directly to students' experience of feedback. Students are asked to make judgements as follows: 'definitely agree', 'mostly agree', 'neither agree nor disagree', 'mostly disagree', 'definitely disagree', or 'not applicable' on each of the following three statements:

7   Feedback on my work has been prompt.
8   I have received detailed comments on my work.
9   Feedback on my work has helped me clarify things I did not understand.

As with the survey results on assessment, students' responses about feedback have continued to show that this is one of the least satisfactory areas in their overall experience of higher education. Many institutions in the UK have taken action to try to improve students' perceptions of the value of feedback, but the problem still continues to perplex staff. It could be argued that:

- Students are right about '7', feedback is often *not* prompt. Even with turn-round times for assessed work being prescribed by institutions, it is often weeks before students get their marked work back. Later in this chapter, I suggest ways of speeding up substantially at least some of the feedback we give to students.

- Staff often defend themselves saying 'But students didn't take any notice of the detailed comments I put on their work', or 'Some of them didn't even bother to collect their marked work'. This is at least partly due to the mark being more important in students' minds than the feedback. Later in this chapter I suggest ways round this problem.

- One of the roles of formative feedback is indeed to help students to clarify things that they did not understand. However, written comments on students' work play only a limited role in this mission. Face-to-face feedback plays a more important role, and in the context of the survey, students may be forgiven for thinking the 'feedback' refers only to the written stuff rather than all the rest of the feedback they get from tutors. Moreover, in the context of the factors underpinning successful learning, feedback is only part of the toolkit available to us for helping students to clarify things they didn't understand. We need to be adopting all of the tactics available to us for helping them to make sense of what they're learning, not least getting *them* to make informed judgements on their work, and not just leave that to us.

Feedback, achievement and failure

There is now a substantial and rich literature on the potential role of feedback in formative assessment contexts. This section of the chapter picks on just a few important sources of wisdom and expertise on using feedback to make learning happen in post-compulsory education. Positive feedback brings few problems to learners or to staff giving it. However, it is the feedback on unsuccessful work which causes most heartache to staff and learners alike. Peelo (2002: 2) writes tellingly on the difficult subject of failure, as follows:

> Failing is not a popular subject. Even though failing, in some shape or form, is an everyday occurrence, it remains a subject rarely discussed. This silence occurs as much in the world of education as in the world generally, even though many educational assessment procedures are intended to discriminate, separating those students deemed unsuccessful from the rest...
>
> To use the word 'failing' seems, superficially, to be a negative approach to education. Indeed, in universities this unpopular word has overtones of the taboo, with the suspicion that using the word itself invites failure. Yet integral to all discussions of standards and access is the practice of failing students. All competitive systems

> have losers. The practice of teaching and examining in universities includes the
> activity of finding some students wanting – it is part of the job…
>
> Just as important as the idea of students failing, is the need to question
> whether or not the system itself is doing the best for its students or is, indeed,
> failing the students it's trying to educate…
>
> Failure in universities, whether of staff or students, is a matter of discomfort
> and embarrassment and yet is seen as an essential demarcator of successful
> work. It is an integral part of institutional structures, yet it is often experienced
> individually and in isolation. (Peelo, 2002: 2)

However, she continues:

> However correctly dealt with by the system, a student who is failing in a system
> which is built on academic success may well experience a sense of isolation and
> strangeness. Similarly, few students suddenly and unexpectedly fail academically –
> there is usually prior warning. For many, *failing is not an event but a series of hesitations,*
> a combination of moments of failure. For others, *experiencing failure is not about*
> *external criteria, but about falling below their own, personal standards.* Externally,
> everything may be fine and they may well be passing their courses successfully. But
> internally, the pressure and striving can be enormous. If something else goes wrong
> in life then the fragile structures which support such students through university
> assignments can begin to crumble. (Peelo, original emphases)

The key to all this is of course timely, helpful and supportive feedback.
Bowl (2003: 93) illustrates poignantly, through student quotes, the need
they have for such feedback. For example, one of the case studies around
which her book is written includes the following scenario:

> Planning assignments is my worst, it's my weakness definitely. I can say what I
> want to put in it, but it's how do I do it? What comes top, second, third? I know
> I can write. It's just that initial help to say that should go first, second or what-
> ever. Once I've got that, I can do an assignment … Some give you guidelines,
> and some don't. It's like, how do you want us to write this? How do you want
> us to do it? I would go out and know how to work practically. But writing, it's
> like – what do you want? … It's getting it structured the way that it suits them
> and suits their needs. (Sandra, first-year student)

But what makes feedback work to make learning happen? Knight and Yorke
(2003: 135) explain it thus:

> Formative assessment can clearly be said to have 'worked' if the student demonstrates
> having learned as a result of the feedback provided. This requires that the student
> has a concept of learning that allows them to take in what the assessor has sought
> to convey and they then act on the basis of this developed understanding.

They also quote Stowell (2001) in discussing the role of formative assessment
as follows:

> Formative assessment is concerned with maximising the learning of each
> individual student. In theory, each student should receive feedback that is most

appropriate to their learning needs. Feedback should therefore be differentiated. The problem occurs on the assessor's side when time and resources
are constrained. The assessor then has to make choices regarding the amount
of feedback that should be given to each individual. The choices they make
will reflect personal value judgements about the purposes of education:
some teachers will opt for 'levelling up' in the interests of social justice, whereas
others will give priority to 'high flyers', seeing their action in Darwinian 'survival
of the fittest' terms.

It is also argued that it is the lower fliers who are most in need of feedback, for example Bandura (1997: 217) argues: 'The less individuals
believe in themselves, the more they need explicit, proximal, and frequent
feedback of progress that provides repeated affirmations of their growing
capabilities.'

Knight and Yorke (2003) have a wealth of useful food for thought concerning
the role of feedback in formative assessment. They argue:

> Complex achievements take time. This implies practice but it also implies
> feedback on practice, whether it be self-generated or comes from other
> learners or experts. Without feedback, the learner is like someone learning
> to play chess blindfolded, wearing earmuffs, and beyond any helpful tactile
> contact. When achievements are complex, careful thought is needed about
> the nature of feedback. When the aim is improving future performances, the
> most useful feedback is about improvement strategies: what are the most
> important two or three things on which to work if performance on a similar
> task is to be improved? Unless there is a requirement that learners master
> particular detail, there is a danger that too much correction of specific detail
> will take attention away from improvement strategies. (Knight and Yorke,
> 2003: 126)

They describe the purposes of formative assessment in general as follows:

> Three purposes of formative assessment
>
> 1 To give credit for what has been done, with reference to the expected standard.
> 2 To correct what is wrong, thereby helping the student to avoid repeating
>   the error (hence merely saying that something is wrong is insufficient).
> 3 To encourage emancipation by alerting the student to possibilities which
>   they may not have hitherto discerned. (Knight and Yorke, 2003: 35)

They also argue that:

> Although all feedback can evoke learning, it is helpful, from the outset, to declare
> an interest in feedback that draws attention to actions that, if taken, have the
> power to make a difference to future work on different topics. Although many
> teachers give a lot of feedback on specifics, it is *general* feedback that has the

> greater power to stimulate learning. If general feedback relates to the learning intentions declared in course and programme specifications, then this is a clear benefit to the coherence of student learning. (Knight and Yorke, 2003: 32–3)

It can be argued that giving learners feedback is just about the most important dimension of the work of teachers in post-compulsory education, second only perhaps to that of making assessment judgements which can affect the future careers and lives of our learners. But perhaps all told, formative feedback is *the* vital dimension as, given at the right time and in the best possible way, it can lead learners steadily towards successful achievement in summative assessment contexts.

Varieties of formative feedback

What sorts of feedback can help to make learning happen more successfully? There are many ways in which feedback can reach learners, each with advantages and disadvantages. Perhaps the more *different* ways we use to get feedback to learners, the more likely we are to ensure that they receive at least some feedback in ways which suit their own personal approaches to learning.

Written, printed and on-screen feedback

All this can be regarded as feedback in the 'read-write' domain of Neil Fleming's 'VARK' inventory. Such feedback can take many forms, including:

- handwritten comments directly entered on to learners' work

- summary overall comments on learners' assignments – handwritten, word-processed or emailed directly to learners

- model answers or specimen solutions, giving feedback to learners on what may have been looked for in their own work

- generic feedback on a batch of learner work, in print, emailed to all learners, or put up on an electronic discussion list, virtual learning environment or computer conference

- sheets listing 'frequently occurring problems' or 'frequently needed explanations' specific to a particular assignment, allowing learners to see feedback on some of the problems they may themselves have encountered, but also alerting them to other potential problems they may not have been aware of themselves, but which may be useful to avoid in their next work.

Face-to-face feedback

This extends feedback into the auditory, visual and kinesthetic areas of Neil Fleming's 'VARK' inventory, and can take several forms, including:

- feedback to whole lecture groups on work that has already been marked and is now being returned to them

- feedback to similar groups, but at the time they have just handed in their work, while it is still fresh in their minds. This feedback of course addresses *anticipated* problems or mistakes, but can be really valuable to learners, still remembering the fine detail of their own attempts at the work

- feedback to small groups of learners, for example, in tutorials, allowing more interaction – for example, learners can probe deeper into what exactly the feedback means

- face-to-face, one-to-one feedback, by appointment, or in other learning contexts such as practical classes or studio work, where tutors can often chat to individual learners in a context less formal than individual appointments.

Feedback on learners' own self-assessments

Where learners are briefed to carry out a self-assessment of their assignments at the point of handing them in for marking, tutors can then not only give learners feedback on the assignments themselves, but also on the self-assessment reflections. In practice, this can help tutors to give learners feedback which is much more focused on learners' real needs than just giving feedback without knowing what learners themselves already thought about their own strengths and weaknesses relating to the assessed work.

Feedback associated with peer assessment

Where groups of learners are assessing each other's work (whether written assignments, essays, reports, presentations, artefacts, exhibitions or posters), learners can get a great deal of feedback from their peer assessors. They also get what is perhaps even more useful feedback individually, directly from the processes of applying assessment criteria to other examples of work – some better than their own, and some not as good. All this helps them to place their own work in context and to work out what they may need to do next time to improve or develop their own future work.

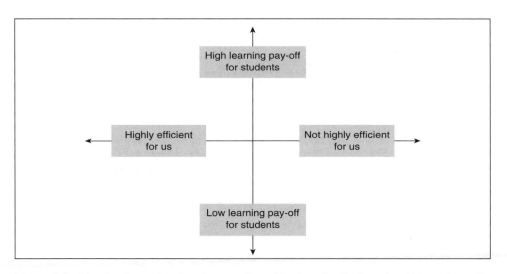

Figure 5.1   Mapping the student learning pay-off resulting from feedback to the efficiency for staff providing it

Feedback, efficiency and learning pay-off

Most tutors and lecturers already know how important feedback is to their learners. Few, however, feel that they have got themselves into a position where the feedback is really working. Ideally, we need to make informed decisions about how best to maximize the learning pay-off associated with our feedback, but at the same time to improve our own efficiency in composing and delivering the feedback. In many workshops, I have asked groups of participants to write down on separate post-its the different ways they use to give their learners feedback (adding also *other* ways learners get feedback – for example, from each other, from web sources, from books and handouts, and so on). I then ask them to place the post-its on to a chart, as shown in Figure 5.1.

The feedback processes which people consider to have the highest learning pay-off are positioned well up the vertical axis. Those which are most efficient for us are placed towards the left of the chart. Those which are most efficient *and* have the highest learning pay-off go towards the top left-hand corner of the chart.

Scales 1 to 5 can then be drawn on each axis, and the product of 'efficiency' × 'learning pay-off' can be worked out for the position of each of the post-its on the chart (Figure 5.2). The highest scoring feedback methods are frequently those involving peer assessment or peer marking, and self-assessment also attracts some high scores. This is not least because the 'efficiency for us' tends to be high, especially when large groups of learners are involved. Further 'high scores' elements emerge, such as 'feedback from clients', 'feedback from

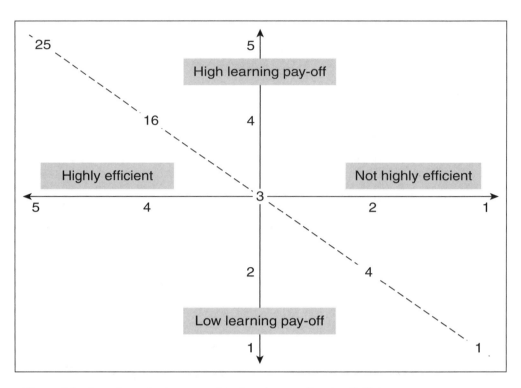

Figure 5.2   A semi-quantitative approach to learning pay-off and staff efficiency

externals', 'feedback from employers', and so on. The lecturers concerned rightly justify these scores along the lines 'Students take far more notice of this feedback than they do of that we give them', and 'It is very efficient for us as it's not us spending the time doing it!'.

'Written comments on students' work' usually scores around 4! One-to-one feedback often attracts low scores, not least because it is inefficient for us, even when the learning pay-off is felt to be high. However, the lowest scoring feedback processes frequently include 'just a mark'. In other words, most tutors know only too well that learners don't learn much from just being given a number or grade for their work. In this exercise, 'no feedback at all' is sometimes an entry, and attracts a score of 5, as it takes no time at all, and is therefore very efficient (in terms of time only, of course), and the learning pay-off is minimal. It can be argued that all feedback methods which score *less* than 5 in this exercise are *worse than useless!*

Working through this kind of discussion about learning pay-off versus efficiency often encourages tutors to make more and better use of peer assessment and self-assessment as tactics in a strategy to provide learners with more and better feedback using existing resources. It also helps tutors to appreciate the limitations of just giving scores or grades.

Just a mark is the least useful form of feedback!

In the 'effectiveness versus efficiency' explorations summarized above, 'just a mark' often scores '1'. In other words, it is very ineffective as feedback for learners, but takes us a lot of time to do! There are problems here.

- Learners *expect* marks – and may complain if we don't give them marks.

- When learners get marks, that is the first thing they look at, and they get blinded by the mark.

- Feedback is often then ignored – or (worse) interpreted in an emotive way, depending on the mark.

- If the mark is high, learners are likely to ignore the feedback, and 'smile and file'. They may well be missing out on finding out *why* the mark was high, and thereby becoming better able to continue in future work to do the things that got them the high mark.

- If the mark is low, learners often bin the assignment concerned, and miss out on all the feedback which might have helped them to work out how to get better marks for similar work next time.

What can we do about these problems? I suggest the following:

1. At a whole-class session, give students back their marked work, but with feedback comments only and no marks (keeping your own record of their scores).

2. Remind them of the assessment criteria and tell them to use the next week to work out their marks from the feedback, and return next week with their scores for the work.

3. Tell the class that their marks count! Suggest that if their scores are within 5% (or one grade) of the scores you've given them, the *higher* score will go forward into their assessment records, but that if they are outside 5%, you will talk individually to them and sort out the score face to face.

4. Suggest that they don't just look at the feedback on their own work, but also the feedback on a few fellow-learners' work. Explain that every time they look at some work which is better than theirs, they will learn something useful, and will be better able to get higher marks next time they do something similar. Also explain that every time they see someone else's work which has attracted critical feedback that their own work missed, they will learn something useful and will be able to *avoid* similar mistakes in future work. In other words, the time spent comparing their work with that of others will always be productive in terms of *making sense* of the subject matter, and (even more importantly) they will

be *learning by making informed judgements* about their own and each other's work (the 'informing' being done through the feedback they see).

5. Next week, pass a board around the group asking everyone to enter their mark against their name. This can be achieved in just a few minutes of a whole-class session, even with hundreds of students there.

6. Two important things have happened over the week, and with no extra cost of time to you: just about all of your learners have read your feedback and many of them have learned from the feedback that some of their classmates have received too.

7. In practice, nine out of ten learners are likely to arrive at scores within 5% of your own scores, and the higher numbers can go forward. This means that nine out of ten of your learners are very satisfied with the marking and feedback, as follows:

   • They have been awarded the mark they awarded themselves, or
   • They have got a small number of extra marks, where either:

     o you gave them a slightly higher mark than they gave themselves, or
     o they got away with a slightly higher mark than you gave them!

8. Make time to talk individually to the remaining one in ten of the learners.

9. Where they underestimated their scores, point out to them where they deserved more marks than they had awarded themselves. Show them where they had in fact achieved the outcomes which they didn't think they had achieved. These learners go away with a spring in their step, even happier than the nine out of ten referred to earlier. After all, they've just found that they're doing better than they thought they were.

10. Where they overestimated their scores, go through their work with them until you find out where the main difference arose. It's usually because of a blind spot – something they thought they'd cracked but which they haven't yet mastered in fact. Talk them through this blind spot until they can see exactly why they lost the marks concerned, and get them to talk you through it so you can check that they have really seen the light about why they lost those marks, and what they can do to avoid losing similar marks ever again. (Don't just say 'Do you understand now?' Make sure they do by getting them to show you.) These learners go away happiest of all – and they are *very* unlikely ever to lose those particular marks again.

Let's just summarize what has been achieved by getting learners to work out their own marks:

A. Learners have taken much more notice of the feedback than if you'd given them marks.

B. 100% of them are very happy with it all.

C. You've spent relatively little additional time achieving all this.

D. You've spent that additional time giving really useful face-to-face feed-back to the one in ten who really needed face-to-face feedback, and you've avoided wasting time with all the learners who don't really need such face-to-face feedback.

E. You've optimized the learning of your students by getting them to *make informed judgements.*

F. You've got something really interesting to add to your teaching portfolio, or to please your external examiner.

In the light of all the benefits of getting students to work out their own marks, the original problem of 'students expect marks' fades somewhat into insignificance. You may, however, come up against the occasional learner who says 'It's your job to assess my work. I'm paying for this course.' My own reply tends to be along the lines 'Fine, I'll give you your mark. But I'm not very good at marking. And you'll miss out on a lot of learning. And you may miss out on some marks you might otherwise have got. But it's up to you.'

Feedback within 24 hours!

At workshops and conferences, I often alarm participants by stating 'Feed-back is of little use unless students get it within 24 hours!' Delegates shake their heads sadly. I remind them of the real-life experiences of a day where things go badly – one may remain upset for the rest of that day, but on wak-ing the following morning, it's rarely quite as bad as it seemed to be. And a few days later, it's faded from the mind quite a lot. It's rather similar with feedback – we need it while our thinking is still fresh in our minds. After a few days, feedback is much less readily received – the work has receded into the past. But there are ways of achieving 24-hour feedback, as discussed in this section and further developed from Race and Pickford (2007).

There's nothing new about the idea that feedback has to be quick to be effective. It is widely accepted that feedback on students' work is most effective when it is received quickly, while they still remember clearly what they were trying to do in their efforts. The work in Australia of Sadler (1989, 1998, 2003, 2009a, 2009b) has consistently emphasized the role of form-ative feedback in leading students towards successful learning. Gibbs and Simpson (2002) look critically at a decline in the quantity and qual-ity of formative feedback which students receive as class sizes grow in a climate of policies about widening participation in higher education. Bowl (2003) provides a wealth of detail about how students react to feedback (or the lack of it) in her book based on interviews with non-traditional entrants to higher education. Yorke (2002) writes convincingly of the role (and speed) of formative feedback in addressing student non-completion, and Knight and Yorke (2003) continue the argument that there are major problems in higher education with assessment and formative feedback, an argument developed further in this book.

Some feedback can be nearly instantaneous, for example when using computer-based or online multiple-choice exercises, where the feedback to choosing distractors (or correct options) can appear on-screen as soon as students select an option. Feedback on practical work can be instantaneous too. However, it is often the case that students get feedback on essays, reports, problems sheets, and so on much too late – it can take weeks to mark their work, particularly if the class size is large. By the time students receive their feedback, they may well have moved on, and then they take very little notice of the feedback. Colleagues in many institutions complain that too many students don't even bother to pick up their marked work. Even when much care and effort and time have been put into writing the feedback, it often ends up entirely wasted! Life is too short to waste time on composing feedback that won't be read or used.

In this section, I suggest processes that enable feedback (on paper and face-to-face with whole groups) to be given to large (or indeed small) groups of students within 24 hours of them engaging with the work they hand in for assessment.

No 'yes, buts ...' please, ... at least not yet. Before you read this discussion, please prepare to abandon any reservations to the ideas you are about to see – at least for the next two pages or so. Then we'll address some of the 'yes, buts...'.

1. You've issued the class with an assignment, including all the usual detail about assessment criteria, links to intended learning outcomes, suggested sources, and so on.

2. Suppose you ask your class to bring the completed assignment (essay, report, whatever) to a particular whole-class session, for example a lecture – say the 10.00–11.00 lecture next Tuesday morning.

3. Explain that the *absolute* deadline for receipt of their work is 10.00 on Tuesday morning, and the (only) place they can hand in that assignment is at this particular lecture during the first minute or two.

4. On the day, ask all students to place their work in a pile on a table at the front of the lecture room, in the first three minutes of the lecture period. By 10.03 or so, you have all their work (and a good attendance).

5. As soon as you've got all of their work (e.g. at 10.03), distribute to everyone in the group copies of a pre-prepared feedback sheet on the assignment concerned – on a coloured sheet of paper (different colours for successive assignments, so you can say 'The green sheet', 'The pink sheet', and so on to refer to particular examples of these feedback sheets). On the sheet, use

numbered points, so you can say 'Point 3 on the green sheet' to refer to a particular explanation, for example. This feedback sheet can contain:

- explanations to anticipated, frequently-occurring problems
- illustrations of components of a good answer to the assignment question
- examples of useful source materials and references
- model solutions of quantitative parts of the assignment (if applicable).

6. Allow your class three minutes to scan through the feedback sheet (e.g. 10.03–10.06). It goes very quiet! Suddenly, lots of students are finding out things about what they missed out of their attempts at the assignment, things they got wrong, but also things that were good about their attempts, and so on. Your class is getting quite intense read–write feedback in these three minutes or so.

7. Next, just for three minutes (10.06–10.09) talk the whole group through only one or two of the most significant of the feedback areas on the sheet, adding tone of voice, body language, eye contact to help the meaning of your feedback to be really clear to the students, augmenting one or two of the paragraphs on your feedback sheet. Don't try to cover the whole sheet – that would be too boring for the class and would take too long. *Which* points should you cover? Watch carefully students near to you between 10.03 and 10.06. See where they look serious as their eyes rest on particular parts of the sheet. These give you clues about which points will be most valuable to expand on between 10.06 and 10.09.

8. Everyone in the class has now had three minutes benefiting from your feedback sheet, and a further three minutes getting some richer feedback on particularly important points about the assignment.

9. Then proceed with the lecture as normal.

The point of all this?

Most of the students will still have been finishing off the assignment – or at least giving it a final check – *within the last 24 hours.* Moreover, more students than you might imagine will in fact have only *started* on the assignment during the last 24 hours – it's worth asking them! These are likely to be the ones who need the feedback the most, and they are very receptive to it at this time. This means they are now getting feedback while they still have a very clear view on what they were trying to do in the assignment and while they remember what their difficulties may have been. They are getting feedback while they still remember very clearly what they were pleased with about their work on the assignment. They are therefore getting a lot of feedback while they really *want* to know how their work will fare in assessment. They are thirsty for feedback at this point.

Now you can mark that assignment in much less time!

When you actually go away to mark your students' work, you can save up to two-thirds of the time you would normally have spent marking it. You save time and energy as follows:

- You don't have to write the same things on many different students' assignments – the common mistakes and difficulties have already been covered by your feedback sheet, and you can simply write 'Please see point 5 on the green sheet', and so on. (Most tutors admit that in 'normal' marking, they get fed up of writing the same explanations time after time on different students' work, and that they get less and less patient doing so!) It is, however, important to take the few seconds needed to write that 'please see...' briefing on the student's work, and not to assume that because the explanation the student needs has already been given out that the student will see the link to his or her own work.

- You can now concentrate in the time you devote to marking the assignment to giving students feedback on particular things they need as individuals – in other words focusing your expertise where it is most helpful to your students.

- If, as you are marking the work of a large class, additional frequently-needed explanations arise (over and above the ones you had on the blue sheet, for example), you can compose a new supplement to the blue sheet (probably just half a page or so in practice), covering perhaps points 8 to 10 to supplement the 7 points already on the blue sheet. You can then, where necessary, abbreviate many of your feedback remarks on students' work to 'Please see point 9 on the blue sheet supplement attached', continuing to save you time and spare you the tedium of repetition.

- Because you've debriefed your students *orally* in the whole group about the most important points in your pre-prepared feedback, there's little need to mention these points in any additional feedback you write on to their assignments, other than to sometimes remind them of your oral debriefing.

- Since you're now marking the pile of assignments in a third of the time it would otherwise have taken, it's likely you'll be able to get the marked work back to the class much more quickly than hitherto, which means that students are getting the rest of the feedback while the assignment has not completely faded from their minds.

- Your growing collection of feedback sheets continues to be available as evidence of your good teaching practice, and can be included in submissions to external examiners, professional bodies and in your appraisal or review documentation.

Now for those 'yes, buts...'!

'But what about students who don't hand it in on time?'

There are no extensions! The real world works on deadlines – for funding bids, conference contributions, job interviews, and so on. It's good to train students to meet deadlines. Deadlines are deadlines are deadlines. A number of universities I know have now abandoned 'mitigating circumstances', 'extensions', and so on. It's worth reminding students that there are quite clear links between punctuality and excellence! Long ago, when marking laboratory scripts, I used to say to my students that 'The marks for the scripts will be more or less in the order you hand them in. First in gets the highest mark, and so on.' In fact, it surprised me how frequently the first scripts to be handed in were the best ones.

You can, however, explain to your students in advance that anyone who misses the deadline is not completely stuffed. They have the opportunity to do 'Alternative Assignment B' instead, which more or less addresses the same learning outcomes as the original but where the coloured feedback sheet is of no help. They then hand the alternative assignment in at another deadline. (You may find ways of giving subtle hints making alternative assignment B somehow less attractive than the original assignment!) Assignments A and B can be issued at the same time, so that students who know they're going to have a real problem with Deadline A (family crisis, illness, whatever) can set their sights on Deadline B.

With a large group, don't be surprised if three students will approach you and say 'Is it OK for me to have a go at both Assignment A *and* Assignment B please?' I always used to reply 'Of course'. And to the one student who will turn back to you after the other two have gone and say 'And can I be credited to whichever assignment I get the best mark for?' I naturally used to reply 'Of course'!! These students are often the higher-fliers in any case.

'If the feedback on the coloured sheet is so valuable, why can't we give out this guidance in advance of students doing the assignment?'

We can indeed give out the guidance in advance – but it doesn't work! Even when students have detailed guidance, many of them read it but soon get so busy doing the assignment that they ignore or forget most of the guidance and still get into the (anticipated) difficulties that the coloured feedback sheet addresses. If in doubt about this, give out the blue sheet three weeks before setting the assignment, simply saying 'Keep this safe, it will be useful to you'. Then at 10.03 on the hand-in date, issue the same blue sheet again, and listen to the chorus of surprised, plaintive comments 'I never noticed *that* on the blue sheet!' Feedback only really seems to work *after* students have done something.

Feedback for high-fliers and for low-fliers

Some feedback processes are much more suitable for successful learners than struggling learners. For example, just a mark or a grade may be all that is needed by high-fliers, while a combination of written and oral feedback may be much more suitable for learners who need significant help. At the same time, learners without any problems may find it irritating to be given detailed feedback on things they have already mastered. However, learners without problems may equally feel short-changed if their less able course mates are seen to be getting more time and attention from tutors. An appropriate balance needs to be struck, where high-fliers get useful feedback too – perhaps a combination of positive comments about their work *and* some constructive suggestions about how they can make their next piece of work even better. It is well known how desolate a learner can feel when, having consistently achieved 'A' grades, an out-of-the-blue 'B' grade hits them. This can all too often be tracked down to a lack of tutors explaining to them *why* they had been achieving 'A' grades to date. 'If you don't know how you did it, you're less likely to be able to do it again.'

Formative and summative feedback

So far in this chapter, most of the discussion has been about feedback in formative assessment contexts. Another dimension which is useful to explore when reviewing the range of feedback approaches available to us is the question of which processes best lend themselves to providing formative feedback and which are more suitable for summative feedback? In some cases, the conclusions are obvious. For example, 'just a mark or grade' serves summative purposes and 'suggestions for your next assignment' serves formative purposes. However, some are much more complex, and the feedback associated with peer assessment, for example, can play a significant formative role even when it is received in contexts where the overt intention is closer to being summative. This is partly because, in some contexts, learners may actually take on board more deeply things they learn from each other, where there is no 'authoritative' agenda present, than from when they receive feedback directly from their tutors.

Formative and summative assessment processes can be regarded as two ends of a continuum. All too often, for example, what sets out to be formative feedback ends up as summative feedback. For example, when learners don't get the feedback until they have already moved on to another topic or another module, they are very unlikely to take any notice of formative feedback given on work from weeks (sometimes months) ago, and the feedback ends up as no more than summative. In other words, learners may notice the mark or grade, but not bother to read the hard-wrought comments their assessors may have added to their work. It can be argued that there is very little point providing detailed formative feedback if no notice will be taken of it, and that it would, in such circumstances, be just as well to limit things to marks or grades and spend the time saved on providing *real* formative feedback on ongoing work, where learners have the opportunity to make good use of the feedback in improving and developing their work accordingly.

Yorke (2002) argues that we need to spend time helping learners to make better use of formative feedback. He suggests:

> There is a case to be made for spending considerable time and resources on students undertaking their first programmes of study to help them understand the purposes of formative feedback and how their own self-beliefs can impact on the ways they receive it. Inevitably this would eat into available time for content delivery, which academic staff no doubt would be unwilling to see slimmed down, but if an institution is serious about retaining students as a key means of survival in an increasingly competitive world, then tough decisions might have to be made. (Yorke, 2002: 39)

One way of helping learners to put feedback to better use is to cause them to reflect on feedback, and evidence their reflections as part of an ongoing process of becoming increasingly conscious of how they learn – and in this case increasing their awareness of how much they can in fact gain from feedback on their assessed work. The following reflective checklists can be used as a starting point to design your own reflection devices to allow learners to develop their approaches to planning their work and making the most of your feedback. It works all the better if you can persuade learners to allow *you* to see copies of their reflections, so that you too can help them further to develop their approaches to assessed work, and improve how you design feedback for them in future.

Designing feedback in response to poor work

This is the most delicate of feedback tasks. Suppose you're in a position of needing to write feedback comments to a learner whose *first* assignment you've just marked. It was a poor assignment. It would be considered a fail. Suppose, furthermore, that circumstances dictate that you have no alternative to giving this feedback in writing (or email) and you've got to put pen to paper or fingers to keyboard to compose a feedback missive to the learner concerned. Under normal circumstances, you would be wise to choose *not* to put this particular element of feedback into writing or print, and to see the learner face to face to handle this difficult situation with all the tact and sensitivity you could muster. But perhaps the learner concerned is away on a work placement, or perhaps there's just no way the two of you can get together for a face-to-face meeting in the immediate future and the feedback needs to be given sooner rather than later. Your choice of words can be critical.

On submitting your first essay on a course

	Please tick one or more columns for each of the options below.	This is what I did.	I would have liked to do this, but didn't manage it.	I didn't think this necessary.	This just was not possible for me.	I'll do this next time.
1	I started thinking about this essay in plenty of time.					
2	I started to collect my reading materials well in advance.					
3	I discussed the ideas associated with this essay with someone, virtually or live, prior to starting writing.					
4	I had a timetable in mind for pre-reading, planning, drafting, writing, checking, doing the references.					
5	I planned out the structure of the essay logically, so my train of thought was continuous.					
6	I made reasonable efforts to clear the decks for the actual writing of the essay.					
7	I made referencing easy for myself by properly noting all of my sources as I did the reading.					
8	I showed someone a draft of my essay before I completed it.					
9	I acted *on* feedback I received to make my essay better.					
10	I wrote a summary/abstract that encapsulated my key points succinctly.					
11	I checked my work over carefully for obvious mistakes, and I used a spellchecker.					

Reflecting on tutor feedback on your essay

	Please tick one or more comments as appropriate.	This is what I did.	I would have liked to do this, but didn't manage it.	I didn't think this necessary.	This just was not possible for me.	I'll do this next time.	This did not apply in this case.
1	I read the tutor's comments carefully.						
2	I read my essay again to see how the tutor's comments applied.						
3	I noted things I needed to do before the next assignment.						
4	I looked back again at the assignment brief to see the extent to which my essay had complied with it.						
5	I looked forward to the next assignment to see which tutor comments might apply to my preparation for the next one.						
6	I followed up tutor advice on further reading.						
7	I used the feedback to check up on the things I did best in my essay, so I can build on my strengths in my next essay.						
8	I followed up tutor advice on my own writing practices.						
9	I shared my feedback with one or more other students to see how the commentary on my work compared with theirs.						

10	I considered aspects of my approach on which I would especially ask for feedback next time.						
11	I asked my tutor for further clarification on comments which I didn't understand.						
12	I identified any feedback comments which I felt were unjustified, so that I could find out more about them from my tutor in discussion.						

At staff development workshops, I often charge participants with this difficult task, and ask them to compose a feedback letter or email dealing with the issue. I then ask them to swap letters so that they now have no idea whose they have in their hands. Next, I ask them to read aloud the letter or email they now have – but with a difference. I ask them to read it out in a sinister, threatening, menacing manner! This is to simulate how the well-intentioned language used in the document might come across to the learner concerned, who may already know the work was poor, may be having a 'bad day' and may be on the point of discontinuing their studies altogether.

It is surprising how threatening some quite ordinary words can be in this context. Words which are often followed by bad news include 'however', 'unfortunately' and even plain 'but'. There is, of course, no way that the use of these 'caution' words can be avoided, but it is worth reminding tutors that such words can cause learners' spirits to fall as they read feedback responses.

Then there's 'power language' which often creeps in. For example 'submit your next attempt' or 'resubmit your assignment after...', and so on. The word 'submit' puts the tutor on a pedestal and the learner much lower down. 'Send me your next version' is so much milder somehow.

And there are the fatal phrases, possibly the worst imaginable of which is 'You've failed to grasp the basics of...'. This position seems beyond all hope, when read out in a sufficiently sinister way! Surprisingly, some well-intentioned ploys to soften the blow of delivering feedback on poor work can also lead to disaster. Phrases such as 'You've obviously put a lot of effort into...' or 'Clearly, you spend a lot of time on...' bring their own dangers. In particular, what if they hadn't? What if they rushed the assignment off at the eleventh hour, and here they find the tutor responding 'Obviously, you've spent a lot of time ...'? There is no quicker or more sure-fire way of losing credibility as a tutor! That learner will never trust you again.

Using feedback to make learning happen: 20 ways forward

This chapter ends with a set of 20 recommendations about feedback. You may well be able to add yet more to this list.

1. *Help learners to* want *feedback.* Spend time and energy helping learners to understand the importance of feedback and the value of spending some time after receiving work back to learn from the experience. Most learners don't do this at the moment, concentrating principally on the mark.

2. *Get the timing right.* Aim to get feedback on work back to learners very quickly, while they still care and while there is still time for them to do something with it. The longer learners have to wait to get work back, especially if they have moved into another semester by the time they receive their returned scripts, the less likely it is that they will do something constructive with the lecturer's hard-written comments. It could be useful to consider a policy not to give detailed written feedback to learners on work that is handed back at the end of the semester if that area of study is no longer being followed by the learner, and to concentrate on giving more incremental feedback throughout the semester.

3. *Provide learners with a list of feedback comments given to a similar assignment or essay prior to them submitting their own.* You can then ask learners, for example, in a large-group session, to attempt to work out what sort of marks an essay with these kinds of comments might be awarded. This helps them to see the links between feedback comments and levels of achievement, and can encourage them to be more receptive to constructive but critical comments on their own future work.

4. *Make feedback interesting!* Learners are much more likely to study feedback properly if they find it stimulating to read and feel it is personal to them, and not just routine or mundane. It takes more time to make feedback interesting, but if it makes the difference between learners making good use of it or not, it is time well spent.

5. *Give at least* some *feedback straight away.* Explore the possibilities of giving learners at least *some* feedback at the time they hand in their work for marking. For example, a page or two of comments responding

to 'frequently occurring problems' with the assignment they are handing in, or illustrative details along the lines 'A good answer would include...' can give learners some useful feedback while their work on the assignment is still fresh in their minds, and can keep them going until they receive the detailed and individual feedback on their own attempts in due course. Giving 'generic' feedback at the time of submission in this way can also reduce the time it takes to mark learners' work, as there is then no need to repeat on script after script the matters that have already been addressed by the generic feedback, and tutors can concentrate their time and energy on responding to the individual learner's work, and giving specific feedback on *their* strengths and weaknesses.

6. *Let learners have feedback comments on their assignments prior to them receiving the actual mark.* Encourage them to use the feedback comments to estimate what kind of mark they will receive. This can then be used as the basis of an individual or group dialogue on how marks or grades are worked out.

7. *Get learners to look back positively after receiving your feedback.* For example, ask them to revisit their work and identify what were their most successful parts of the assignment on the basis of having now read your feedback. Sometimes learners are so busy reading and feeling depressed by the negative comments that they fail to see that there are positive aspects too.

8. *Ask learners to respond selectively to your feedback on their assignments.* This can, for example, include asking them to complete sentences such as:

   • 'The part of the feedback that puzzled me most was...'
   • 'The comment that rang most true for me was...'
   • 'I don't get what you mean when you say...'
   • 'I would welcome some advice on...'.

9. *Ask learners to send you, confidentially, an email after they have received your feedback, focusing on their feelings.* In particular, this might help you to understand what emotional impact your feedback is having on individual learners. It can be useful to give them a menu of words and phrases to underline or ring, perhaps including: 'exhilarated', 'very pleased', 'miserable', 'shocked', 'surprised', 'encouraged', 'disappointed', 'helped', 'daunted', 'relieved', and others.

10. *Don't miss out on noticing the difference.* Comment positively where you can see that learners have incorporated action resulting from your advice given on their previous assignment. This will encourage them to see the learning and assessment processes as continuous.

11. *Make use of the speed and power of technology.* Explore the uses of computer-assisted formative assessment. While a number of universities,

including Bedfordshire, Plymouth and the Open University, are using computer-assisted assessment summatively, many would argue that it is currently most powerfully used to support formative feedback, often automatically generated by email. Learners seem to really like having the chance to find out how they are doing, and attempt tests several times in an environment where no one else is watching how they do. They may be more willing to maximize the benefits of learning through mistakes when their errors can be made in the comfort of privacy, and when they can get quick feedback on these before they have built them into their work. Of course, many computer-assisted assessment systems allow you to monitor what is going on across a cohort, enabling you to concentrate your energies either on learners who are repeatedly doing badly or those who are not engaging at all in the activity.

12. *Link feedback directly to the achievement of intended learning outcomes.* Explore ways in which formative assessment can be made integral to learning. Too often assessment is bolted on, but the more we can constructively align (Biggs, 2003) assignments with planned learning outcomes and the curriculum taught, the more learners are likely to perceive them as authentic and worth bothering with. Giving learners feedback specifically on the level of their achievement of learning outcomes helps them to develop the habit of making better use of the learning outcomes as targets, as they continue to study.

13. *Provide most feedback at the beginning.* Investigate how learning can be advanced in small steps using a 'scaffolding' approach. This means providing lots of support in the early stages which can then be progressively removed as learners become more confident in their own abilities.

14. *Use feedback to let learners know what style of work is expected of them.* Devote energy to helping learners understand what is required of them in terms of writing, that is, work with them to understand the various academic discourses that are employed within the institution, and help them to understand when writing needs to be personal and based on individual experience, such as in a reflective log, and when it needs to be formal and use academic conventions such as passive voice and third person, as in written reports and essays.

15. *Use feedback to help learners learn how best to use different kinds of source materials.* Help them also to understand that there are different kinds of approaches needed for reading, depending on whether they are reading for pleasure, for information, for understanding or reading around a topic. Help them to become active readers, with a pen and post-its in hand, rather than passive readers, fitting the task in alongside television and other noisy distractions.

16. *Take care with the important words.* Ensure that the language you use when giving feedback to learners avoids destructive criticism of the

person rather than the work being assessed. Boud (1995) talks about the disadvantages of using 'final language', that is, language that is judgemental to the point of leaving learners nowhere to go. Words like 'appalling', 'disastrous' and 'incompetent' fall into this area, but so also do words like 'incomparable' and 'unimprovable' if they don't also help outstanding learners to develop ipsatively – i.e. build yet further on their already high achievements.

17. *When possible, use feedback in rehearsal contexts.* Consider providing opportunities for resubmissions of work as part of a planned programme. Learners often feel they could do better work once they have seen the formative feedback and would like the chance to have another go. Particularly at the early stages of a programme, consider offering them the chance to use formative feedback productively. Feedback often involves a change of orientation, not just the remediation of errors.

18. *Get learners giving feedback, not just receiving it.* Think about ways of getting learners to give each other formative feedback. The act of giving feedback often causes deeper thinking than just receiving feedback. Involve learners in their own and each other's assessment. Reflection is not a luxury; it is the best means available to help them really get inside the criteria and understand the often hidden 'rules of the game' of higher education. In particular, asking learners to review each other's draft material prior to submission can be really helpful for all learners, but particularly those who lack confidence about what kinds of things are expected of them.

19. *Cause learners to build on your feedback.* For example, ask them to include with their next assignment an indication of how they have incorporated your feedback from the last one into the present one.

20. *Encourage learners to analyse, systematically, all the feedback they get.* Explain how useful it is for them to identify recurring trends, for example similar comments given to them by different tutors. Above all, encourage learners to identify their strengths, as indicated by recurring feedback, so that they can aim to demonstrate these strengths again and again quite purposefully.

Making Learning Happen in Large Groups

Why have learners in large groups?

There are many reasons why large-group teaching is increasingly important in post-compulsory education. Not least, with policies to widen participation, there are many more learners in our systems, and it is clearly cost-effective to try to work with them in large groups for at least some of the time. But perhaps the most significant reasons for making good use of large-group teaching is to give whole cohorts of learners shared experiences, so that each learner feels part of the group and knows what is expected of them. Feedback from students on their experience of higher education (not least that gathered annually since 2005 in the National Student Survey in the UK) shows that students want more contact with lecturers. Making the most of such contact in large-group contexts is a very significant way we can enhance students' perceptions of the quality of our higher education provision.

What are the differences between the kinds of learning which happen best in a large group and those which go on in all the other facets of higher education, such as tutorials, seminars, laboratories or problem classes? In some subject disciplines, subject coverage is split carefully between large-group sessions and various kinds of small-group sessions. Probably the most important features of the learning which we should strive to engender in large groups are:

- giving students a sense of 'belonging' to a course or module cohort, and making the large-group experience so positive that they feel valued and cared for

- helping learners to see the big picture, including exactly where tutorials, seminars and other teaching–learning elements contribute to the overall context

- giving the whole group shared experiences – for example, developing attitudes and feelings towards the subject matter and the various sources and resources available to deepen the learning experience

- providing the overall information map – for example, using handouts, downloadable files from the intranet, reading lists, specific references and so on

- helping learners to set their sights regarding the real meaning of the intended learning outcomes, and the ways in which learners' achievement of these outcomes will be assessed in due course

- sharing expectations about what learners are required to do on their own, so all members of the whole group are aware of the expected scope of reading around the subject they are intended to do

- providing an opportunity for clarification, so that collectively learners can have their questions answered

- helping learners to gain a real sense of identity in the cohort and to see the links between the different subject areas they are studying.

Tutorials, seminars and other small-group learning contexts are necessarily not identical learning experiences for different sub-groups of the whole cohort, so large-group sessions need to address all the things that *all* members of the whole group need to share, particularly explanations about the evidence of achievement students are required to meet to reach the targets specified in assessment criteria.

How important is large-group teaching?

In the UK National Student Survey, the whole of the first section of the survey (the first four of 22 statements) have links to large-group teaching. The section is called 'The teaching on my course', and students are asked to make judgements as follows: 'definitely agree', 'mostly agree', 'neither agree nor disagree', 'mostly disagree', 'definitely disagree', or 'not applicable' on each of the following statements:

1   Staff are good at explaining things.
2   Staff have made the subject interesting.
3   Staff are enthusiastic about what they are teaching.
4   The course is intellectually stimulating.

These statements apply not just to large-group teaching, but to all the other aspects of a course. However, I am sure that when most students make their judgements on statements '1' to '4' above, the first thing to cross their minds is the most public form of teaching – lectures.

These statements link in turn to how well we have managed to address the factors underpinning successful learning. Students are likely to think we're good at explaining things if we have made it straightforward for them to make sense of difficult concepts and get their heads around fundamental principles. Students are likely to think we have made the subject interesting if we have kept them actively engaged in their learning, including in large-group contexts. Conversely, if we have bored them in lectures, we are unlikely to get a vote of confidence on statement '2'.

In particular, large-group contexts are probably our most important occasions to demonstrate our enthusiasm about what we're teaching. If *we* look bored with what we're teaching, we can hardly expect to enthuse our students about it. It's not just enthusiasm about the subject matter we need – it's also enthusiasm about *students*. If we give the impression of being really pleased to be there with them in lectures, and we're really keen to ensure that they succeed, we're far more likely to get a vote of confidence with statement '3'. Moreover, if we really show that we care that our students succeed, that vote of confidence will be enhanced. That's where helping students to get a real grip on what we're looking for as *evidence of achievement* of the learning outcomes comes in. Similarly, if we do everything in our power to help students *learn by assessing* so that in due course they can prepare successfully for assessment, we're winning.

Statement '4' is rather more complex. What do we mean by 'intellectually stimulating'? Naturally, if we've got ourselves into the position of giving lectures on a topic, we might be expected to find it intellectually stimulating ourselves. But in the UK's National Student Survey, statement '4' is about whether *students* find the subjects intellectually stimulating.

Furthermore, later in the Survey, under the title 'Academic Support', statements 10 and 11 are:

10   I have received sufficient support and advice with my studies.
11   I have been able to contact staff when I needed to.

When students respond to these statements, they are likely to think of their lecturers, and at least some of the support and advice should link to large-group teaching. Students are also likely to think of whether their lecturers were sufficiently available for contact when needed too, even though when groups are very large, it may be intended that they contact other staff (for example, personal tutors) rather than lecturers for most things.

Making learning happen in large groups

There is no 'best' way of working effectively with a large group of learners. There is no best way of lecturing – though lecturing in the traditional sense is unlikely to be the best way of making learning happen, when the learning will in due course be measured and accredited. Furthermore, if all lecturers did the same things in lectures, it would be very boring for students. Indeed, the most common criticism students make about the lectures they find least useful is summed up in one dreaded word in their feedback to us – 'boring'!

There are as many ways of working excellently with large groups as there are skilled lecturers. Many of them do it successfully in their own ways, and others trying to imitate them just can't do it – it's a very personal thing, excellence in teaching large groups. We can, however, improve what we do in large groups through two main approaches:

- observing how many, many colleagues go about it, and noting things to try to emulate and, particularly, things to avoid doing ourselves – Chapter 11 on 'Reflective observation' includes an overview of how we can use peer observation to enhance our own teaching

- paying attention to the *learning* which is happening in large-group contexts, and consciously addressing the seven factors underpinning successful learning outlined in Chapter 2 of this book.

In the discussion which follows, I will address each of these factors in turn.

1 Wanting to learn

What can we do to enhance the *want* to learn in large groups? Ideally, each large-group session should result in as many as possible of the group members going away fired up to continue their learning. Different lecturers achieve this in completely different ways. Probably the most important common factor is enthusiasm. If we seem bored with a subject, there's not much chance we will inspire others to go and learn more about it. But it's not just enthusiasm for the subject that matters. Learners are quick to pick up the vibrations of our enthusiasm for *themselves as people*. Lecturers who come across as really *liking* learners – and respecting them and treating them accordingly – do much to inspire learners to learn. If we enhance the *wanting to learn* dimension, attendance at large-group sessions improves, students look forward to our lectures, and try not to miss them.

One factor we can play with is students' *curiosity*. If they're curious about the topic, they want to learn it – they want to find out answers to the questions about the topic which are in their minds. It's therefore very useful to us to find out what questions students want to explore. Even with hundreds of learners in a lecture theatre, in just a few minutes we can ask everyone to jot down on a post-it 'What I really want to find out about is…'. We can count up the number of times the most popular questions occur and make slides containing these questions. We can then proceed to address these, knowing that many members of the audience wanted to find out more about these aspects of the topic.

Another aspect worth addressing is the *learning incomes* of the students. Another post-it scenario: ask everyone to jot down their response to the statement 'The most important thing I already know about "x" is…'. Students often surprise themselves (and indeed surprise us too) with how much a large group collectively knows about a topic before we've even started a lecture on it. Students are more likely to come to a large-group session if they know that we'll take into account and build upon what they already know about the topic, rather than them having to sit there being told things they already know.

2 Ownership of the *need* to learn

How best can we clarify the need to learn in large groups – sharing the standards we expect regarding students' evidence of achievement, putting the intended learning outcomes to work? Large-group teaching contexts are our best shot at clarifying the need to learn, not least because it is the *fairest* context in which to give learners information about exactly what we expect of them. This is the context where it is fair to tell everyone at once about the assessment standards which underpin the achievement of the intended learning outcomes. Large-group sessions are occasions when we can give cues and clues about the sorts of exam questions which would be reasonable ways to measure learners' achievement of the intended outcomes – much better than giving such clues to only *some* of the learners in particular small-group tutorials or in response to individual questions privately. We can collect learners' individual enquiries about the standards expected of them from all sorts of contexts, but the best chance to clarify our expectations is when *all* the learners in a cohort are present. Indeed, if we make a habit of using large-group contexts to let learners into the fine detail of our expectations, large-group session attendance is improved.

It's useful to start each and every large-group session by going through the intended learning outcomes for that particular session. There are normally only three or four of these. It is also useful to remind students of what they should already be able to do as a result of past lectures. Where possible, arrange that the intended learning outcomes remain visible for the whole of the lecture – for example, by showing them on an overhead projector continuously, while doing other visual things on PowerPoint slides. This allows us to make it quite clear now and then through the session exactly which outcome we're addressing, and it helps students to keep the overall picture of the session in mind throughout.

3 Learning by doing in large groups

Brown and Race (2002) listed things learners actually do in lectures, and added some further things their lecturers *hope* that they may be doing. I have summarized the two lists in Table 6.1, which shows actions which can be linked in straightforward ways to

- wanting to learn (W)
- taking ownership of the need to learn (N)
- learning by doing (D)

- learning through feedback (F)

- making sense of what is being learned (M)

- learning through explaining (E)

- learning through assessing – making informed judgements (A).

You might find it useful to mark up the activities in Table 6.1 with the codes 'W', 'N', ... 'A' as a way of mapping the learner activities you wish to happen during a large-group session, and of trying to ensure that what students do during the session addresses as many of the underpinning factors as realistically possible.

You can then concentrate in your own large-group sessions on facilitating those learner actions which have the highest learning pay-off. Some of the learner actions 'hit' more than one of W, N, D, F, M, E and A, and it is all the more worthwhile to make space for these in large-group teaching. 'Understanding the subject' is not included in the list as it takes a combination of several of the most productive actions to make this a reality. I should also point out that Table 6.1 shows only *some* of the things which learners do in large-group teaching sessions!

Table 6.1 Some things learners do in large group teaching sessions

Adding important points to the handouts	Admiring the cool, calm way the lecturer handles awkward questions
Answering each other's questions	Answering the lecturer's questions
Asking each other questions	Asking the lecturer questions
Being bored	Chatting to the next learner
Copying down important things from the screen	Copying things down (or trying to) that the lecturer says
Discussing things with each other	Explaining things to fellow learners
Feeling embarrassed that they couldn't answer the question	Feeling the light dawning – and trying to capture it
Fretting about their relationships	Getting annoyed at the learner in front busy texting on a mobile
Having misconceptions debunked	Hearing a range of opinions
Highlighting things in the handouts	Itching to get to their books to get into the topic deeper
Jotting down their own answers to the lecturer's questions	Jotting their notes on to the handout materials
Looking for cues about how to tackle the assignment	Making judgements
Making links with things they had learned previously	Making mistakes in buzz group tasks and learning from them
Making notes	Picking up cues about what's important
Practising things	Showing fellow learners how to do something

Table 6.1 (Continued)

Summarizing what's being discussed	Taking down notes
Trying to sort out what's important and what's just background	Waiting, and waiting for some of the class to get things down and for the whole thing to move on
Wanting to leave, but not daring to	Wanting to talk to their neighbour to check out whether they are the only one who can't see the point
Watching the lecturer	Wishing they'd looked at the last two sets of notes
Working out what seems likely to be coming up in the exam	Writing down their own questions for later study
Writing down their own questions so that they can check them out later.	

What can *we* do in large groups?

As already said, there is no one best way of running a successful large-group teaching session – different people do it well in quite different ways. Asking workshop participants to identify the most important large-group teaching behaviours gives a wide range of responses, all of which have their place. But each works best for different people in different ways. Table 6.2 shows a list of such behaviours.

Table 6.2 Some things teachers can do to make learning happen in large-group teaching sessions

Adapting the session to the actual needs of the group at that time	Initiating discussion
Asking learners questions	Inspiring learners
Asking learners to identify issues	Listening to the learners
Being accessible and approachable	Making it relevant to learners – personalizing it
Being enthusiastic	Managing the time well
Being flexible	Orientating and guiding
Causing learners to revise	Providing notes
Challenging learners' thinking	Questioning
Developing learners' study skills	Quizzing learners
Doing a variety of things	Relating their work to the forthcoming or ongoing assignment
Encouraging them to ask questions	Reviewing material they have previously learned
Encouraging feedback	Setting learners challenges
Encouraging participation	Setting the scene – placing the present bit into context
Entertaining	Setting the scene about how learning should happen
Explaining concepts	Signposting the intended learning
Explaining outcomes/objectives	Stimulating interest
Facilitating learners working in groups	Storytelling
Facilitating processing of material	Testing learners

Table 6.2 (Continued)

Getting feedback from learners	Using humour where appropriate
Getting learners to do things with handouts	Using mixed methods
Getting learners to make individual learning plans	Using real examples
Giving learners feedback on their work	Using their experience
Giving learners practical examples	Using visually attractive material
Giving value-added to person who bothers to turn up	
Having prepared properly	

All these processes can be regarded as contributing to making learning happen in large groups. Note how many of these actions go well beyond just 'lecturing' or 'telling learners things'. The more different things we can include in any large-group session, the less likely it is that it will be found to be boring by learners.

As before, it is interesting to run through lecturer activities such as those in Table 6.2, thinking about which of these are most likely to address the factors underpinning successful learning, for example by marking them 'W', 'N' and so on in the same way as you did for the student activities in Table 6.1.

4 Learning through feedback in large groups

How best can we make use of large groups as a feedback-rich environment? Too often, the value of lectures as feedback-receiving opportunities is underused. We can give each and every learner in even the largest group feedback, but only if we have got them to do something – decision-making, problem-solving, and so on. Feedback only really works after action.

How *not* to do it (1)

- **Lecturer**: asks class a question. Waits seven seconds. Then answers own question.

- **Students**: sit there thinking 'Just been asked another question. I'll hang on for seven seconds, then he'll answer it, and I'll write down the answer.'

I've seen somewhere a figure for how long the average lecturer waits after posing a question before proceeding to answer it – 1.8 seconds!

How *not* to do it (2)

- **Lecturer**: asks class a question. Waits seven seconds. Picks a student to try to answer the question.

- **Students**: sit there thinking 'He's just asked another question. I'll hang on for seven seconds, and keep my head down, avoid eye contact. With a bit of luck, he'll pick someone else to answer the question, and if they get it right, I'll write down their answer.'

How to do it?

- **Lecturer**: asks class a question, showing it on a slide so students don't forget what was said. Then he/she says 'Everyone jot down privately your own answer to the question.'
- **Most students**: jot down their answers.
- **Some students**: do nothing.
- **Lecturer**: 'Hands up anyone who is sitting *next to* someone who hasn't jotted down their answer.'
- **Many students raise hands.** (*But all students have now had the feedback of seeing others' answers.*)
- **Lecturer**: 'OK, nothing more happens until you've all jotted down your answer to the question.'
- **Remaining students**: shamed into jotting down their answers to the question.
- **Lecturer**: 'Many of you will have written down a good answer to this question. Volunteer to share your answer?' (Picks volunteer, who reads out answer.)
- **Lecturer**: 'Well done – that's great. How many of you wrote down a similar answer?'
- **Several students raise hands.** (*All students have received feedback now – those whose answers were correct and those whose were not.*)

We can get much more feedback to each member of a large group if we include buzz-group episodes, and get them arguing, debating, speculating, practising, explaining things to each other, and so on *during* the large-group session. It is worth remembering how valuable it is for each learner not just to receive feedback, but to give it to fellow learners. Both processes link strongly to making sense of what is being covered.

We can pave the way towards making optimum use of the feedback-rich environment of large groups by taking away the perceived pressure we often feel, that we must use the precious time to cover as much as possible of the syllabus content prescribed. We can make time to use in feedback by using handouts to provide learners with the information they need, rather than allowing them to simply gather it from us in a one-way process, or wasting their time merely copying down the information from our slides or from what we say. We can then get learners working individually or collectively *processing* the information in their handout materials, making sense of it as they proceed.

5 Making sense in large groups

How can we help learners to get their heads around things in large-group contexts? Ideally, we need to make learning happen *in* large groups, not just some time later when learners revise the contents of a session for exams or assignments. The more we succeed in making large-group sessions occasions where learners feel that they're making sense of the subject matter, the better the attendance will be – in all senses of the word. The case study above of getting them to jot down their own answers to questions, then compare, then volunteer, helps to allow everyone in a large group to get feedback on their own thinking, helping them to make sense of the question and its answer. Helping learners to get their heads round ideas and concepts *during* large-group sessions is best done by making sure that there are plenty of learning-by-doing episodes during the session, each followed by feedback (from fellow learners and from us) so that each learner has the opportunity to find out how much making sense has so far occurred.

Our best chance to help learners to make sense of things is when they have us with them, with all the extra dimensions of tone of voice, body language, eye contact, repetition, emphasis, and so on. Few of these dimensions can be taken away by learners from the large-group session itself, unless they have distilled these into their notes and handouts.

We can, however, cause further making sense to occur by setting tasks for learners to do between one session and the next, so that they engage in further learning by doing, practice, trial and error, and so on. This is made all the better if we can arrange that they get feedback as quickly as possible – for example, by encouraging them to do some of the tasks in small groups with discussion. Alternatively, we can, for example, issue a problems sheet at the end of the session, with a marking scheme and model answers in a sealed envelope. Few learners fall into the temptation of opening the envelope before they have had a go at the problems. The feedback they get when they do their self-marking and compare their work to the model answers is much more rapid than if they had to wait until the next teaching session. We can put some pressure, where necessary, on learners to make sure that they actually *do* the between-sessions work by quizzing the whole group about the work in the opening minutes of the forthcoming session, choosing names at random to shame any learners who have not got round to the task. That said, we've got to be really careful not to shame any learners too much – otherwise next time they haven't done the task, they won't come to the lecture to avoid the risk of humiliation.

6 Learning through explaining, coaching or teaching

At first sight, we can be forgiven for thinking that explaining, coaching and teaching are *our* job in large-group contexts. Indeed, we might feel under pressure to do most of the talking in such contexts. However, we can reverse the situation, allowing learners to deepen their learning, for example by explaining things to each other. For example, suppose you've just gone through a rather complex explanation of a difficult concept with a large lecture group. You might then ask 'How many of you are still with me at this point? Raise your hand if you reckon you've made sense of what we've just been thinking about.' Suppose a third of the class raise their hands. You can now invite them to get into threes or fours, each cluster containing one student who has mastered the concept. Then ask that person in each group to spend a few minutes explaining the concept to those who haven't yet 'got it', until they have all made sense of it. This has enormous benefits for the 'explainers'. The act of explaining something about which the 'light has just dawned' is a very memorable activity, and the explainers retain it strongly. Those being explained to are also advantaged, as this time the concept is being explained by someone who remembers the light dawning. Lecturers may have known the concept so long that they can't remember the feeling of the light dawning.

'But what about using my precious time in this way?', lecturers may ask. 'It is well worth it in terms of students' learning pay-off' is my response. Students remember what *they do* in large groups much more than they might remember what *we say*. We can go further than this, and actively encourage learners to spend time out of the lecture context coaching each other. Many institutions go as far as to have 'supplemental instruction' or 'peer teaching' provision, where (for example) third-year students are given the responsibility of supporting first-year students in chosen aspects of the curriculum. As before, the greatest value of this is to the 'explainers'. The third-year students develop a strong mastery of the fundamentals they are teaching to the first-year students, who in turn feel more relaxed learning difficult concepts from a fellow-student than from a lecturer, and are more willing to ask questions as necessary until the 'making sense' has been achieved.

7 Learning through assessing – making informed judgements

This is one of the most powerful things we can do in large-group teaching contexts. For example, we can use a whole large-group session as follows.

1. Give everyone in the room three handouts on different colours of paper, for example of an essay or report or assignment, or examples of an answer to a past exam question. Make one of them an excellent example, one a poor example and one an intermediate one. Ensure that the three examples don't immediately *look* excellent, poor and intermediate, but that they need to be studied quite carefully before it becomes apparent which is which.

2. Ask everyone in the class to work independently for a few minutes, looking through the three examples, and deciding which is the excellent one, which is the poor one and which is the intermediate one.

3. Get the class to vote – for example, 'Hands up those who think the pink handout is the poor one', and so on.

4. Then get students into clusters, to work out *why* the yellow one is better than the blue one, and why the blue one is better than the pink one.

5. Ask different clusters for the *criteria* that distinguish the excellent one from the intermediate one, and so on, writing up these criteria (in the students' own words) on to a slide, board or chart.

6. Now show students a marking scheme for the piece of work they have been judging, and ask the clusters to apply the marking scheme to the three examples. The students are now *making informed judgements* on the pieces of work they are examining. Moreover, they are making these judgements in the same ways that will be used for their own work in due course – they are getting their heads around the assessment culture in which they are studying.

7. Finally, remind the class about how the same sort of criteria will be used to judge the students' own work on a forthcoming assignment or exam answer.

A whole lecture period spent in this way has a really high learning pay-off. It is a way of:

A. Showing students details of the *evidence of achievement* which in due course will be expected of them.

B. Illustrating what the related learning outcomes actually mean in practice.

C. Helping students to see the standards expected of them so that they take increased ownership of the need to achieve the learning outcomes and produce suitable evidence to demonstrate this.

D. Allowing students to experience the assessment criteria they will in turn be judged against, and to apply these criteria to examples of essays (or reports or exam answers, and so on) so that they get their heads around exactly how their own work will in due course be assessed.

In fact, there are few ways of achieving such a high amount of learning pay-off with a large group in a single lecture period. Just giving yet another lecture would only have achieved a fraction of that learning pay-off for the students. It can be argued that getting a class to make judgements in this kind of way is one of the best things to do in whole-group contexts. Furthermore, when students see that they find out in such a lecture a great deal of useful information about how their work will be assessed, their motivation increases, and they are far less likely to risk missing a lecture in case they should miss such valuable information relating to their future assessment.

At the same time, they are still learning about the topic concerned, but in a much deeper way than if they were simply being told about it in 'lecture mode'.

Making learning happen by *not lecturing!*

You will have seen from the discussion so far in this chapter, that large-group teaching–learning contexts can play a really vital part in making learning happen for our students – particularly if we don't fill these sessions with the sound of our voices merely *telling* students things. We can, as you've seen above, purposefully address in large-group contexts each and every one of the seven factors underpinning successful learning as outlined in Chapter 2. Lectures are no longer just to give students information – if that's all we want to do, we may as well give each of them a data stick full of information. Lectures are for helping students to get their heads around information and begin turning it into their own knowledge or linking it to what they already know.

This in no way detracts from the value of the old-fashioned sort of lecture as enlightenment or entertainment. Going to that sort of lecture for pure pleasure remains one of the attractions of the experience of university or college life. But when there is the serious business of *learning*, followed by the even more serious business of *assessment*, we can argue that the primary purpose of a large-group session is that the students should leave the session with much more in their heads than when they entered the room, and that mere 'lecturing' has little part to play.

How can we use handouts to make learning happen?

The evolution of handouts

Only two or three decades ago, handouts were relatively rare. Learners in lectures needed to make notes if they were to take away from the lecture the content that had been covered by the lecturer. Typically, this meant that in an hour they could only acquire a few pages worth of information. If they had just been furiously writing out all they could capture from the lecture, this information may have been mainly unprocessed when they took it away, but at least the task of going through it again and turning it into their own knowledge was manageable. Nowadays, it is common for a great deal more information to be placed directly into learners' hands (or more often on to their computer screens) than they could ever have written down in a lecture. They may even be able to download the information upon which a lecture focuses from the intranet before the lecture, and then work with it, adding to it ideas they gained from the lecture itself, and build into the material their thinking after the lecture. So it is not uncommon for learners to receive one way or another 10 or 20 pages or screens of information around a lecture – and printed pages contain many more words (numbers, pictures, graphs, diagrams, and so on) than could be written or drawn by any learner in an hour.

Similarly, where formerly learners needed to make their own notes from books in libraries, nowadays they are likely to make photocopies of the information they believe to be most relevant or important, and take the information away with them, or scan the originals and transfer the files to their computers. Cue-seeking learners are probably the best at deciding which extracts are important enough for them to make their own copies, and cue-oblivious learners run the greatest risk of copying everything which *might* turn out to be relevant – this is in fact simply postponing (often indefinitely) the task of getting down to making sense of the information and turning it into their own knowledge.

For a while, handouts became increasingly important in the context of large-group teaching, and were important not only to learners, but as elements of the evidence used to assess the quality of post-compulsory education. More recently, however, the number of actual handouts issued in lectures has decreased quite dramatically, for reasons that include the following:

- Handouts are costly to produce and groups are often much larger these days than they used to be.

- It is onerous for lecturers to organize the production of handouts in time for a given session, and tedious to carry around large bundles of these for big classes.

- It is much easier to put up the handout materials on an intranet or on the web, and they can be put their just before the lecture, with the request that students look at them as preparation, or even print them and bring copies to the lecture to annotate during the session.

- Handouts can be annotated immediately after the lecture (usually quite quickly) before putting them up on the web, reflecting issues which emerged during the session.

- Students are impressed that a spontaneous discussion which took place in the lecture was summarized shortly afterwards in the web-based handout – 'I was part of this', they may think.

Nevertheless, the accompanying handout materials remain an important aspect of large-group teaching, even when no paper is involved. I have reflected the importance of handouts by discussing their use in some detail below, linking them to the factors underpinning successful learning quite overtly.

While feedback may be considered to be the lifeblood of making learning happen in post-compulsory education, handouts can be thought of as the arteries controlling the flow of information to learners' hands. However, perhaps handouts are not an entirely successful means of getting the information processed in students' brains. Returning to Einstein's idea that 'learning is experience, everything else is just information', it is easy to see that the main danger associated with handouts is that they give learners information which is not, in due course, processed by them to become their own knowledge.

Some problems with handouts

- Some learners take the view 'I don't need to go to the class, I can simply get a copy of the handout'. The same applies, of course, if the handout material is made available on the web. It is true that learners can get the *information* in this way, but with an element of good teaching, just having the information does not equate to actually *being there*. Learners who miss out on the tone of voice, body language, facial expression, emphasis, clarification and often *inspiration* of participating in a class are seriously disadvantaged. But frequently they do not realize this until too late, thinking that they've 'got it all' in their copied handout or web file. Indeed, in many an effective face-to-face session, a handout is more of an *adjunct* to the intended learning than a summary of it.

- 'I've already *got* the handout, therefore there's no point in me going to the class.' This happens all too often when handout materials are issued in advance or made available on an intranet before the relevant teaching session.

- 'I don't need to pay attention now. I've already got the information so I can sit back and switch off now.' This can be the view of learners sitting in a class with their own copy of a handout safely in their possession. True, they may already have got the *information*, but they are then missing out on the best chance to turn that information into the beginnings of their own *making sense* of that information, using tone of voice and so on as cues and clues.

- 'What am I expected to *do* with this handout – read it now, revise from it later, do things with it now and soon after now, just file it, collect handouts until I've got all of them and *then* do something with them...?' This list is endless. In fact, all such reactions to handouts can be regarded as handout-using avoidance tactics – excuses for putting off doing some *real* learning until later.

Increasing students' *ownership* of handouts

Whose handout is it? Is it simply the lecturer's? With paper-based handouts, when learners have *done* a lot with a handout *during* a class, the ownership is very much more *theirs*. When there's a lot of *their* writing on the handout, they feel quite differently about it than when it was exactly the same as everyone else's copy of the handout. In fact, they're then much less likely to loan it to a friend who missed the session so that they can copy it – they might lose *their* thoughts in the process. Indeed, they may feel 'Why should so-and-so benefit from the work *I've* done on these pages?'

I have included below an example of a self-assessment checklist which learners can be given with the aim to get them thinking exactly how they are making use of handout materials. The example I chose for the checklist refers to a handout accompanying a particular lecture, but the idea of making such a checklist can easily be extended to help learners to self-evaluate how they are making use of *any* handout – any collection of information, exercises, subject matter, and so on.

Checklist on using a handout during and after a lecture

Please tick one or more columns as appropriate for each choice below.	This is what I did.	I would have liked to do this, but didn't manage it.	I didn't think this necessary.	This just was not possible for me.	I'll do this next time.	This was not possible for this handout.
1 I filed the handout together with other handouts from this course, but haven't yet *done* anything with the handout itself.						
2 I read through this handout within three days of getting it.						
3 I marked up the handout with my own ideas during the lecture.						
4 I marked up the handout with my own ideas within a few days of the lecture.						
5 I wrote on the handout my own questions about the topic, so that I would not forget these questions.						

6	I compared *my* questions and notes on the handout with at least one other learner's thoughts.						
7	I have tried the tasks and exercises in the handout now, and learned useful things through doing this.						
8	I have followed up the handout by reading suggested reference materials.						
9	I have used the handout as a framework to add further notes from other sources I have consulted.						
10	I found that the intended learning outcomes gave me a useful frame of reference, helping me to structure my work on the handout effectively.						
11	I missed the lecture concerned, but have now got a copy of the handout.						
12	I feel that I have mastered the handout, and that there is nothing further I now need to do with this bit of subject matter to be ready for any aspect of it that will come up in assessments.						

Using handouts to make learning happen in lectures

How, then, can we make best use of pieces of paper with information already reproduced on them, or electronic files for learners to view on-screen or print out for themselves, to maximize the associated learning pay-off learners derive from them?

1 Handouts and wanting to learn

For a start, if handouts *look* interesting, there's more chance that they will be used and not just filed away. Making handouts look interesting can be done in several ways, including:

- making the subject matter interesting to read and study

- making the information on handouts *digestible* rather than dry and forbidding

- using paper or screen images to capture diagrams, graphs, pictures, and so on to bring to life the ideas concerned

- even simply paying attention to layout, choice of font, and so on.

However, the most important way of ensuring that handouts enhance learners' *want* to learn is to make sure that learners find them really *useful*. This can be partly achieved by paying attention to the content of the handouts, and helping learners to feel that at least some of the work has already been done for them. By narrowing down the subject content so that everything on their handouts can already be regarded as important, learners will be encouraged to invest time and energy following up the subject matters.

2 Handouts and taking ownership of the need to learn

Perhaps the most direct way that handout materials can help learners to take ownership of their need to learn is including (prominently) the relevant intended learning outcomes and, where necessary, translating these into language which learners can readily relate to. In other words, it is useful to give learners some guidance about what in due course they need to become able to *do* with the content of the handouts – how learners will be expected to become able to *evidence* their achievement of the intended learning outcomes.

This does not assume that all the intended outcomes can be achieved just by studying the information on a given handout. The intended outcomes can range outward and link to what learners are expected to be able to do through their work on reference sources listed in a handout, along with guidance about how best to approach each individual source. Rather than, for example, suggest 'Now read Chapter 4 of Smith and Jones', a handout is much more useful if it suggests 'Consult Chapter 4, particularly sections 3 and 5, looking for answers to the following questions...'. In addition, including a self-assessment exercise will help learners to focus their work on the source so that they do indeed get the most important things out of the handout. This sort of guidance can also include advice such as 'You don't need to bother with sections 2 or 7 unless you really want to – these are not directly relevant to your own particular intended learning outcomes relating to this source'.

3 Handouts and learning by doing

Throughout this book I have stressed the importance of learning by doing – particularly practice, repetition of relevant activities, and learning by trial and error. When handout materials are designed quite overtly as learning-by-doing devices, the chances of them just being filed away are dramatically reduced. Handouts (including those supplied electronically) which contain several tasks and exercises are likely to be used, not just stored. When it can be *seen* that a handout is something to do things with – for example, with boxes to be filled in, spaces for calculations to be done, and so on – at least learners know that simply leaving these boxes unfilled is not going to be sufficient. If it is made clear that the activities in a handout relate directly to the achievement of relevant aspects of the intended learning outcomes, learners are all the more likely to engage with the material. If it is also made very clear that *doing* the handout will relate well to the sorts of *doing* which will in due course be assessed (exam questions, assignments, essays, essay plans, and so on), learners become much more aware that they need to engage with the activities in a handout.

Cue-seeking learners are in their element here, of course, but cue-conscious learners find this way of highlighting what is important (and what isn't) useful too, and cue-oblivious learners are still able to benefit to the extent that the things they *do* using the handout are already designed to be relevant and important, saving them perhaps from spending too much time or energy going off on tangents, or straying too far away from the intended learning outcomes which will form the basis of their assessment further down the line.

4 Handouts and making sense of what is learned

There are several things we can do to design handouts which help learners to get their heads round ideas and concepts. As indicated above, we can design into handouts relevant learning by doing, so that learners get the chance to apply their minds to the information in the handout and process it as part of the journey towards building their own knowledge using the hand-out. Also as noted above, careful use of intended learning outcomes can assist learners in finding out *what exactly* they should be trying to make sense of, and alerting them to the ways in which they will need to become able to demonstrate that they have made sense of the material in the handout.

Moreover, handout materials are really useful as study guides, referencing a wide range of print-based and web-based sources and resources. Such handouts help learners to see exactly which parts of these sources are most relevant to them, and how they can use these sources to evidence their own achievement of the intended learning outcomes.

5 Handouts and learning through feedback

When the primary intention of handout material is to give learners feedback on things they have already done, handouts can be particularly useful in making learning happen. For example, when learners have struggled with something, a handout showing them how best to go about it may be eagerly used. However, one of the best ways of coupling learning by doing with feedback is to include in handout materials self-assessment exercises of one kind or another, where learners can have a go at a task or problem, then find elsewhere in the handout the means to judge their own efforts. In this way, they find out the extent to which they 'got it right', and, more importantly, they address the 'if not, why not?' question. Clearly, there are disadvantages in making the feedback *too* easy to find. If learners can see it at the same time as seeing the tasks themselves, the temptation for eyes to stray towards the answers remains great. Only the most conscientious learners will resist looking straight at the solutions. Other learners who skip having a go at the problems may *feel* that looking immediately at the solutions is good enough, but we all know that being able to do something is not the same as *feeling* that one can do it correctly.

6 Handouts and explaining, coaching, teaching

One of the dangers with handouts, whether they are paper-based or electronic, is that learners tend to study them in solitary silence. We can encourage learners to explain things to each other using handouts as a resource, for example by setting group tasks based on handout materials. We can encourage learners to coach each other in the deeper points of material addressed in handouts, and we can start off such processes *during* lectures, so that learners get the message that this is a valuable thing to continue doing afterwards.

7 Handouts and assessing – making informed judgements

This is perhaps where handout materials really reap the greatest rewards in terms of making learning happen. For example, when students are using handouts to apply assessment criteria to work similar to work they will themselves do later, the handout materials can achieve a high learning pay-off. It is again useful to start students off doing this kind of activity with handout materials in the lecture room, to whet their appetites to continue doing the same sorts of things on their own – and, more importantly, in groups.

Should I give students handouts of my slides?

Having explored handouts in general terms, the following discussion is about one particular variety of handout: copies of PowerPoint slides. There is a tendency in many institutions to issue students with handout materials of PowerPoint slides using the 3-per-page or 6-per-page options. Many institutions now have policies to address students' special needs, often including the availability (in advance) of PowerPoint presentations and handouts. I argue here that this process, although having some advantages, is not a good idea, and that there are better ways of addressing the special needs of students.

Ten reasons not to issue handouts of PowerPoint slides

1. Learners are likely to switch off when they have the slides before them in a handout. They think 'There's no real need to pay attention now. I can look at this again anytime.'

2. In practice, many learners never look at the handouts of the slides ever again! I've now asked thousands of learners how often they have revisited such handouts, and very few claim to have done so – and even then, only to recapture the odd strange fact or joke. Students rarely file slides (and handouts in general) in a systematic way.

3. Too often, slides are effectively just information. Learning only happens when people process information, and do things with it, apply it, argue with it, extrapolate from it, compare and contrast it, and so on. Therefore it is very unsafe to assume that just because everyone has the information, all will have learned.

4. Students *want* copies of the slides, but not everything that they want is good for them. This is partly because they seek the safety of ensuring that they get all the relevant information. While it is good to avoid letting them simply copy down information from a screen in a lecture theatre into their own notes, it remains important that they engage actively during lectures, and are getting their heads round information rather than just looking at it on the screen or on their own copy of what's on the screen.

5. It is environmentally unsound: if the paper ends up not being used, it's a waste of paper. If we want to give people the chance to revisit slides, it is much more sound environmentally to put the presentation on the web or on to an intranet, or to email it to them.

6. When people have paper copies of the slides, they get dissatisfied when several slides are 'missed' in the session. It is good to keep the choice to skip particular sections of a prepared presentation, and concentrate on the key issues, especially when time is taken to address questions and follow up the emergent interests or needs of the particular audience.

7. While it may be better to have 3-per-page with space to make notes alongside each slide, this is rarely done well in practice. Not least, the lined nature of the boxes alongside the slides does not allow people to make detailed notes alongside some key slides.

8. Making copies of the slides available tempts students to miss sessions. Many lecturers have now realized that attendance drops as students just photocopy the handouts of the slides (and other handouts too) rather than coming to the lecture. The students who miss the lecture usually fare much worse in coursework assessment or exams, and just give back the information which was in the slides or handouts, whereas those who were present learn a lot more through the actual discussion, where communication is aided by tone of voice, body language, eye contact, emphasis in speech, repetition of important points from different perspectives, and so on. Words or pictures on paper (or on screen) can never compete with normal full human communication.

9. It can be even more environmentally unsound when the presentations are made available in advance. The keen people come with their print-out of the slides, often in colour, and at considerable expense.

10. Making slides available in advance greatly restricts flexibility in presentations and lectures. It is often a good idea to make the presentations available electronically *after* the event. This gives you freedom to choose which slides to use during the event and allows you to add slide sequences to address matters that arose in the lecture, for example questions from the audience. Making the slides available after the event also allows you to delete any slides you chose not to show or didn't show because time ran out.

How can we get learners in large groups to ask us questions?

In many teaching–learning contexts, not least lectures and small-group sessions, one of the most productive ways of making learning happen is to cause learners to ask questions and provide answers to their questions. When they are working out what questions to ask, they are exploring their own *need* to learn, and at the same time they are often working on what they *want* to find out. Asking questions is one kind of *learning by doing*. Receiving answers to their own questions is, of course, *learning through feedback*, as is hearing answers to other people's questions. Ideally, all of these processes should help them to *make sense* or *digest* the topics which are the basis of the questions.

While it is relatively easy to get learners to fire their questions at us in small groups or in one-to-one contexts, it is harder to achieve this with hundreds of learners at a time. One thing that can help is to ask everyone to jot down two or three questions. Give them a couple of minutes to do so. Then ask them to compare their questions with those of their immediate neighbours. Then ask the class for some of the questions. This way, there is more chance of you being asked the questions that are more widely owned, and are thus more important. It is also a way of getting everyone to think about at least some questions, so that even the learners who don't get answers to their questions during the session are still able to take the questions away with them. If you'd just got learners to *think* of some questions and call them out, many of the questions in their minds would have evaporated away very soon after the session. However, there can be another problem – dominant learners. Read on.

How can we avoid a few students dominating questioning?

How can we enable all learners to get answers to their questions in large-group sessions without the sessions being monopolized by a few vociferous learners? Following on from my response to the previous question, it remains worthwhile trying to get all the learners to write down a question or two in the first instance. However, when you know that it will be the same learners who voice their questions, possibly because they are more confident than their course mates, some alternative tactics can come in handy.

For example, pass out post-its so the whole group can have one each, and ask everyone to jot down one or two questions on their post-it. Then ask for the post-its to be passed to you and stick them on a flipchart, whiteboard, window or suitable wall. With really large groups, get the learners themselves to do this, it's quicker. You can then scan through the questions, picking off a post-it at a time, and reading out the question so everyone knows what you're going to be answering. Then you can answer the question, filing the post-it so you have an accurate record of which questions you have answered.

Normally it is worth concentrating on those questions which you can readily see to be relatively common ones, so that you are satisfying the needs of a reasonable cross-section of the large group. However, it is also worth taking away with you *all* the post-its, so you can look through them in your own time. You can then create an 'FAQ' (frequently asked questions) sheet containing other important questions and headline answers to give out at your next meeting with the large group, or you can post a *frequently needed answers* bulletin on the web.

How can we manage inappropriate behaviours in large groups?

This is a frequently asked question at workshops on dealing with large groups! I often use a '30-second theatre' technique with workshop participants. Working in threes, one makes an 'inappropriate behaviour incident', another responds as the teacher or lecturer for no more than 30 seconds, then the third, who has been observing, leads a discussion on how well the exchange might have gone in a real situation and explores alternative ploys. Two of the most frequent 'inappropriate behaviours' are discussed below.

Learners coming in late

This is increasingly common, not least because many learners have commitments which sometimes conflict with their college programmes – childcare, work-related matters, and so on. It can be very infuriating, however, especially when latecomers disrupt a large group as they make their way to the remaining seats. Indeed, some latecomers seem to be only too happy to be disruptive in such circumstances.

Confronting them publicly is not the best idea. If they are indulging in attention-seeking behaviours, that would just reward them. Moreover, when latecomers have good reasons for being late, making them feel uncomfortable is not likely to increase their confidence to turn up late ever again, and they are quite likely to miss your next session entirely rather than risk further embarrassment.

The safest option is probably to ignore latecomers. Pausing while they settle themselves in is better than trying to carry on talking when learners are being distracted by the latecomers' entry. But sometimes you can't just ignore them, and it would take too long to wait until they have settled down. If there are successive interruptions of this kind, it can be wearing both on yourself and on all the other learners in the group. Peer pressure under such circumstances can often come to bear on regular offenders.

Some lecturers can't resist a touch of irony. 'So glad you could join us', and so on. But this can sometimes hit hard at the odd learner who is hardly ever late or who on this occasion has a really good reason for being late. When you are able to use their names, it can be useful to say something to them by name, for example, 'There are still some seats down here, John', and this can at least have the effect that the latecomer knows that you know who he or she is.

One tactic which can reduce the incidence of latecomers is to always start as soon as reasonably possible, but with something particularly useful to learners. For example, preceding the intended learning outcomes for *this* session with five important points to carry forward from the *last* session can reward those who are punctual, particularly when these points contain useful advice relating to a forthcoming assessment based on the last session.

Learners chatting to each other

This is often a sign that they are bored – or, at least, that their motivation is low. However, sometimes learners are talking to each other in more productive ways, such as:

- explaining a point to a neighbour who missed it

- clarifying what something you said actually means

- translating something into a different language for someone whose first language isn't English.

Whatever the context, however, it is unwise to continue trying to talk above a growing level of background chatter. Sometimes, going closer to the people who are chatting stops them. Alternatively, asking them 'Is there a problem here?' can help you to find out what's going on. Sometimes, gradually *lowering* your voice can work and actually cause learners to cut down the amount of chatter.

It is more difficult to decide what to do when the problem is simply that some learners are not interested in what is going on and are being deliberately disruptive! Asking them to leave may be an option, but if they refuse to leave it becomes a real problem. Never get into the situation of having done something irreversible like this.

Sometimes, a level of background chatter can be a signal to do something quite different with the large group. Options include:

- Give them a task where they are *intended* to talk to the people sitting closest to them for a few minutes. For example, put up a slide asking them to argue a case with each other, or make a decision, or think of some causes for a phenomenon. When learners are getting restless, and one of the symptoms is talking to each other, *causing* them to talk to each other for a few minutes can help them to get it out of their system.

- Make it more interesting. This is where it can be useful to inject a little humour, for example, by having a hidden action button on a PowerPoint slide which you can use to summon up an amusing picture, or something else to restore learners' concentration.

- Give them a written task to do individually first, then discuss with each other. If some learners continue chatting, you at least know that you may need to push them a little harder to get down to the task before continuing to talk to each other, as intended.

- If it's near the scheduled end of the session, bring it to a close anyway, rather than press on against all the odds to cover everything you had intended to cover in that particular session. Complaints about lecturers ending a lecture ahead of time are extremely rare – I've never heard such a complaint!

How can you help learners to be heard in large-group sessions?

We've already explored some ways to get questions from individual learners, for example, using post-its. However, it's useful to be able to respond to spontaneous questions from learners too. Always try to repeat the question back to the whole group before proceeding to answer it, as people behind the questioner may not have been able to hear the question when first posed. If the question is a long one, a complex one or an unclear one, it can be worth clarifying the question, for example, by asking 'Is your question really about... ?', or suggesting 'Let's break this question into three parts...' and then breaking it down into a logical sequence before continuing to answer it. Repeating the question back to the whole group also gives you a little longer to mentally rehearse how you're going to respond to it.

Sometimes, a dialogue happens between one particular learner and yourself. In such cases, if the room allows, it can improve things if you can move closer to the questioner, so that it is easier for you to interact well with this learner and so that they are better able to make sense of your responses to them. If, however, the dialogue becomes too protracted, it may be necessary to explain to the whole group that 'I think this is a matter for the two of us to explore outside this session', so that they don't feel that they are being ignored.

What do learners do that hinders learning?

We've already explored some learners' actions which hinder learning – coming in late and chatting inappropriately. There are many other things they may do which get in the way of their learning. These include:

- *Taking notes rather than making notes.* At one level, this is not a problem; if they're busy copying things down from the screen or board or writing down what you are saying to them, they're unlikely to be disruptive in other ways. However, *taking* notes is usually very passive; *making* notes is much better for learning. *Making* notes can include making their own summaries of what has been covered in the last few minutes, or annotating a handout with the main points that you have covered which are not already presented there, and so on. It is important to help learners to make notes by building in suitable time spans (e.g. two minutes) to give them an opportunity to do this. It can also be useful to allow another minute or two for them to compare the notes they made with each other and add further ideas to their own notes. 'Now steal your classmates' best ideas for a minute' is irresistible to many learners.

- *Just sitting passively.* This is all too easy. Unless we *cause* learners to be active in large-group sessions, many will just sit there waiting until they're told to do something. They may look as though they're listening – even quite attentively – but may have already found out that as long as they *look* as though they are there in spirit, they can switch off mentally! The answer is for us to continue to take control of what they do, so they have a variety of things to do and are less likely to sink into passivity. We can alternate between getting them to answer questions, discuss points with each other, make notes, solve problems, apply what they've just learned to a case study scenario, explain things to each other, make judgements on things we give them to assess, and so on. Students very rarely complain in evaluation feedback 'I was kept too busy during lectures!' They much more often complain of being bored.

- *Going to sleep and snoring!* This is many lecturers' worst-case scenario of things going wrong in large groups. It has to be said that for things to get this far, they must have been passive for rather too long in the first place, and we need to look to what *we* have done – or not done – to cause them to slumber. That said, it is worth remembering that at least some learners in any large group will be in *need* of sleep. Some may have worked late or early shifts, and may be already deprived of sleep. Others may have enjoyed themselves into the early hours, to the same effect. Sitting still for a long time in a relatively warm comfortable environment, especially if the lights are dimmed for slides to be seen, fulfils fairly ideal conditions for human sleep! It does not help to make anyone who has nodded off feel seriously embarrassed – that may have the effect of causing them not to bother turning up at all next time they are tired and in danger of falling asleep. The kindest thing to do is perhaps to change the activity, for example getting *everyone* to discuss a point with their nearest neighbours – even if they have to wake up the odd neighbour in the process.

What do lecturers do that hinders learning?

Learners themselves can tell us a lot about this. The worst, and all too frequent, comments that learners make about unsatisfactory experiences of large-group teaching feature one word – 'boring'. Their feedback includes:

- droning on and on

- going right over our heads

- not looking at us – or ignoring us

- going too fast – or going too slow (this is a problem in any large group, with people learning at their own speeds, of course, and we need to try to vary the pace accordingly, with 'catch-up' time for the slower learners but also giving the faster ones something extra to think about so that they don't become bored)

- telling us things we already know
- not linking the topic to what *we* know about it
- doing things that seem irrelevant
- forgetting to explain *why* a particular topic will be useful
- failing to make things relevant to our own experience
- not responding to our questions or giving us the chance to ask them
- not giving us anything to do.

Some of this feedback warns us to sharpen up our own act, to make things as interesting as we can, checking regularly that the large group is 'with us' and keeping each and every member of the large group as active as we can. However, there are many well-intentioned lecturer actions which can hinder learning too. These include:

- going off on lengthy tangents to the main purpose of the session, sometimes out of a will to make a topic more interesting
- explaining things in detail when most of the group already need no further explanation
- presenting too much information without giving learners the chance to do something with the information
- sticking too closely to the agenda for the session when all the signs are that learners need a few minutes rest from thinking about a difficult concept
- doing *anything* for too long at a time and failing to bring some variety to learners
- being too predictable!

It is helpful to us to continuously gather feedback from our learners about what they like about our large-group sessions and what they dislike. We can't please all of them all of the time, but the more we find out about their likes and dislikes, the better we can strike a balance. It is also really useful to sit in on colleagues' large-group sessions as often as possible. In someone else's lecture, whatever the topic, we can usually come out with two lists:

- Things that seemed to work well for them, that I can try in my own large-group sessions.
- Things I noticed which didn't work and which I'll try to avoid in my sessions.

This can all be done quite informally and, where team teaching is the norm, lecturers find it very useful simply to learn informally from each others' approaches in this way. Many institutions nowadays have systems of peer observation (more detail in Chapter 11), and it is then useful to have direct feedback from different colleagues about how they find our individual approaches to large-group teaching.

How can we increase the *takeaway* from lectures?

I've already referred to the differences between *making* notes and just *taking* notes. It can be useful to help learners themselves to take owner-ship of the need to capture much more than just the information which is covered in large-group sessions. Remind them that even just an hour or two after a lecture, especially if they have already been in two or three other lectures, much of the fine detail will have evaporated away. Suggest that learners consciously try to capture questions which go through their minds all the way through large-group sessions, and jot these questions down in their notes (perhaps in a different colour). These questions can include things they would have liked to have asked in the lecture but didn't, questions other learners asked, questions about things not yet understood, and so on. Even when questions are jotted down only to be fol-lowed by the answers becoming clear, it is valuable to have written down the question, and then perhaps ticked it or drawn an arrow to where the answer is now written down.

A wise and experienced colleague told me how a couple of years ago he fell in with his institution's policies and put all his lecture handouts and PowerPoint slides on the intranet. He did this a couple of weeks ahead of each lecture, for the sake of any learners with special needs. But two things happened:

- attendance fell off at his lectures

- exam performance in due course worsened dramatically.

He analysed this. The learners who *didn't* come to his lectures only gave him back in exam answers that which he'd given them in the handouts and PowerPoint slides, nothing more. The learners who *did* attend his lectures gave back much more, from the thinking which he got them to do *during* his lectures, and the reading around the subject that he inspired them to do *after* his lectures. Yet many colleagues continue to put up all of the informa-tion for learners in similar ways, and it is often now institutional policy to do so. We need to make sure that our best efforts to respond to learners with special needs do not end up disadvantaging many more learners.

How can we use lectures to build appropriate study skills?

What kinds of briefing do learners need to help them understand how best to learn in large-group contexts? In particular, learners need guidance on what to do in lectures. Especially in first-year courses, they may feel strangely alone even in a packed lecture theatre, with no idea what they are expected to do. Write it all down? Sit there and think about it? Try to look as intelligent as possible? Be quiet and 'good' and not interrupt by asking questions?

Some guidance on the differences between note-taking and note-making can be very welcome. It is best if this kind of guidance is regarded as everyone's business, and not just the remit of a specialist in learning support services. When we all share our suggestions about how to make the most of large-group sessions, learners pick up a much more balanced picture of the possibilities open to them and the different ways their lecturers themselves found successful when studying. I've tried to address the study skills side of large-group teaching in Race (2007), written directly for learners themselves.

In particular, learners need to be well briefed on the importance of intended learning outcomes as a framework for their learning and as the basis of a specifications framework laying down the standards of the evidence that they themselves need to become able to provide for their learning in the different kinds of assessment which will follow.

Left to themselves, learners often simply add their notes and handouts to piles of similar information-bearing papers. Sometimes, it's only when revising for exams or tests that they return to these original materials and, unsurprisingly, it is then often not at all easy to make sense of the materials. All the *extra* impact of tone of voice, emphasis, body language, repetition, clarification and so on has evaporated away from the information in the notes and handouts. Learners often ask themselves 'Was I actually *there* for this session? Did I copy the notes from someone who was there?', and sometimes: 'Is this really my handwriting?'

We can advise learners how useful it is to follow up each large-group session within two or three days, to edit and improve the notes and handouts while the memory of the session itself is still present. One way of helping learners to realize for themselves the importance of not losing the experience of large-group teaching is to get them to reflect on what they do after the average lecture. The self-assessment checklist shown below is one way of alerting learners to what we hope they will be doing after each lecture. Furthermore, if we can persuade learners to give us copies of filled-in self-assessment questionnaires of this kind, we too can find out a lot more about what they are actually doing after each large-group session. This may make our expectations rather more realistic.

Self-assessment checklist to use after a lecture

Please tick one or more columns for each of the options below.	This is what I did.	I would have liked to do this, but didn't manage it.	I didn't think this necessary.	This just was not possible for me.	I'll do this next time.
1	I've looked through my notes to check I understood everything.					
2	I've re-read the handout, and made extra notes *on* it to help me to remember what seemed clear at the time.					
3	I've jotted down questions where I don't yet understand something, on my notes and handouts for me to follow up later.					
4	I've filed my notes carefully where I can find them easily later.					
5	I've followed up reading suggestions made by the lecturer.					
6	I've noted down for revision purposes the three most important things from the lecture.					
7	I've looked back at the course outline to see how this lecture fits into the programme as a whole.					
8	I've looked forward on the course outline to see what will be coming up in the next lecture.					
9	I've made sure that the intended learning outcomes for the lecture are included in or with my notes.					
10	I've checked how well I reckon I've already achieved each of the intended learning outcomes, and marked these decisions against the outcomes for future reference.					
11	I've asked my fellow learners for their reactions to what we learned in the lecture.					
12	I've compared my notes with those of at least one fellow *learner*, and added in things I missed.					
13	I've self-tested myself on what I remember from the lecture, and to find those parts that are in danger of slipping away again.					

Summing up: making lectures unmissable!

Giving learners information is only part of the business of designing a lecture, so we've got to make sure that lectures are learning experiences and not just information distribution events. In particular that *first* lecture in any series is a make or break occasion for many a learner. In other words, we've got to try to make lectures unmissable! It's got to be worth *being* there. This chapter has been about making learning happen in large-group contexts – usually called 'lectures' on timetables. We've seen that the act of *lecturing* is rarely the best way of making learning happen, and that we need to be thinking carefully about what learners are doing while sitting in lecture theatres or large classrooms. In this final section of the chapter, I would like to condense some of my main suggestions, linking them particularly to the context of starting off a lecture series – there's no second chance to make that vital first impression. Every new lecturer's nightmare is getting a lecture series off to a bad start, and learner attendance falling off as the series goes on – or worse, lots of learners later failing the related exam and the blame coming back to the lecturer. This isn't confined to new lecturers. The following suggestions may help you to make your lectures unmissable.

1. *Start reasonably punctually.* When most of the group is there, get started. Remind learners of some of the things they should already know but that you will discuss in more depth. Ask those present a few questions to find out more about what they already know. Don't be unkind to people drifting in late – that won't encourage them to come to your next lecture if they are late again. Don't punish the people who are punctual by making them wait too long for their less punctual colleagues. Gently allow the people who are coming in late to feel that they may have missed something useful.

2. *Make good use of intended learning outcomes.* Near the start of the lecture, let learners in on what *they* should be able to do by the end of that particular lecture. At the end of the lecture, show the intended outcomes again, and check to what extent learners now feel that they have cracked the learning outcomes. Help them to *feel* the added value of having been there. Bring each lecture to a close – don't just stop.

3. *Always link lectures to assessment.* Give learners cues and clues about how this particular lecture 'counts' when it comes to assessment. Whenever you say 'You'll need today's material for exam questions like so-and-so' you'll notice learners jotting something down!

4. *Lecturers should be seen and heard.* Use a microphone if it helps. Don't just say 'Can you hear me at the back?' Ask someone in the back row a question and find out. And don't dim the lights to show your slides at the expense of learners no longer being able to see *you*. Remind yourself that low lighting for too long at a time is one of the components of the natural conditions to induce human sleep!

5. *Don't keep slides up too long.* Learners will keep looking at the screen, even when that screenful is quite finished with. Get them to look at *you* now and then. For example, when using PowerPoint, on most systems pressing 'B' on the keyboard makes the screen go black. Pressing 'B' again brings it back.

6. *Avoid death by bullet point.* Make different slides *look* different. Include some charts or pictures where possible. If you're confident with technology, put in some optional very short video clips now and then – but nothing that would matter if it didn't work straight away.

7. *Try to make the learners like you.* Smile. Be human. Look at them. Respond to them. If they like you, they're more likely to come to your *next* lecture too. Remember that the feedback students will give on your course depends rather a lot on how much they actually like you.

8. *Think of what learners will be* doing *during the lecture.* Don't worry too much about what *you* will be doing, plan to get your learners' brains engaged. Get them making decisions, guessing causes of phenomena, applying ideas, solving problems, and so on. They'll learn more from what they *do* than from what you tell them.

9. *Get learners note-making, not just note-taking.* For example, try to get learners to put down *their* views and ideas, not just write out yours. You can give them *your* ideas on a handout or on the intranet. Note-making is unmissable, note-taking isn't. And mere note-taking can be a very low learning pay-off activity.

10. *Don't put too much into that first lecture.* It's better to get learners thinking deeply about a couple of important things than to tell them about half-a-dozen things and lose their attention.

11. *Be kind to learners' brains.* Concentration spans are measured in minutes, not hours. Break up each lecture into at least three parts, with something lighter in between the tougher bits.

12. *Bring in some appropriate humour.* The odd funny slide, amusing anecdote or play on words can work wonders at restoring learners' concentration levels. Then follow something funny up with an important point, while you've still got their full attention.

13. *But don't use humour if it's not working!* Watch their faces and respond accordingly. If they're liking the funny bits, keep putting them in, but if they're not, don't!

14. *Give learners something to take away.* But not just a printed handout. Learners who miss the lecture will easily get copies of these, but that's just information, not knowledge. Make handouts something that learners will give *thought to.* For example, use a 'gapped' handout, where learners themselves add in the most important points from time

to time, in their own words. And give them time in the lecture to do this. Something that they have *made* is seen as much more important than something everyone was simply given.

15. *Flag up related sessions.* For example, if you're lecturing to a large group and learners will be going later into tutorial sessions to follow-up the content of the lecture, show learners some of the questions which will be covered in the tutorials. This will get them started on thinking about them.

16. *Think twice about giving out handout copies of your PowerPoint slides.* When this is done, learners can switch off their brains, thinking 'I've already got what's on the screen, I don't need to think about it now'. And if you give out copies of 24 slides, and only get through 16 in your lecture, learners will get the wrong impression. Leave yourself the luxury of being able to choose *which* slides you will show. When time is running out, miss out some less important ones to make space for that important closure.

17. *Keep yourself tuned into WIIFM.* 'What's in it for me?' is a perfectly intelligent question for any learner to have in mind. Always make time to remind learners about *why* a topic is included and *how* it will help them in due course.

18. *Don't be unkind to learners who missed your previous lecture.* They're here now. Giving them a bad time won't encourage them to come again. And at least *some* learners will have very good reasons for not having been able to be there last time – illness, crises, whatever. The more unmissable your lectures are, the more learners will try not to miss them whatever else is happening in their lives.

19. *Don't overrun.* At least some of your learners are likely to have something else to go to after your lecture, and perhaps with not much of a margin for error. If you come to a good stopping place and there are 15 minutes left, do your closing bit and stop. Learners actually *like* lectures which finish early now and then.

20. *Pave the way towards your next lecture.* After reviewing what learners should have got out of the present lecture, show (for example) a slide with three questions which will be covered in next week's instalment.

7

Making Learning Happen in Small Groups

Short measure for small-group teaching?

This chapter is a lot shorter than its predecessor on large-group teaching, but not because small-group teaching is less important. The reason is that Chapter 6 included a wide range of ideas about turning large-group sessions into individual learning experiences for all present, *and* getting learners in large groups to work with each other in smaller groups. Many of the suggestions offered in Chapter 6 continue to apply to groups which are intentionally small, for example contexts including tutorials and seminars, particularly the comments on helping students to ask questions and on finding out what they already know. Therefore, in the present chapter, I will focus on a few particular features of small-group teaching. That said, it is worth reminding ourselves that in many parts of the world, higher education functioned for hundreds of years in what we would now regard as small-group teaching/ learning contexts, and hundreds of learners in the presence of one teacher would have been hard to imagine for most of the history of higher education until relatively recently.

Why have small-group teaching and learning?

One answer to the question is that a great deal of normal human learning takes place in what can be regarded as small-group contexts – families and friends. For most people, that is how learning first happened. Therefore, it should continue to be a natural part of any wider learning environment. Moreover, small-group contexts can be much more 'social' than studying alone – and more personal than large-group contexts like lectures, where there is usually less room for social interchange.

Small-group teaching does not always get an easy ride, however, not just in students' eyes, but also in the view of their lecturers. 'Why do we persist in pretending that small-group teaching is as good or better than other methods?'

is the sort of question asked by those who don't like small-group teaching – or are not very good at doing it. Indeed, when small-group teaching is done badly, it might be better if it had been abandoned. Sadly, too many learners report unsatisfactory experiences of learning in small-group contexts.

Further light is thrown on the value of small-group work from cases where class sizes have increased to such an extent that small-group work (particularly tutorials and seminars) has had to be discontinued, and manifestations such as the following develop:

- increased drop-out and failure statistics because learners don't have enough opportunity to have help with their difficulties

- more time being taken trying to help those learners who make appointments for one-to-one help with particular problems – often the same problem many times over

- more interruptions to the flow of large-group teaching, when it is no longer possible in a lecture to reply to a question 'This is just the right sort of question to discuss in detail in your next tutorial – bring it along then and make sure that it is sorted out to your satisfaction'

- increased risk of learners succeeding satisfactorily in written assessment scenarios, but not having gained the level of mastery of the subject matter that comes from discussing it, arguing about it and explaining it to other people

- increased risk of lecturers remaining unaware of significant problems which learners were experiencing until too late – when the problems have turned into assessment failures.

Where is the real pay-off from small-group teaching?

The real learning pay-off from small-group teaching is linked to the following factors:

- increased opportunity for learners to ask us questions

- more time for us to spend answering specific questions

- the opportunity for us to make ourselves approachable to learners and get to know them as individuals

- the chance to give high-quality feedback to individuals in the group, where eye contact, tone of voice, body language and emphasis can all clarify our feedback – much more than just written, printed or emailed comments ever can

- the chance for learners to learn from the feedback *others* are receiving

- the opportunity for learners to explain things to each other, helping them to make sense of difficult parts of the subject matter

- the opportunity for learners to find out how their learning is going by comparing the level to which they are making sense of concepts and ideas with each other

- the opportunity for learners to make informed judgements about their own work, and about each other's work, helping them to deepen their learning and find out more about the assessment culture surrounding them

- the opportunity for us to gain feedback about how their learning is progressing, allowing us to make adjustments where necessary to other teaching contexts, including large-group sessions.

What *else* are we trying to do in small groups?

Among the most significant reasons for using small-group teaching are the benefits learners acquire that lie beyond the curriculum as expressed through intended learning outcomes. The *emergent* learning outcomes associated with small-group work help learners to equip themselves with the skills and attitudes they will need for the next stages of their careers – and lives.

I've referred in earlier chapters to the National Student Survey used in the UK since 2005 to find out about the experience of final-year students. None of the statements in the questionnaire refers directly to small-group teaching and learning, but three of them (numbers 19–21) under the heading 'Personal Development' have strong links:

19   The course has helped me to present myself with confidence.
20   My communication skills have improved.
21   As a result of the course, I feel confident to tackle unfamiliar problems.

Each one of these aspects of the student experience links to small-group learning contexts. This at least partly explains why the overall results of the survey tend to be better for smaller higher education institutions, where group size is likely to be lower in general, and where it may be argued staff and students get to know each other better.

Ideally, we should be using small-group teaching to achieve as many as possible of the things we wish to do to help learners to succeed, but which can't be directly incorporated into large-group teaching or resource-based learning. This is why it can be so wasteful if small-group sessions just degenerate into a continuation of what we're doing in large-group contexts. Among the additional outcomes of successful small-group work are the following (which of course also link strongly to the 'personal development' agenda of the National Student Survey in the UK):

- the opportunity for learners to develop their confidence in speaking, presenting, arguing, discussing, debating, and so on
- the opportunity for learners to practise and develop their oral communications skills, such as those they will need for job interviews or oral exams
- the chance for learners to develop and practise their interpersonal skills, learning how best to work collaboratively with different people
- the chance for learners to reflect together on how their learning is going and to find out more about how they stand compared to their peers
- the opportunity to get learners deepening their own learning by explaining difficult ideas and concepts to each other.

Addressing the seven factors in small-group contexts

Deep learning is most likely to happen in small-group contexts when as many as possible of the seven factors underpinning successful learning are involved. In other words, when students:

- are motivated to the extent that they *want* to learn from the small-group setting
- have clear targets so they know what they *need* to be getting out of the session
- have plenty of opportunity for learning by doing, practice, trial and error and participation
- gain useful feedback from each other as well as from the tutor
- realize that they are making sense of the subject matter being addressed in the session
- get their heads round key concepts by explaining them to each other
- make informed judgements about their evidence of achievement of the learning outcomes, deepening their learning.

I will expand on the links between small-group settings and the seven factors below.

1 Wanting to learn

What can we do to help learners *want* to learn in small groups? The best we can do is to make small-group sessions so enjoyable that learners can't wait to come along to them! However, this is perhaps rather harder to achieve if the session is a problems class on applications of the second law of thermodynamics, or some other element of 'troublesome knowledge' in your own discipline.

It is a measure of the success of small-group teaching sessions if learners always feel that it is worth coming along and joining in, and that they leave with things they simply wouldn't have got if they'd missed the session – handouts, explanations, answers to their own questions, ideas and, particularly, the feeling that during the session they had made sense of parts of the subject matter. If they feel they've not got anything more than some extra information, the want to learn is hardly likely to be enhanced. We can easily gather feedback from learners, for example, asking them to rate small-group sessions in terms of how much they feel them 'time well spent'. When learners feel that they have progressed their own learning faster as a result of participating in a small-group session than they would have done simply studying the topic on their own, they are likely to come to the sessions with greater expectations and increased willingness to take part actively.

2 Taking ownership of the need to learn

How best can we use small-group contexts to clarify the learning need and to help students take ownership of this need? Small-group sessions are ideal occasions to spend extra time clarifying the intended learning out-comes so that learners gain a greater awareness regarding what exactly we are, in due course, going to expect them to do to evidence their achievement of the outcomes. While we should be doing this in large-group contexts too, small-group sessions can allow us to let learners *get their hand on* examples of the kind of evidence we're looking for, for example, portfolios, disserta-tions, past essays or assignments, and subject-specific artefacts such as drawings, photos, posters and so on.

Small-group contexts are also an opportunity to gather learners' ques-tions about how exactly assessment works, though for fairness it is best for us to *respond* to these questions in a large-group context so that particular small-groups do not become advantaged regarding their insight into assessment expectations. We can use small-group sessions to get learners themselves applying assessment criteria to past work or their own work, and we can clarify for them how the criteria are used in practice.

3 Learning by doing in small groups

What actions do learners learn most from in small groups? Table 7.1 lists some actions we can help learners to do in small groups to maximize their learning pay-off. There are, of course, countless other subject-specific things we can get learners doing in small groups, but it is useful to ask learners from time to time exactly what they are finding works well for them in terms of learning pay-off.

Table 7.1 What we can help learners to do in small groups to maximize their learning pay-off

Agreeing solutions	Engaging	Reviewing
Analysing	Explaining	Selecting
Arguing	Guessing	Sharing
Assessing	Helping	Sketching
Connecting	Listening	Solving problems
Debating	Note-making	Succeeding
Demonstrating	Participating	Summarizing
Designing	Questioning	Talking
Discussing	Remembering	Watching others

4 Making sense of things in small groups

As mentioned throughout this book, *making sense* of ideas, concepts, theories and so on has to be done by learners themselves – we can't do this for them. We can, however, strive to ensure that small-group contexts provide them with ideal environments for getting their heads round things, not least by allowing them to compare their own grasp on a subject with that of other group members, alerting them to exactly where the blocks may be, and encouraging them to feel good about the things they've mastered successfully. In particular, ways of helping learners to make sense of things in small groups link strongly to the remaining three factors underpinning successful learning – getting them to give and receive a lot of feedback in small groups, helping them to explain things to each other, and involving them in making informed judgements about their own and each other's work by using small-group contexts for self-assessment and peer-assessment activities.

5 Making the most of feedback in small groups

How best can we maximize the feedback learners get from each other in small groups? Feedback is most useful when it is about something learners have just done. We can therefore give them tasks to do in small groups (and before the sessions), then get them reviewing each other's efforts and explaining what they think about them.

It is useful to discuss with learners how best to receive feedback from each other (and, indeed, from ourselves). For example, learners often need to be encouraged not just to shrug off positive comments or praise, but to allow themselves to *accept* such feedback, swell with pride about it and take on board exactly what they have done well, not least so that they can continue to build on their achievements. They also need to be helped to receive critical feedback well, not become defensive and try to justify their actions, but listen carefully to the feedback and see what they can learn from it so that mistakes or deficiencies can be useful learning experiences for them.

6 Explaining, coaching and teaching in small groups

There is enormous potential for using small-group contexts to help students to learn by explaining things to each other, coaching each other, and even teaching each other. This is, of course, dependent on us as tutors refraining from doing all that explaining, coaching and teaching ourselves! There is a balance to be struck. Learners may indeed expect us to do most of the work in small groups, not least answering their questions and helping them to solve their problems with the subject concerned. We can, however, invite fellow learners to answer questions first, and only step in when we are really needed. We need to be honest with learners about our intention to help them get the most out of working with each other in small groups, to reduce any feeling that they are not getting full value out of us in the sessions. We may need to propose to learners how valuable it is to practise explaining difficult ideas to each other, as a precursor to them becoming able to explain them quickly and confidently in assessment contexts such as exam answers or coursework assignments.

In the case of seminars, where it is normal to ask one or more students to take the lead in presenting a particular topic which they have researched, we can strengthen the learning pay-off they derive from the exercise by suggesting that they not only *present* the topic, but do so in a way designed to help their audience to *learn* significantly as a result. This necessarily helps them to see their presentation from the point of view of the audience, improving the presentation, and better still perhaps, designing questions or exercises which will involve the audience.

Moreover, when learners leave a small-group session feeling that it was well worth their time having been there, they are more likely to invest in such sessions more earnestly, not least doing any work we have suggested as preparation for their participation in the session. In addition, when learners get to know each other by explaining things to each other, they are much more likely to continue to make the most of working with each other outside the timetabled curriculum – all the more learning then happens without any additional effort on our part. So it is in our interest to help learners to become more dependent on learning from each other.

7 Learning by assessing in small groups

We can, as mentioned in Chapter 6, help our students to learn by assessing in large-group contexts, but we can often achieve this even better in small-group contexts where we can oversee how they apply assessment criteria to their own and each other's work. Where necessary we can explain exactly what the criteria really mean. For example, we can ask learners to bring along to small-group sessions work they have prepared, then ask them to exchange scripts, and mark the work of a fellow learner, talking them through the marking scheme, and helping them to make judgements on the quality of the work. This allows all present to:

- learn from things a fellow learner may have done better, and thereby become able to emulate the better performance in future work

- learn from mistakes a fellow learner may have made, and more consciously avoid making similar mistakes in future work

- get their heads around the finer detail regarding how their work may be assessed when exam answers or formal coursework are assessed by tutors – in other words, find out important detail about the assessment culture in which they are working.

The last of these is particularly important. When learners realize that if they miss a small-group session, they are losing out on finding out valuable information about how assessment will work for them, they are less likely to choose to miss such a session in future. If it was just some *information* they would miss, they could copy that from those who were there, but if it was an important *experience* they would miss, they soon realize the importance of such small-group sessions.

What sorts of small-group teaching are there?

There are many contexts that can be thought of as small-group teaching. *Tutorials* in some institutions are scheduled meetings between a tutor and a few learners, often used to follow up the content of lectures and to get learners applying what they are meant to do with theories and concepts. One problem is that learners don't necessarily know what is expected of them in tutorials. Sally Brown says of her first experiences of tutorials as a learner, 'I tried to be good, and sit quietly and listen to what the tutor had to say'. Tutorials are ideal occasions for learners to bring their own individual questions and problems and to seek help from the tutor. In some institutions, the word 'tutorial' is used to describe face-to-face meetings between a tutor and one learner at a time. With increasing class sizes, however, it is not uncommon to find the term 'tutorial' used for groups of as many as 20 learners.

Seminars are often confused with tutorials. Learners often don't know what they're supposed to do in these sessions. The essential difference between a seminar and a tutorial in many tutors' minds is that in seminars, learners themselves contribute most of the content. For example, they prepare to talk as individuals or small groups about pre-allocated topics, then open the topics up for discussion.

Other kinds of small-group teaching include laboratory work, studio work, problems classes, and practical work of various kinds where learners work independently or in twos and threes, with individual support from time to time from tutors.

How can we shut the teacher up in small groups?

Probably the most significant danger in most small-group learning contexts is that teachers just continue to teach, and learners are not involved as much as they should be. Sometimes the blame goes to the teacher, but often teachers continue to talk to fill the silence caused by learners *not* being ready, willing or able to contribute.

It takes a little nerve for a teacher to pose a question to a small group of learners and wait for them to answer it. Silence is threatening, and it's all too easy for teachers to go for the comfort of filling the silence. It can be better to wait a while, and if the silence is still continuing, to clarify the question, putting it into other words or breaking it down into more manageable sub-questions. One of the best ways to cause learners to participate is to give them a little time, individually or in twos or threes, to jot down notes in response to a question, *then* ask them to give their answers orally. Armed with some jottings, most learners feel more confident to speak. We also need to encourage learners to participate, particularly by not ridiculing their contributions when they are wrong, and always trying to find something positive to say in response to their efforts.

What tutor behaviours are *least* likely to make learning happen in small groups?

I've already mentioned that just continuing to teach (or lecture!) can damage the learning pay-off which might have resulted from small-group work. However, the most damaging tutor behaviour is not taking small-group teaching as seriously as large-group teaching. For example, it is relatively rare for a large-class session to be cancelled or postponed, but much more common for small-group sessions to be cancelled at short notice. This infuriates part-time learners who may have travelled to the institution just for the cancelled tutorial. Learners are quick to get the message that if small-group sessions are not valued by their tutors, the sessions can't be very important.

Another tutor behaviour that can easily damage small-group teaching is to put learners down. If they arrive late, for example (perhaps for unavoidable reasons), a sharp retort from a tutor can make them feel really bad about being there at all, and sometimes they don't return to small-group sessions again. More often, however, tutors demotivate learners by responding inappropriately to their comments and questions. This is likely to make learners less likely to participate and undermines the whole rationale of the less formal communication between tutors and learners which small-group teaching should allow.

How big is a small group?

It all depends. In some subjects, a small group is no more than about four learners. However, seminar groups are often much bigger, for example a cohort of 300 learners may be broken into seminar groups of around 20. Problems classes in maths, science and engineering may be as large as 40. This increases the danger that they become a continuation of large-group teaching unless tutors take care to keep the focus on learner activity, for example, by dividing the group up into fours or fives so that every learner has an opportunity to discuss things and gain feedback from peers. With group sizes of 3–6 or so, there is less chance of passenger or bystander behaviours, and it is fairly straightforward to get everyone to contribute. With larger groups, however, it becomes more difficult to keep everyone engaged.

Where can small-group learning happen?

Small-group sessions can occur just about anywhere. Small teaching rooms are often heavily timetabled in institutions, and it is all too common for a tutor and small group to be seen wandering the corridors looking for a suitable venue, particularly if a tutorial or seminar has had to be rescheduled. Small-group sessions often spill over into other areas, including lounges, dining areas and even the nearest comfortable pub (but we need to remember that if the group contains members whose religion prohibits alcohol that this venue would be entirely inappropriate).

By common consent, small-group sessions on late Friday afternoons or early Monday mornings, for example, are often rescheduled, but this can add to the difficulties of finding suitable space. In most institutions, staff are urged only to book rooms for sessions that definitely will take place, rather than make block bookings for a whole semester, even when some of the small-group sessions are going to happen in alternative places such as computer suites, laboratories or field visits.

Making learners feel at home in small groups

How can we ensure in small groups that learners don't feel marginalized, alienated and ignored? Using learners' names can help. The simplest and most effective way of getting to know learners' names in small groups is to give learners self-adhesive labels, ask them to write down what they prefer to be called, and stick the labels to their clothing. This has the advantage of revealing what they *really* want to be called – at least some of their chosen names will be different from those printed on a class list. Addressing learners by name makes a surprisingly big difference, especially when asking questions or giving feedback. When learners spend much of their contact time in very large groups, where they can easily feel just one of a crowd, small-group teaching can compensate.

It is up to tutors to ensure that learners don't feel alienated in a small group. Where there is just one female learner in a group, or one male learner, care needs to be taken not to allow this to cause them to feel exposed in any way. Similarly, ethnic background differences need to be handled sensitively. The best way of checking that all is going well in small-group sessions is to have a sufficiently relaxed and informal atmosphere so that it is easy to keep asking 'How are you finding these sessions?' and 'Is there anything we can do to improve these sessions for you?' and so on.

What gets in the way of effective small-group learning?

The principal factors getting in the way of effective small-group learning include:

- Learners not turning up, perhaps because they don't feel small-group contexts are as important as large-group sessions. This is often because learners think that all the important material will be linked to large-group sessions such as lectures, and we need to make it very clear to them all that, although most of the *information* may be given out in large-group sessions, the *making sense* of the information by applying it and practising with it is often best done in small groups, where there can be quick and individual feedback to all present, helping them to turn the information into their own knowledge.

- Tutors not taking small-group teaching as seriously as they take large-group teaching, and arriving for small-group sessions relatively unprepared.

- Sometimes learners are shy and embarrassed about being expected to join in discussions in small groups. However, as tutors we need to help them to gain the confidence to contribute actively, and it is important that they don't feel 'put down' if they get things wrong or don't communicate their ideas effectively at first.

- Small-group teaching being viewed in institutions as not very cost-effective compared to large-group teaching.

- Insufficient attention being paid by tutors to what is *best* covered by small-group work compared with what should be covered by large-group teaching.

- Learners not doing their part in preparing for small-group sessions.

- Failure to adjust group membership and composition when particular groups fail to work well together.

- Failure to clarify the intended learning outcomes for small-group sessions.

- Tutors continuing to teach in a non-participative way.

- Difficulties in finding suitable spaces and environments for small-group teaching.

- Dominant learners being allowed too much air time in discussions.

- Passive learners being allowed to remain passive. Human nature being what it is, it is easier to be passive in small-group learning situations than to take the risk of being active but wrong. The words 'passenger' and 'bystander' are often used to describe the behaviours that can lead learners to get nothing out of small-group work.

- Difficulties in achieving equity of the learning experience when a large group is divided into several small groups, and particularly when different group sessions are facilitated by different tutors.

As indicated in some elements of the list above, most of these factors can be addressed directly by tutors, provided they themselves are indeed convinced of the benefits for learners of small-group teaching contexts. There are, however, some institutional factors which can be harder to address. These include:

- difficulties finding sufficient suitable small-group learning venues when very large groups are split up into a lot of small ones

- timetabling difficulties: finding sufficient tutors to facilitate parallel small-group sessions

- tutors who lack the experience or expertise in the subject matter, especially when other parallel sessions are being facilitated by the lecturer responsible for the associated large-group sessions

- tensions between research and teaching getting in the way of researchers putting enough time and effort into preparing for their small-group teaching work

- the institutional ethos regarding small-group teaching, if it is regarded as not very important or 'a bit of a luxury' or 'just the icing on the cake'

- lack of feedback from learners on their experience of small-group teaching when, as often happens, monitoring and evaluation tends to focus on large-group teaching.

How long should small-group sessions be?

In practice, the duration of small-group sessions is less important than how well the time is spent. A well-facilitated small group can achieve in as little as half an hour much more than a poorly facilitated group achieves in a couple of hours. The problem with short duration sessions is that the time can all too easily be eroded if it takes some minutes to get everyone there. Where small-group sessions last for an hour or two, it is important to build in a variety of processes and get learners involved in different tasks and activities. When small-group learning is working well, learners often comment that the time has flown by, even when the session lasts a day or half-day.

Can learners lead small-group learning sessions?

They *can*. Getting learners to lead sessions develops just the kind of confidence that the National Student Survey is looking for. Learners are helped to lead small-group sessions (seminars in particular) if they have clear, manageable briefings about what exactly is expected of them, sufficient time to prepare to take the lead and are not interrupted too often by tutors! It remains important that the task of leading sessions is not made too daunting for any shy or retiring learners, nor just given to the vociferous ones. Tutor interventions need to be restricted to when the learner leading a session really needs to be rescued or helped out – but even then it can be better to facilitate other learners coming to their aid.

Towards better small-group learning

To summarize this short chapter on small-group teaching and learning, I offer the following suggestions.

1. *Be seen to take small-group sessions seriously.* Learners will take cues from how important you treat small-group sessions. Be as punctual for small-group sessions as you are for lectures.

2. *Don't just fill small-group sessions by continuing to lecture!* Avoid the temptation to fill a silence just by providing yet more information. Get the students doing something instead.

3. *Link sessions to intended learning outcomes.* This helps learners to see that small-group sessions are just as important as lectures. Sometimes it's worth flagging up a particular intended learning outcome in a lecture,

then explaining that this one will be addressed *only* in related small-group teaching, but that evidence of achievement will still be assessed in the normal ways through coursework or exam questions.

4. *Gather the emergent learning outcomes from small-group sessions.* Ask learners *what else* did you learn as a result of this seminar (or tutorial, or team meeting, and so on). Then flag up typical emergent outcomes in large-group sessions so that learners realize that the additional learning which accompanies small-group learning is important and relevant to them.

5. *Address purposefully the seven factors underpinning successful learning.* In particular, make optimum use of small-group contexts to allow students to *learn by explaining* and to *make informed judgements* so that they *make sense* of important concepts and ideas, and deepen their grasp of the subject concerned.

6. *Make small-group learning a personal experience for learners.* Help learners to get to know you better in small-group contexts and (more importantly) to get to know each other so that they can learn more from each other.

7. *Ensure that learners feel it was worthwhile turning up for each small-group session.* If they can see the value of being present, they are less likely to choose to miss future sessions.

8. *Don't grumble to those who turn up about those who don't!* Make each small-group session a positive and useful learning experience for those who *are* present.

9. *Take care with learners' feelings.* Some learners may be intimidated having so much more attention from someone as scholarly and important as *you* in a small-group context, and may be easily damaged by criticism. (Others won't be nearly so fragile, of course.)

10. *Use small-group sessions to feed into large-group sessions.* For example, when important questions relating to assessment come up in small-group contexts, bring the questions to the attention of the whole group, rather than deal with them solely with the small group.

8

Responding to Diversity and Widening Participation

Colleagues in post-compulsory education are only too aware of the ways in which the student communities in educational institutions are changing as a greater proportion of the population continues education beyond school. However, it is quite difficult for college teachers to pin down what they should be doing to try to respond to the increasing diversity that results from widening participation. There is also a greater awareness of the importance of addressing special educational needs as a result of legislation such as the Special Educational Needs and Disabilities Act 2002 (SENDA) in the UK, and its subsequent amendments.

Responding to special needs

'Making learning happen' is essentially about responding to the needs of *all* learners, and in various ways this is addressed throughout the book. This section, however, is focused on responding to learners' *special* needs. In other words, the particular needs of various categories of learner that are present in differing proportions among the wider populations of learners in further and higher education.

What's changed regarding special needs?

People with special needs have been among our learners throughout the evolution of post-compulsory education, but in recent years a number of trends and developments have highlighted the problems which some of them face, and the need for us to respond appropriately to their various needs. In addition, over the last twenty years in particular, significant advances have been made regarding detecting and identifying many special needs, and how best to make adjustments to teaching, learning environments and assessment instruments and processes so as to minimize any disadvantages which can arise for at least some of the manifestations of special need. For example, a great deal more is now known about detecting and responding to dyslexia.

Widening participation policies are gradually transforming the spectrum of learners in post-compulsory education. It now seems a distant past where only about five per cent of the population entered post-compulsory education. Nowadays in the UK, for example, recent targets have revolved around 50 per cent of the population having at least some experience of higher education. This target has already been exceeded in Scotland. In addition, with the recession at the time of writing this edition, more learners are trying to get into higher education, but funding constraints militate against achieving a leap in participation. Nevertheless, a different 'slice' of the overall population is now present on post-compulsory education programmes and courses. That in turn means that the population in any large lecture group, for example, now contains a proportion of learners who previously would not have been there. At least some of these learners will have special needs of some description. For example, any large group of learners is likely to have at least some who are affected by some degree of dyslexia. Also, post-compulsory education has become much more accessible to learners with visual impairments, hearing impairments, limited mobility and other sources of special need. There are significant proportions of any population affected by such conditions as diabetes and epilepsy, and these too are naturally represented in educational contexts.

In addition, however, a wide range of what could be considered as mental health needs are now represented among any large group of learners. Perhaps we have become more aware of these needs because we now know a lot more about their causes, symptoms and treatment? Perhaps the student (and staff) population in higher education is living in more stressful times than used to be the case? Mental health needs don't just relate to conditions which are directly associated with cognitive processing, but also include short-term or long-term manifestations of stress, anxiety, depression and the various conditions resulting from exposure to mind-altering agents, not least alcohol, but also other drugs and medicines.

Learner attitudes have also changed significantly in recent years, reflecting the tendency for society as a whole to be more aware of rights. People are more likely to resort to law if injustice is felt to have happened. Learners are more litigious. Lack of appropriate attention to any identified special need may end up disadvantaging particular learners when they come to be assessed. Appeals and even legal action can come as no surprise.

A further dimension of change is the increased attention paid to feedback from all learners, and the ways that quality assurance processes and systems make use of this feedback. In UK higher education, the data from the National Student Survey (relating to final-year students), collected since 2005, is turned into league tables and is studied carefully by institutions and intending students. External accountability links firmly now to funding provision in one way or another in most post-compulsory education systems and contexts. Within all the feedback from learners that is collected, collated and analysed is at least some feedback that reflects how those learners with special needs have fared alongside those without such needs. We need to be ready to interpret all feedback as yet one more source of information about such needs.

We need also to be aware that not all special needs have anything to do with something which is 'wrong'. For example, anyone learning in a second language in which they are not reasonably fluent, can be regarded as working under conditions of a special need. We may make every effort to help them to improve their fluency in the language concerned, but this often does not allow them to develop their language skills fast enough to keep pace with the growing complexity of language which may arise in the subject matter, or in the wording and design of assessment tasks and activities.

We need to remember not to ignore or undervalue the most significant source of expertise in how best special needs can be addressed – namely, the owners of the needs. Learners themselves usually know a great deal about any special need they have lived with over the years. They know what works for them, and what doesn't. We need to keep asking them 'How best can I help you?' in as many contexts as possible – lectures, group work, individual work, practical work and preparation for assessment. Very often their answers can not only help us to make adjustments which are really effective for them, but can spare us wasting time and energy making changes which we *imagine* are going to be useful but which are often of limited value in practice.

When special needs remain undiagnosed, the problems are more profound. Some special needs evolve quite gradually, not least some of those of the mental health variety. When a learner has a physical accident and ends up, for example, with mobility problems, at least the problems are apparent, and it is relatively clear what sorts of help may be needed. However, it is the invisible onset of special needs which poses the greatest problems for learners and tutors alike. Sometimes learners may begin a programme of study with no knowledge of having any special needs, and then it gradually emerges that problems exist. The most frequent triggers are to do with assessment of one kind or another. When learners underperform in assessment contexts, the causes frequently include the effects of one or more special needs.

While there is already a wealth of experience relating to how best to accommodate the most commonly identified special needs, it remains an uphill struggle for subject-based teachers in post-compulsory education to respond to the considerable spectrum of such needs that may be present simultaneously in a given group of learners. It is also important to ensure that learners *without* any special needs are not themselves significantly disadvantaged by the steps which are taken to respond to special needs. The phrase 'inclusive practice' is increasingly used to describe attempts to design teaching, learning and assessment for the whole range of learners in a group. In fact, it can be argued that in many cases, whatever helps learners with identified special needs can indeed be of help to *all* learners, as will be shown in the analysis of particular contexts which follows in this chapter.

Expert help with special needs

Most institutions of post-compulsory education have expert help available both to learners with special needs and to those teaching them, responding to them and supporting their learning. Large institutions are often able to provide or arrange quite elaborate levels of support when needed, ranging all the way to 24-hour assistance when really needed. The 'disabilities unit' or 'equality unit' in a large institution will usually contain personnel trained in identifying and responding to specific learning needs, and such people can provide a great deal of help to tutors and lecturers regarding how best to approach handling particular teaching contexts when special needs are known to be present. It is important that the dimension of special needs is addressed in staff development and induction programmes, so that, at the very least, staff become aware of where to find expert help when needed and, at best, become able to make reasonable adjustments to all their teaching approaches to anticipate the presence of the more common special needs.

Special needs and the factors underpinning learning

My argument here is that it is useful to think about various special needs in terms of how the seven factors underpinning successful learning are affected in each individual context. In other words, some or all of these factors can be considered to be 'damaged' or 'limited' by particular special needs. If, then, we can identify which factors are impeded in a given context, we are in a better position to explore how best we may be able to compensate for the 'damage', and respond directly to each factor underpinning successful learning.

The following is intended just to be a starting point on our journey towards being able to make adjustments to teaching, learning and assessment to respond to learners with selected special needs. Not least, we need to continue to ask learners themselves how best we can respond – almost invariably they know more about their own special needs than anyone else. That said, I believe it is particularly useful to look at which one or more of the underpinning factors could be damaged, as a way of fine-tuning our own thinking about how we may start to go about compensating for the damage.

The rest of this chapter offers a systematic approach to identifying and addressing the following special needs categories:

1. Dyslexia

2. Visual impairment

3. Auditory impairment

4. Mental health needs.

1 Dyslexia

A great deal is now known about dyslexia, both in terms of how to detect its effects and how to respond. In short, however, dyslexia can be regarded as making it harder for learners to process information and turn it into their own knowledge, particularly when the information they are working with is in written or printed form, or where they need to be capturing information into written form from lectures, libraries or the web.

Which factors underpinning successful learning may be damaged, and how?

1. *Wanting to learn*: possibly the most significant way that dyslexic learners may have the 'want' damaged is the increased fear of failure which they may be bringing forward from their past educational experience, for example, when they may have underachieved due to their special needs.

2. *Needing to learn*: it can be harder for dyslexic learners to take on board ownership of targets when these are printed on handouts or in course handbooks. For example, they may find it harder to interpret exactly what is meant by intended learning outcomes and information about assessment processes, instruments and criteria.

3. *Learning by doing*: practice, trial and error, repetition, and so on are less likely to be problematic for learners with dyslexia so long as the 'doing' is not overly based on materials which are linguistically challenging. Indeed, learners with dyslexia tend to have found already the increased value of learning by doing, and are usually ready to invest in it.

4. *Making sense*: words and sentences can be regarded as 'getting in the way' of making sense, particularly when the language level is complex or the amount of printed and/or written information to be handled is great.

5. *Learning through feedback*: it may be more difficult for learners to make sense of written feedback. This is all the more problematic when the main vehicle for giving students feedback about their work is written communication from tutors.

6. *Learning by explaining*: learners with dyslexia may be just as good as their peers – sometimes even better – at explaining things orally to fellow learners. As always, the learning pay-off of explaining remains high. It can be very motivating to allow dyslexic learners who are accomplished at explaining concepts and theories orally to do so to learners without special needs – increasing the confidence and self-esteem of the explainers themselves as well as allowing them to deepen their learning.

7. *Learning by assessing*: using self-assessment and peer assessment can, when facilitated sensitively, be really useful to learners with dyslexia, as it gives them opportunities to *make sense* of the nature of the assessment criteria that they need to meet to succeed. The face-to-face practice of peer assessment can allow the discussion to take place orally rather than entirely 'on the page'.

What adjustments may we be able to make to compensate?

1. *Wanting to learn*: one of the best things we can do is to try to help learners to develop their confidence as early as possible, for example, by building in the opportunity for some 'early success' so that dyslexic learners feel that they are up to the tasks which will follow.

2. *Needing to learn*: using face-to-face opportunities to explain intended learning outcomes can help, adding tone of voice, emphasis and the opportunity for learners to seek clarification when they are not yet sure exactly what they are intended to become able to do or how exactly the evidence of achievement they produce will be assessed in due course. Explaining the intended learning outcomes all along the learning pathway is of course very useful for *all* learners, not just those affected by dyslexia, and is just one element of best inclusive practice.

3. *Learning by doing*: we can sometimes help by ensuring that we keep tasks based on reading and information retrieval to manageable proportions. Helping *all* learners to gain an idea about which are the really important sources and which are for background reading can pave the way for dyslexic learners to ensure that they don't dissipate unreasonable amounts of time and energy on the less relevant materials.

4. *Making sense*: using shorter sentences in our teaching can help. Using shorter rather than longer words can help. In particular, in task briefings and exam questions, doing both of these things can prevent learners from misinterpreting tasks and wasting time and energy by going off on tangents.

   We need also to make as much use as possible of the non-textual aspects of learning, for example making full use of the power of communication available in face-to-face teaching and learning contexts, where tone of voice, body language, facial expression, and so on can all contribute strongly to learners making sense of what they are thinking about. Similarly, group work can help learners affected by dyslexia to make the most of the learning, giving them an opportunity to watch other learners making sense of the subject matter being learned. As always, it is useful to ask learners 'How best can I help you to make sense of this bit?'

5. *Learning through feedback*: face-to-face feedback can improve the picture by again making the most of tone of voice, emphasis, and repetition where necessary. Where everyone is being given written feedback (whether handwritten, printed or emailed), it can be particularly necessary for us to find ways of debriefing learners affected by dyslexia on what exactly we are intending them to get out of each element of feedback, and using face-to-face communication to ensure that they are interpreting our feedback appropriately. Group learning contexts can also be helpful. Here dyslexic learners can also learn from feedback from their peers and from the feedback we give their peers.

6. *Learning through explaining*: we can maximize the benefit to dyslexic learners by allowing them to gain confidence by explaining things orally. We can also adjust our assessment processes so that less weight is placed on written work and more weight is given to face-to-face ways of demonstrating evidence of achievement of learning outcomes.

7. *Learning through assessing*: involving dyslexic learners in self-assessment can help them to get a better grip on the standards underpinning assessment criteria. In self-assessment they can also handle the criteria at their own pace, and be assisted face to face when necessary to interpret the wording of the criteria. Peer-assessing the work of non-dyslexic learners can also help them to see the differences between fellow learners' work and their own work, and to work towards bridging any gaps in standards.

2 Visual impairment

As with dyslexia, visual impairment ranges from a mild effect on learning to a very significant one. Where the effects are really significant, learners have usually a lot of knowledge about how best they can be assisted in day-do-day learning contexts. Turning information into knowledge is clearly harder when much of the information concerned is visual. Depending on the extent of the impairment, some sources can be much easier to handle than others. For example, material in electronic formats, which can be turned into sound by computer software, can be much more accessible than material that is only available in print.

Which factors underpinning successful learning may be damaged, and how?

1. *Wanting to learn*: unsurprisingly, this can be reduced in situations where, for everyone else, there is considerable enjoyment in the visual side of learning. Similarly, when visual means are used to help learners make sense of things (e.g. mind-maps, flow charts and so on), the motivation of

visually impaired learners can be significantly reduced, especially when they find it more difficult to make sense of the subject matter concerned.

2. *Needing to learn*: it is easy to forget how easy it is for students *without* any visual impairments to look at intended learning outcomes at any time – on the screen in lectures, in handouts, in course or module handbooks, and so on. Indeed, we *intend* the learning outcomes to be a frame of reference to help learners set their targets and take ownership of what they are preparing to be able to do to demonstrate their achievement. Students with visual impairments can all too easily miss out on the essentially *visual* nature of the ways we usually communicate learning outcomes to learners. Similar considerations arise in coursework task briefings and so on.

3. *Learning by doing*: some tasks may simply not be possible for learners with particular levels of visual impairment. When dealing with practical work, there may also be safety implications.

4. *Making sense*: it is often surprising to people without visual impairment just how much *making sense* happens by a combination of thinking about information and stimuli gathered visually. For example, all sorts of handouts, screen-based learning materials and, indeed, learners' own notes are often improved by the inclusion of pictures, flow charts, mindmaps, and so on. For visually impaired learners, it may be difficult to compensate for the roles that these illustrations play in making sense of the subject matter concerned. Also, in face-to-face sessions, learners without visual impairment gain a great deal quite subconsciously from our facial expression, body language, and so on.

5. *Learning through feedback*: this can be mainly impaired by the lack of being able to see facial expression and body language accompanying face-to-face feedback from tutors, and also from fellow learners. Also, where written or printed feedback is issued to learners, those with visual impairments cannot revisit it as easily as those who can just glance at it again. Even though the feedback may be able to be turned into audio, it is still more time-consuming to return to a particular point when required.

6. *Learning through explaining*: this may work very well for learners with visual impairments, who are often very competent not just at explaining what they know orally, but also at listening skilfully to others' explanations.

7. *Learning through assessing*: this can be problematic when the assessment is dependent on vision – such as involving written work.

What adjustments may we be able to make to compensate?

1. *Wanting to learn*: since the extent of, and effects of, visual impairment vary so widely, probably the wisest way to set about compensating for damaged 'want to learn' is simply to keep asking visually impaired

learners straightforward, open-ended questions such as 'How can I make this topic better for you?' As always, learners with disabilities are likely to know very well what will be of particular help in their own individual contexts.

2. *Needing to learn*: it can help to make the intended learning outcomes and coursework task briefings available in sound, so that visually impaired learners can hear them at will. It can, in fact, help *all* learners to make full use of the clues and cues which we can build into intended learning outcomes through tone of voice, emphasis, and so on. It is important that all learners know what we really mean by each intended learning outcome, and it is much more satisfactory to communicate these using both sound as well as vision when possible.

3. *Learning by doing*: we need here to concentrate on designing *other* tasks so that visually impaired learners can achieve the relevant intended learning outcomes, and other means so that they can demonstrate their achievement of the outcomes. This is directly what legislation such as SENDA in the UK requires, making 'reasonable adjustments' in an anticipatory manner so that we don't have to stop and think for too long before being able to provide suitable alternative tasks for visually impaired learners.

4. *Making sense*: it can be useful to seek expert advice on the most appropriate design of illustrations and flow charts in handouts and screen-based materials. 'TechDis', a UK government agency advising on teaching those with special needs (see www.techdis.ac.uk for more information), is a source of such advice. Visual impairment can range widely in scope and severity, and most visually impaired learners already know a great deal about what works best for them in compensating for their difficulties. It is useful to ask them individually directly how best we can make adjustments to our learning materials to minimize their problems.

5. *Learning through feedback*: sound can again compensate to at least some extent for difficulties in receiving feedback visually. It can be useful to check with learners that they really have received the feedback we intend to give them, elaborate where necessary on points they had not quite understood in our feedback, and compensate for aspects where they need more detail.

6. *Learning through explaining*: there can be significant benefits for those with visual impairments to involve them in explaining things orally to other people, particularly fellow learners without impairments. This not only increases the extent to which the explainers make sense of the topics concerned, but also increases their confidence and self-esteem, and promotes better bonding between them and their non-impaired fellow learners.

7. *Learning through assessing*: while it may be difficult to involve learners with visual impairments in assessing other learners' written work, the reverse may still be possible, with non-impaired learners helping to peer-assess the products of the work of those with impairments. This can also allow those with impairments to receive useful advice from fellow learners about any ways that the products of their work may be improved to meet assessment criteria more closely.

3 Auditory impairment

There are several ways in which hearing difficulties can impede learning. Turning information into knowledge becomes harder when significant dimensions of the information come from tone of voice, emphasis, and so on. In lectures, even though induction loops may help learners to hear the lecturer, hearing-impaired learners may find it particularly difficult to hear other learners' questions. Many commonsense approaches can reduce the problems for most hearing-impaired learners. For example, making sure that the lecturer's face is well lit (particularly when dimming lights to show slides) and clearly visible to them will help them with lip-reading. A simple desk lamp placed at an appropriate position on the lecture bench or podium can make a big difference in this respect.

Which factors underpinning successful learning may be damaged, and how?

1. *Wanting to learn*: this can be damaged and undermined by the embarrassment associated with hearing impairments. This is at least partly caused by what seems to be an all too common reaction to people who don't latch on to what we say to them – that they are 'slower' or 'more challenged' by the subject matter. As any hearing-impaired learner will confirm to you, slowing down your speech or shouting is not the best way forward. (Similar frustrations are often expressed by wheelchair users, who are sometimes treated as if their hearing must be impaired.)

2. *Needing to learn*: hearing-impaired learners may miss out on much of the informal face-to-face explanation of – and clarification of – intended learning outcomes in lectures and other face-to-face contexts. They therefore may be less well informed about the targets they are heading towards, and less clear about the kinds of evidence of achievement that in due course will be expected of them.

3. *Learning by doing*: some aspects of learning by doing may not be available to learners with hearing impairment, for example, due to safety requirements. Also, when they are engaged in practical work, they may not be able to attend to instructions at the same time as performing operations, as they may need to watch the person giving the instructions to lip-read.

4. *Making sense*: hearing-impaired learners are in danger of missing out on some or all of the clarification which other learners gain from explanations where tone of voice, emphasis and so on convey much of the meaning.

5. *Learning through feedback*: when learners are restricted in gaining feedback auditorily, for example, in face-to-face contexts, there is the danger that they may place too much emphasis on written, printed or online feedback without having the same opportunity to probe what it *really means*, which is available to learners who can ask about it and hear the responses. Hearing-impaired learners may also miss out on the informal feedback which comes through discussions with fellow learners, and may not themselves realize how much this can be disadvantaging them.

6. *Learning through explaining*: it remains useful where possible to get hearing-impaired learners to benefit from the deepening of their learning which accompanies explaining things orally to fellow learners. If their speech is significantly impaired as well, however, this is less likely to be an option. In addition, patience is needed in that they may not be able to receive the auditory clues that their explanations are being received properly – although visual feedback may well be enough for this.

7. *Learning through assessing*: in many cases, hearing-impaired learners are well able to peer-assess the work (particularly written work) of learners without impairments, and can benefit significantly from internalizing the assessment criteria and becoming better able to work towards meeting these criteria in their own work.

What adjustments may we be able to make to compensate?

1. *Wanting to learn*: the most significant way of helping to avoid damaging hearing-impaired learners' 'want' to learn is to educate both teachers and fellow learners to respond sensitively and successfully to the real needs associated with auditory difficulties. Perhaps everyone should from time to time sit through a colleague's lecture with ear plugs in place, just to remind them of the effects of hearing impairments and to clarify which aspects of presentation can compensate for at least some parts of the problem.

2. *Needing to learn*: it can help to make intended learning outcomes, evidence descriptors and assessment criteria really speak for themselves in print, whether in course handbooks, on-screen or in handout materials. This of course helps *all* learners, but can be particularly valuable to those who may be missing out on the tone-of-voice clarifications which arise in face-to-face teaching–learning contexts and group-work contexts.

3. *Learning by doing*: in most cases, it is possible, with some forethought, to design tasks and briefings which allow learners with

hearing impairments to achieve the same learning outcomes, perhaps by slightly different routes.

4. *Making sense*: There are so many contexts where loss of auditorily received information can affect learners' ability to make sense of concepts and ideas as they turn information into their own knowledge. The most satisfactory way of compensating for this is to keep helping them to find out how well (or not) they are making sense of important elements of subject matter, and asking them 'How can I help you to make sense of this?'

5. *Learning through feedback*: it is worth checking that hearing-impaired learners are really understanding the feedback that we give them. When we find that a particular point has not yet got across in print or on-screen, at least we can try to use other ways of addressing that point or clarifying it.

   To compensate for peer-group informal feedback, it can be worth finding out more about who *can* be heard more easily among the peer learner group, and making best use of those who have a natural ability to 'be heard' more readily than others. This is not, of course, to be confused with mere *loudness*. Some people are much easier to lip-read than others, some have much clearer diction, and so on.

6. *Learning by explaining*: where hearing-impaired learners are able to explain things to non-impaired fellow learners, they are able to benefit from the additional deepening of their learning this brings, but also from the increased understanding which develops between them and their fellow learners.

7. *Learning through assessing*: hearing-impaired learners may well be able to peer-assess the work of non-impaired learners, deepening their own grasp of the subject matter involved. They are also usually able to self-assess their own work, making informed judgements about the extent to which they are evidencing their achievement to the standards required for success in their studies, and can benefit significantly from tutor feedback on the effectiveness of their self-assessment.

4 Mental health needs

This general heading in fact covers a very wide range of needs and conditions, ranging from depression, anxiety, Asperger's syndrome and mania to schizophrenia – any of which can have significant or even profound effects on learners' ability to handle various teaching–learning situations. Also, there are the much more common effects that can affect a learner's 'state of mind' in one way or another, including fatigue (often due to working shifts at night to support study) and conditions relating to consuming alcohol or other mind-altering agents. Furthermore, most learners at some time (and some learners for most of the time) are affected by various levels of stress. Stress can be attributable to a wide range of sources – financial issues, emotional problems, low self-esteem, and so on. Some mental health conditions can be slow-onset, and grow in intensity so gradually that they are not noticed for some time – by others or even by the individuals themselves. Other conditions can be precipitated very rapidly by life-changing events or crises.

As with other special needs, mental health needs of most kinds lie on a continuum ranging from what we would regard as 'normal', including occasional stress or anxiety, to more intensive or what we might call 'abnormal' needs. The latter frequently require expert help and support. Borderline needs are very difficult to define.

Perhaps the most important difference between mental health needs and physical ones is that learners affected by mental health conditions are *not* necessarily able to give realistic responses to our question 'How can I best help you with this?' Some learners may have a firm grasp on exactly how their special needs can best be addressed, but others may be quite wrong in their view of what is likely to be best for them. That is why it is so important for anyone whose job is about making learning happen in post-compulsory education to know where to find the nearest sources of expert help to address the more significant mental health problems. Experts include counsellors and other appropriately trained personnel, who invariably have their own links to the specialists who may be needed on occasion.

While it can be safely assumed that in a lecture theatre full of students, at any given time some will be impeded by one or more mental health needs or conditions, it is quite impossible for a lecturer to know exactly which conditions may need to be addressed. One can't really ask the students 'Hands up those of you who have mental health problems today please'!

Which factors underpinning successful learning may be damaged, and how?

1. *Wanting to learn*: this can become seriously undermined when learners with mental health needs tend to retreat into a world of their own problems and difficulties. Conversely, sometimes learners with particular mental health needs can be found to be setting their own self-expectations unrealistically high, causing problems when they fail to live up to their own demands on themselves.

2. *Needing to learn*: the most general risk is that learners with mental health needs are in danger of not taking ownership of the standards as intended. They may make their own interpretations of what is meant by the intended learning outcomes, evidence descriptors and assessment criteria, only to find in due course that they've made incorrect judgements about them.

3. *Learning by doing*: some learners may be unable to sustain effort for as long as their fellow learners. Some may find it particularly difficult to focus properly on a given task.

4. *Making sense*: the effects here can range very widely. In some cases, learners may be able to make sense of some things perfectly well – even exceptionally well – while other topics or subject areas may come to be distinct blocks.

5. *Learning through feedback*: some learners may be unreceptive to feedback, both from tutors and peers. Others may take feedback too seriously, and get it entirely out of proportion, especially when it happens to be critical. This can turn out to be a useful clue to tutors that not all is well, leading to more sensitive approaches to giving feedback where necessary.

6. *Learning through explaining*: in most cases, the benefits of learning through explaining are just as significant for learners with mental health problems as for any learners. Problems may arise, however, regarding those who are at the receiving ends of the explanations, who may lack sensitivity regarding how to respond to the explanations they receive, and may give inappropriate feedback regarding the explanations which could damage the self-esteem or confidence of those explaining.

7. *Learning through assessing*: at best, the internalizing of standards accompanying self-assessment and peer assessment can be just as useful to learners with mental health needs as to any other learners. However, depending on the nature of the mental health needs, the degree or intensity of self-assessment or peer assessment may get out of proportion, detracting from the potential benefits of learning by making informed judgements. In other words, as tutors, we probably have to keep a close eye on learners we know have mental health issues in the context of learning through assessing. Or, indeed, keep an eye on 'normal' learners for signs of this sort of activity beginning to happen abnormally.

What adjustments may we be able to make to compensate?

It is not possible to offer point-by-point advice on how to respond where there is such a wide spectrum of mental health needs that can undermine successful learning. However, there are some general ways to respond to the possibility – indeed, probability – that in any group of learners at any time there will be some mental health needs.

An obvious, but nonetheless important, aim is to avoid conflict, temper, distress or highly charged emotional exchanges for all learners at all times. For example, it is worth refraining from overreacting to challenging or unexpected behaviours from any learners, however irritating they may be to us – and, indeed to the rest of the learners in a group. While 'normal' learners may weather such minor storms perfectly adequately, those with particular mental health needs may get them quite out of proportion.

Conclusions

This chapter as a whole has ranged around some consequences of widening participation, particularly the increased presence of various special needs. We need to try to adjust the educational environment to be more suitable to all the learners whose needs it is intended to address. This is all the more achievable by continuing to think of how best to design our learning environments to address the factors underpinning successful learning. In other words, inclusive teaching could be described as follows:

- Doing everything we can to enhance the *want* to learn of all participants in post-compulsory education.

- Clarifying as well as we can the *need* to learn, as spelled out by the intended learning outcomes we formulate to define our curriculum.

- Adjusting the *learning by doing* tasks and activities we design for learners, to allow all learners to have suitable opportunities to practise, learn through mistakes, and learn from their individual experiences.

- Helping all learners to *make sense* or *digest* the information they encounter, and respond to their different ways of doing this.

- Maximizing the *feedback* that all learners gain both from us and from each other, and adjust the feedback processes towards those techniques that are most effective for learners as individuals.

- Using *learning through explaining and coaching* appropriately and sensitively, not only to help learners to deepen their own learning, but to bridge the gap between those with and without disabilities or special needs.

- Carefully using *learning through assessing* to monitor which learners with disabilities are indeed helped by doing this, and making sure that the experience does indeed deepen their learning without damaging their confidence or self-esteem.

To achieve these aims, we need to continue to seek feedback from all our learners, not just on their experience of our teaching, but also in their individual experience of learning in the context of their own particular needs. Learning, after all, is done by individuals. Each learner learns in a particular way. Inclusive teaching is about helping all learners to optimize their own individual learning, where possible allowing them to learn productively from and with each other.

Addressing Employability

'With the changing economy, no one has lifetime employment, but community colleges provide lifetime employability' (President Barack Obama, 2009). In the recession we are experiencing at the time of preparing this edition, it is encouraging that the importance of employability, and our role in trying to develop it, is recognized by such a world leader.

Part of the purpose of post-compulsory education in the grand scheme of things is to help learners become ready for what is likely to be one of the main features of the rest of their lives – getting a job and staying in employment. For the last two decades and more, there has been a lot of discussion about the balance we need to strike in our educational provision between deepening learners' knowledge and understanding of the subjects they are studying and developing the skills they will need for their careers, and indeed the rest of their lives. Many aspects of becoming more employable can be developed alongside the subject-related knowledge and skills which are the basis of the main intended learning outcomes of our provision, and indeed can be regarded as important 'intended learning outgoings', as mentioned in Chapter 3. Indeed, it is perfectly possible to formulate intended learning outcomes and outgoings for the whole field of 'becoming more employable', and to assess learners' evidence of achievement of the former alongside the subject-based curriculum.

What do we mean by employability?

It is useful to try to establish exactly how wide the field of employability is. This short list illustrates how different people think of different things when asked to explain what they mean by employability:

- Having demonstrable intellectual curiosity, generosity of spirit, understanding of purpose, and adaptability.

- Being positive, responsive, thoughtful, well informed, organized, sociable and, above all, able to listen and try to fit in while also contributing to the workplace.

- The ability to say 'yes'!
- The ability to interpret appropriately your role within an organization.

What else is 'employability'?

- 'Earnability'? Many, perhaps most, learners in post-compulsory education already have some measure of this, through various part-time jobs they engage in to afford to continue with their education.

- 'Hold down a job' ability? Some learners are perfectly satisfactory at getting a job every now and then, but are not so good at keeping it. Sometimes boredom sets in.

- 'Have a satisfying life' ability? This is more about making wise choices in the first place regarding what sort of employment suits individual learners.

How can we help learners to *show* that they are employable?

There are many good reasons for building into our curriculum opportunities for learners to evidence their employability. Employers themselves know better than to rely simply on academic results when choosing the right candidate for a post. They seek evidence of employability from letters of application, CVs and, above all, from interviews with job applicants.

Evidence of employability needs to arise from purposefully designed learning by doing activities, including plenty of opportunity to learn by trial and error in safe environments – mock interview panels, CV selection panels, and so on. Therefore, it is useful to think, when designing learning by doing towards the achievement of subject-based intended learning outcomes, to what extent the same activities can embrace the skills and attributes associated with employability. This gives learners practice at evidencing their employability, and in contexts where it is not just seen as an add-on, but as a process directly linked to the mainstream curriculum.

How can we help learners to *feel* that they are employable?

This is not least about helping learners to develop their confidence and self-esteem. In the National Student Survey used in the UK since 2005 to gather data about students' experience of higher education, the section entitled 'personal development' comprises these statements.

19 The course has helped me to present myself with confidence.
20 My communications skills have improved.
21 As a result of the course, I feel confident in tackling unfamiliar problems.

These three statements certainly elicit feedback from students on how well they feel that employability-related skills and confidence are developed through their courses. Also, because the Survey is used throughout the higher education sector and the data arising from it are turned into league tables for use by students and institutions, making students *feel* they are more employable has been given increased attention in the sector.

How, then, can we help students to feel positively about these aspects of their studies? As always, feelings are developed most quickly by feedback. In particular, when learners engage in activities where they are evidencing aspects of their own development relating to employability, they can gain a great deal of feedback from each other, often informally, but also purposefully, for instance, in the context of peer assessment. For example, getting learners to role-play interviewers and candidates in interview simulations, and capturing the process on video, can help learners to see themselves as future employers might see them, and learn by trial and error in a safe context.

We can get learners to put together applications for fictitious posts, and allow them to learn by judging each other's applications as 'shortlisting committees', prior to using these applications as part of the basis for the interview simulations. They then learn a great deal about which aspects of an application may lead to good (or difficult) interview questions. The whole process develops their written and oral communication skills by practice, and trial and error, in a safe environment and can do a lot to help them to feel that they can succeed in making a good job of preparing to be seen to be employable.

Should we also be preparing learners for 'unemployability'?

I do not, of course, mean here 'unable to be employed', but rather 'able to survive being unemployed' temporarily. This question seems ever more crucial in light of the current recession, but even in times of prosperity, in many people's lives nowadays there are episodes *between* employment of one kind or another. It is a valuable life skill to be prepared to survive without employment for a while, and not just sink into a morass of despair and gloom. For many learners, the time *before* the first significant employment opportunity can seem like an age. We need to equip learners to work constructively at not just filling their time when out of employment, but at heading purposefully towards the next employment opportunity, and continuing to build up their employability.

Should we also equip learners regarding 'sackability'?

Perhaps this is just as important as many aspects of employability, in a world where very significant numbers of people lose their jobs through no direct fault of their own, through redundancy, restructuring of organizations, mergers and takeovers, fixed-term contracts coming to an end, expected renewal of contracts not happening, and so on. Few education programmes really prepare learners for the trauma associated with losing a job – something they are quite likely to experience at least sometime in their lives.

Developing employability by building on learners' own experiences

Many learners in post-compulsory education already know a lot about employability. It is far from unusual for learners themselves to have had more varied experience at being employed than their tutors in post-compulsory education, many of whom have had a relatively stable and trouble-free pathway through only a few posts during their careers. It is important that we don't fail to recognize the breadth and diversity of the experience of at least some of our learners, and help them to value it, share it with their less-experienced colleagues and build on it.

Mapping aspects of employability

Knight and Yorke (2003: 151–2) commented on a range of 'aspects of employability' drawn from the 'Skills *plus*' project. This project ran in four varied universities in the North-west of England between 2000 and 2002, and sought to bring fresh thinking into the incorporation of skills in curricula in higher education. Knight and Yorke noted that in the table of 'aspects of employability' they presented, the acquisition of disciplinary understanding of skills is assumed, and that the *application* of these skills is included as '30' of the 39 aspects listed in their table, which is reproduced below. It is interesting to see how far the table ranges beyond discipline-related skills and knowledge, and it is challenging to ponder how we, as educators, might set about using our subject teaching and learning as a vehicle to develop so much wider a range of human skills and attributes.

A: **Personal Qualities**
  1 **Malleable self-theory:** belief that attributes (e.g. intelligence) are not fixed and can be developed.
  2 **Self-awareness:** awareness of own strengths and weaknesses, aims and values.

3 **Self-confidence:** confidence in dealing with the challenges that employment and life throw up.
4 **Independence:** ability to work without supervision.
5 **Emotional intelligence:** sensitivity to others' emotions and the effects that they can have.
6 **Adaptability:** ability to respond positively to changing circumstances and new challenges.
7 **Stress tolerance:** ability to retain effectiveness under pressure.
8 **Initiative:** ability to take action unprompted.
9 **Willingness to learn:** commitment to ongoing learning to meet the needs of employment and life.
10 **Reflectiveness:** the disposition to reflect evaluatively on the performance of oneself and others.

B: Core Skills
11 **Reading effectiveness:** the recognition and retention of key points.
12 **Numeracy:** ability to use numbers at an appropriate level of accuracy.
13 **Information retrieval:** ability to access different sources.
14 **Language skills:** possession of more than one language.
15 **Self-management:** ability to work in an efficient and structured manner.
16 **Critical analysis:** ability to 'deconstruct' a problem or situation.
17 **Creativity:** ability to be original or inventive and to apply lateral thinking.
18 **Listening:** focused attention in which key points are recognized.
19 **Written communication:** clear reports, letters, etc., written specifically for the reader.
20 **Oral presentations:** clear and confident presentation of information to a group.
21 **Explaining:** orally and in writing.
22 **Global awareness:** in terms both of cultures and of economics.

C: Process Skills
23 **Computer literacy:** ability to use a range of software.
24 **Commercial awareness:** understanding of business issues and priorities.
25 **Political sensitivity:** appreciates how organizations work and acts accordingly.
26 **Ability to work cross-culturally:** both within and beyond the UK.
27 **Ethical sensitivity:** appreciates ethical aspects of employment and acts accordingly.
28 **Prioritizing:** ability to rank tasks according to importance.
29 **Planning:** setting of achievable goals and structuring action.
30 **Applying subject understanding:** use of disciplinary understanding from the higher education programme.
31 **Acting morally:** has a moral code and acts accordingly.
32 **Coping with ambiguity and complexity:** ability to handle ambiguous and complex situations.
33 **Problem-solving:** selection and use of appropriate methods to find solutions.

34 **Influencing:** convincing others of the validity of one's point of view.

35 **Arguing for and/or justifying a point of view of a course of action**.

36 **Resolving conflict:** both intrapersonally and in relationships with others.

37 **Decision-making:** choice of the best option from a range of alternatives.

38 **Negotiating:** discussion to achieve mutually satisfactory resolution of contentious issues.

39 **Teamwork:** can work constructively with others on a common task.

Knight and Yorke (2003: 203) concluded that:

> If progress was to be made in encouraging employability throughout a programme, then, especially in highly modularized programmes, it is necessary to look away from summative assessment practices with their own often unrealistic demands for reliability, and towards other ways of providing developmental feedback and helping students to make claims to achievements.

Striking the balance between independence, collaboration and followership

There is much discussion of the importance of using post-compulsory education to develop learner autonomy and independence, but the ways that learning is driven by assessment often pushes us in the reverse direction towards conformity and uniformity. One aspect of employability which attracts a lot of attention is the development of leadership. However, particularly in the early stages of employment, perhaps an even more important set of skills and attributes to be identified are those linked to the concept of 'followership' – at any time there need to be more followers around than leaders, even when some perfectly capable leaders are present. Looking back at Knight and Yorke's 'aspects of employability', it is interesting to note how many of the factors link to decision-making, communication and leadership attributes. Perhaps we also need to consider some attributes which can be thought of as more conformist, perhaps including the following:

- recognizing when *not* to air one's own views, in the interests of getting things done and promoting teamwork

- listening without giving one's disagreement away by body language, facial expression and so on, when disagreement is not important – or, indeed, when it needs to be shelved for the purposes of the task in hand

- accepting action plans that are not quite as good as those in one's own mind, so that others continue with the increased momentum which comes from their sense of ownership of the action plan

- allowing others to do things which one could have done better to aid everyone's contribution to a task.

Beyond employability – enterprise and entrepreneurship

In recent years, several higher education institutions have addressed purposefully the development of these attributes in students, alongside their subject-related studies. In times of recession, it is likely to be these qualities which are needed to move us back towards prosperity.

It is very clear that we can't develop these qualities *for* our students – only *they* can do this. This is similar to *making sense* in the context of their subject-related learning. It is also clear that developing enterprise skills and entrepreneurship qualities is not likely to be achieved in a 'conformist' environment. We need to allow students the time and space to learn these skills by trial and error (giving plenty of feedback) and, above all, by a great deal of interpersonal interaction – interaction with other students, with tutors and, more importantly perhaps, interaction with real-life entrepreneurs from outside the relatively conservative confines of higher education.

As ever, when learning is driven substantially by assessment, we face the challenging task of designing assessment processes and instruments which will serve as targets to students, so that they develop their enterprise and entrepreneurship qualities along the way. By their very nature, however, there are no 'right answers' to assess, and our traditional assessment methods are far from fit for purpose as means of measuring these qualities.

Perhaps if a future version of an instrument such as the National Student Survey should probe final-year students' experiences of the extent to which their courses helped them to develop enterprise and entrepreneurship, we would see much greater attention paid by institutions to providing students with the opportunity, time, space and feedback needed to achieve these qualities alongside their studies in higher education.

Conclusions: seven factors underpinning developing successful employability?

All seven of the factors underpinning successful learning discussed throughout this book can be considered to link strongly to developing learners' employability (and indeed can link to enterprise and entrepreneurship development too). You might also notice that collectively, addressing these seven factors links well to just about everything in the list from Knight and Yorke (2003), and more.

1 *Wanting to learn*: this links closely to the sort of motivation employers value. Getting learners to think consciously about their 'want' to learn during their studies at college paves the way to them being conscious of their own driving forces in general, and helps them to remain more

aware of what they want in employment. This, in turn, helps them quickly to communicate their ambitions both to prospective employers at interview – helping to secure a job in the first place – and to their actual employers when in post – helping them perhaps to justify some training or development they would like, or indeed to secure promotion as 'someone who knows their own mind'.

2 *Taking ownership of the need to learn*: working towards targets is necessary in the day-to-day life of being employed. Working towards other people's targets, in particular, is very important in the early stages of any post. Skills gained from working out what intended learning outcomes actually boil down to in practice are usefully extended to breaking overall targets in post into achievable manageable steps. Enterprise and entrepreneurship can be regarded as including setting *new* targets, and planning how to reach them.

3 *Learning by doing*: any job can be regarded as an extension of practice, repetition, learning through mistakes, and so on. If we can help learners to be more conscious of their learning by doing while in post-compulsory education, they are likely to remain so as they move into employment, and continue to be more willing and able to 'have a go' at new problems, even when some trial and error will be involved – linking, of course, to enterprise and entrepreneurship.

4 *Making sense*: helping learners become aware of how best they achieve this paves the way for them to continue to become better at it during employment. The more conscious we help them to be about what works best for them in getting their heads round new scenarios and concepts, the better they can take charge of understanding the employment contexts they find themselves in, and the less likely they are to rush into things having only thought through the consequences at a superficial level.

5 *Learning through feedback*: this is perhaps the most important of the factors underpinning successful learning when we consider the links to employability. Employers value highly the skills of good listeners. However, *receptive* listeners are those who take feedback on board rapidly and easily, and adjust their actions accordingly. Similarly, the skills of *giving* feedback constructively are very important in work-based contexts, and employees who experience least difficulty supervising other employees are all the more valued by employers. Helping learners to become really conscious about how they respond to feedback, and how best to give feedback to others, are useful aspects of the overall purposes of post-compulsory education. There are further strong links to feedback in the remaining two factors below.

6 *Learning through explaining, coaching, teaching*: skills gained through these processes are very close to many of the skills needed for employability in the wider sense, and vital for many particular kinds of job. Essentially, we

can do a great deal to develop learners' communication and interpersonal skills by giving them time, space and reason to deepen their learning in these ways. This does sometimes mean us as tutors stepping back from the temptation to do most of the explaining, coaching and teaching, and realizing that while it may be somewhat slower to allow learners to do this with each other, the end results are much more profound.

7 *Learning through assessing – making informed judgements*: the pay-off resulting from involving learners in self-assessment and peer assessment have huge relevance to developing employability. People who have the ability to assess their own activities 'during the doing of them' (cf. Sadler, 1989) are likely to do a much better job. Practice gained through peer assessment not only develops judgement-related skills, but also the accompanying interpersonal and communication skills to convey these judgements effectively and sensitively to fellow human beings in workplace environments.

Overall, learners who become skilled at learning, and consciously reflecting about their own learning, are in a strong position to continue to develop as learners long after leaving post-compulsory education. Equipping learners to be able to get the most from their brains paves their way towards lifelong learning – employers value 'a good learner' possibly more than anything else. Therefore, when a primary purpose of post-compulsory education is to equip learners for their future careers, there is nothing better we can do for them than help them to take conscious control of how they learn best, and help them to become well-practised in exercising key communication and interpersonal skills during their time with us. Furthermore, we need to allow learners opportunities to 'step out of the box of higher education' and exercise their own minds in ways which prepare at least some of them to be enterprising and entrepreneurial.

10

What Can I Do When...?

This chapter contains a selection of answers to frequently occurring problems. A few of these are adapted from suggestions which proved popular in editions of *In at the Deep End* which I wrote for Leeds Metropolitan University in 2006, and revised in 2009, but most are entirely new. I sought 'difficult questions' from a number of web lists, including those of the National Teaching Fellows in the UK, the members of the All Ireland Society for Higher Education (AISHE), the mailing list of the Higher Education Research and Development Society of Australasia (HERDSA), and the members of the Staff and Educational Development Association (SEDA). From over 200 questions, I've chosen here to try to provide some answers to the most commonly occurring ones.

What can I do when I'm feeling very nervous?

You're not alone. Even many very experienced lecturers are quite nervous, especially with a new group, or with a subject they don't know particularly well. Some tactics that can help include:

- Smile! You'll notice that at least some of the students will smile back – this immediately makes you feel better.

- Have good prompts available. It's reassuring to have (for example) a list of your slides, so that you won't be nervous about losing your place in the lecture.

- If they all have copies of a handout, ask them to study a short section of it for two minutes. For a while, just about all eyes are off you.

- Ad-lib an explanation of the importance of a point you've just recently been making. Sometimes the very fact that you're making a spontaneous addition is relaxing in its own right.

- Bring in your students. For example, ask them a question along the lines: 'How many of you have already come across ...?' or 'How many of you have never yet heard of ...?'

- Don't be afraid to pause for a short while, and take a deep (quiet) breath.

- Act courageous even when you feel ghastly. Stage performers do this all the time, and it works.

What can I do when I forget where I am in my lecture?

This happens to most lecturers now and then, so don't feel that there's something wrong with you if it happens to you. Your choices include:

- Give your students something to do for a couple of minutes. For example, have a slide or overhead already prepared for such an eventuality. Make the activity seem a perfectly natural step for your students, for example by saying: 'Now would be a really good time for you to think for a minute or two about...' and then put up your task briefing. While the students are doing the task, you've got time to sort out where *you* are and get ready to resume your lecture after debriefing students' work on the short task.

- Minimize the chance of losing where you are by having a print-out of your slides so that you can quickly *see* what you've done and what you were talking about.

- Ask students to jot down the two most important things they've learned so far from your lecture. Then ask them to compare with those sitting close to them. Then ask for volunteers to tell you what they chose as these things. This often helps you to regain a feel for exactly what had been happening in *their* minds up to the point at which you lost your way.

- If you're very confident, you could say: 'Oops, I've lost it! Anyone like to remind me what I was going to say next?' At least then, you'll have the full attention of your students for a moment – and they normally respond well to you just being human.

What can I do when I don't know the answer to a student's question?

A common nightmare. You'll feel less concerned about this as you gain experience, but the following tactics can take away some of the worries you may have about this.

- Give yourself time to think. Repeat the question to everyone, as other students may not have heard the question. Sometimes this extra time is enough to give you a chance to think of how you may respond.

- Don't try to make an answer up! If it turns out to be wrong, or if you get stuck in the process, you will soon have the full attention of all the students – not what you really want at this stage!

- Say: 'This is a really good question. How many of *you* can respond to this?' and look for volunteers. Quite often, there will be someone there who is willing answer it.

- Break it down into smaller bits. Then start by responding to one of the bits where you *do* have something to say. If it's a question that your students don't actually *need* to know an answer to, say so. 'Interesting, but not actually needed for your course', and so on.

- Admit that at this point you don't have an answer to the question, but you will find one by the time of the next lecture. Invite the student who asked the question to jot it down on a post-it, with their email address, so that you know *exactly* what the question was and can respond to the questioner directly as soon as you've located an answer. But don't forget to share the answer with the whole group at the next lecture too.

What can I do when students repeatedly come in late and disrupt my lecture?

This is a balancing act. There will usually be *some* students who arrive late, but sometimes the problem becomes more significant in certain time slots and at particular times in a module.

- Don't keep the punctual students waiting until they're fed up. Start the session with something that will be useful or interesting to them.

- Don't gradually get more and more annoyed with latecomers! The *next* student to arrive may have a very good reason for being late.

- Resist the temptation to be sarcastic (e.g. 'How good of you to join us today'). Mostly, students who come in late don't actually enjoy being late, and if they get a rough ride from you, next time they're late they may well decide not to risk coming in at all.

- If the late-coming is noisy (loud doors, shoes on floors, and so on), pause until it will be possible for everyone to hear you properly again. The students themselves will get tired of having to wait for latecomers, and will often show their own disapproval, sparing you the need to do so.

- If necessary, agree some ground rules with the whole group. For example, if quite a lot of the students have had to come from another session at the other end of the campus, negotiate to start promptly five minutes *after* the normal time.

- Build in a little 'warm-up' time at the start of each lecture. In other words, start doing something useful with the students (for example reminding them of three important points from last week, or quizzing them gently).

What can I do when the technology lets me down?

For example, your PowerPoint slides disappear, or freeze! The thing *not* to do is to struggle for ages, with the undivided attention of the whole group, with a mouse, a remote control, a keyboard, or any other piece of technology. Alternatives include:

- Smile, rather than sweat! Even if inside you're quite tense about it, it's best to give the impression of being cool about it.

- Give your students a discussion task to do – something to talk about to those sitting next to them, for example a decision to reach, a problem to solve, and so on. It's a good idea *always* to have such a task ready and waiting. Then when they're all busy and eyes are off you, you can try to rescue the technology.

- Ask for help. 'Anyone know how to fix this please?' quite often brings a competent volunteer from the floor. Sometimes, you can ring up technical support, but it remains advisable to give the students something else to do until help materializes.

- Recognize when the problem is terminal – for example, when the bulb has failed in a ceiling-mounted data projector.

- Improvise a quiz. This can be good revision, particularly if you are really on top of the subject matter (but don't try this if you don't know the material well).

- If it's towards the end of a session, wind up. Remind your students of the intended learning outcomes, and promise to cover anything important that remains outstanding on a future occasion or to put the relevant slides on to the web. Your students won't mind you stopping early!

What can I do when attendance drops off during a series of lectures?

It could be, of course, that your students are getting bored – or tired – or are busy trying to catch up ready for someone else's assignment deadline. Whatever the cause of absenteeism, one or more of the following tactics may help:

- Don't wait an inordinate time for more students to appear. Those who came punctually deserve to be getting some value, so get started even if the audience is sparse.

- Don't take it out on the students who *do* attend. Make it well worth their while coming to the lectures.

- Probe the causes. For example, if students are taking handouts for their absent friends, only bring enough handouts for those who do attend, and send a message to those who have missed the handout to come and collect it from you at a given time, and ask them why they missed the session.

- Find ways outside the lecture room to ask a few students why they missed a particular session. However, don't rail on them and tell them how unwise they are being – keep to fact-finding until you know more about what's going on.

- Link each and every lecture firmly to the assessment agenda. Students don't like to miss (for example) clarification of what a typical exam question could reasonably ask of them.

- Include some activities for students in groups in some lectures, with a small proportion of the coursework marks allocated to participation in the lectures. Students don't like to miss any opportunity to gain marks.

- Try for added value. Make sure that the students who do turn up feel that it's been well worth doing so. Give them a useful and enjoyable learning experience – and things they would have missed if they had not turned up.

What can I do when students do not attend lectures but get the notes from the VLE?

This is a problem which is increasing rapidly in scale. The following tactics may help:

- Remind the students that what is on the VLE is essentially *information* not knowledge, and is only part of the story. Explain to the class that the purposes of the lectures include to help them to *navigate* all of that information, so that they can make sense of it all much faster and more efficiently.

- Include in every lecture some details relating to how students' mastery of what's on the VLE will in due course be assessed. Ensure that students know that they need to come to lectures to find out what they are going to be expected to show for their studies using the information on the VLE.

- Include things for students to *do* in lectures, which get them making sense of concepts and ideas, and making judgements to deepen their learning. Make it clear to students that coming to lectures will help them to get their heads round topics much faster than just reading all about it on the VLE.

What can I do if I get very critical comments from students in the annual feedback?

We *all* get very critical comments sometimes, and often we've earned them! But it's easy to get things out of perspective when it comes to critical comments, and one or more of the following tactics may help you in such a position.

- Don't let one or two savage comments prey on your mind unduly. If the overall comments are much more favourable on the whole, it could be the case that a few students really didn't like you very much, and much as we all wish to be liked, we can't achieve that all the time with everyone.

- Work out whether the criticism is justified. If it is, think of what you could do next time round to address the criticism and the issue behind it.

- Balance the picture by searching out the favourable comments you attracted at the same time. Think of how you can build on these, and get more of these next time.

- Take opportunities to find out more about the teaching of any colleagues who attracted more favourable comments than you did. Watching others teach regularly is an excellent opportunity to learn from others. There may be things you can emulate.

What can I do if I'm near the end but have only got through half my material?

This can happen to any of us. Any number of good things can cause this, not least going into detail answering important questions which arose during the session. It's only really a problem if you've got no more lectures coming up. General tactics which may help include the following.

- Don't overrun. That would annoy whoever is booked into the room next, and many of the students may have other places to go at the scheduled close of your session.

- Come to a sensible stopping place at the scheduled time, and re-plan your next session to pick up the ground which wasn't covered, and if necessary to delete something less important from that session.

- Alternatively, set the students a task which gets *them* to explore some of the ground you are not able to cover, and pick this up next time.

- In any case, it's probably only *you* who knows that you've only got through half of your material – the students only know what *was* covered.

- If it *was* your only lecture with the group, spend the last few minutes explaining that you will issue a self-study resource package on paper or on the web in a week or two, to enable your students to find out even more about the topic than you were able to cover in just one lecture with them. There's no need to tell them that you only got through half of your stuff!

What can I do if students are sitting like puddings and not responding?

One distinguished and experienced teacher recalls how he explained to the class that he was bored with their lack of response, and was going to have a short sleep, and lay down at the front of the room for half-a-minute, after which the class continued with much more gusto! Less risky tactics include:

- Remind yourself that this is human nature – it's easier to sit like a pudding and not respond than to think about something or actually do something. Think of what *you* do in a lecture, if you're not enthralled by it? It's probably time to give your students something to do, for example...

- Ask all of the students to jot something down. For example, 'See if you can jot down three things that could cause...'. Then get them to compare notes with their neighbours, and ask for some of the things thought of by students who you can see have something to say about it.

- Amuse them for a moment or two. It's useful to have a hidden action button at the bottom of each slide which can link you to a 'fun' menu – little video clips, cartoons, witty puns, and so on. Students (and staff) are often easier to engage after a little lightheartedness.

- Look for links between the topic of the lecture and contemporary issues, and cross-refer your material, inviting discussion.

What can I do if students are texting or checking Facebook online in my lecture?

This is just about the most common 'What can I do when...?' question posed nowadays. We can't turn the clock back – students *will have* laptops and i-phones with them in lectures, and they *will* have them turned on, even when requested not to do so. Many students live life with one eye on the laptop or i-phone screen, and one ear with an ear-piece in it, and the other eye/ear on the rest of the world, whether watching TV, or in pubs and clubs. We're not going to succeed in getting them all to switch these things off in our lectures. Tactics at dealing with this situation include:

- Set out your own ground rules and ask your students to abide by them.

- Don't threaten them that you'll ask them to leave unless they stop doing these things. It would just take one student to *refuse* to leave to give you a much more serious problem with the class.

- As best as you can, ignore those students you notice doing these things. If they're totally captivated by your lecture, they'll stop doing such things. Try to be more captivating.

- Now and then, give them something to *do* with these devices. For example, in groups see what the most important three things you can find on the web about 'x' is. Then quiz the class about what they've found. This can get the 'using gadgets' to a more productive activity.

> ## What can I do if students have not done the necessary preparation before their small-group sessions?

This is a really common 'What can I do if...?' question! Here are some thoughts.

- Don't give those who have not prepared a hard time. If you do, next time they haven't prepared, they will probably choose not to come at all – that is worse in the long run.

- Try to capitalize on the work of those who *have* prepared. For example, divide the small group into threes, and ask each trio to find answers to half-a-dozen questions based on their preparation, if you think that each trio is likely to have at least one member who has done some preparation. It will actually do the students who did prepare some good, explaining what they found to the others.

- Where possible, have handout material available so that the small group can do some further preparation at the start of the session (including those who have and have not done the advance work) and build on this.

- Next time, try to make the prepared work more engaging?

> ## What can I do to encourage online participation in a discussion?

This is a common question. Here are some thoughts.

- Make participation count. For example, tell the class that some of their coursework marks will arise from the extent and quality of contributions to the discussion. In practice, this is not actually difficult to estimate (albeit rather roughly), for example, all 5 marks for really good contribution, exactly zero for no contribution, and somewhere between for at least some contribution. Students don't like to risk losing even the odd mark or two.

- Use email to give positive, short, encouraging responses to those who do participate. Help them to feel that their efforts are worthwhile.

- In the nicest possible way, cool off the odd student who contributes too much, in case they put others off joining in. 'Great stuff, Tasmin, but could you ease off now and let some of the others catch up?'

- Report some of the main findings of those who did participate to the whole group at a lecture. Gently allow those who didn't participate to feel that they missed something useful.

- Make the discussion irresistible! Choose something suitable, and get a real debate going in a lecture, then say 'we'll continue this online'.

What can I do to ensure all the students in the group feel confident to ask questions or join in the discussion?

It's not surprising that some students are shy, especially in their first year, and in large groups. They don't want to say anything that may make them look or feel stupid. Some international students may also feel uncomfortable about 'putting themselves forward' as they may see it. The following ways of helping them join in with more confidence may help you to get them all contributing.

- Use the old adage 'better to look silly for a moment than to remain ignorant for a lifetime' – please do ask me questions.

- Never make a student who does ask a question feel silly.

- Accept that at least some students will remain very shy, and will be unlikely to feel confident enough to ask questions. Sometimes it may be because they are learning in a second language, and are embarrassed that they aren't yet as fluent as students around them.

- Get them all to jot down a question or two, for example on post-its, and then share their questions with their near neighbours, then invite students to ask *someone else's* question.

- For greater 'comfort of anonymity' in a big group, ask students to write questions on post-its and send the post-its down to you.

- Use a 'question box' to collect queries, and reply via the course web page.

- Suggest that students email you with *short* questions, and then answer some of them in the next whole-class session.

What can I do to inspire students (and myself) when I'm getting bored with delivering the same content year after year?

Boredom is as infectious as enthusiasm. If we radiate boredom with a topic, students will catch it. The following tactics may help you increase your enthusiasm for the content which is currently beginning to bore you.

- Remind yourself that the content may be the same, but the students are different. They will already know different things this year, and will have at least some different problems with the content.

- Avoid just turning up with the same notes and slides as you used last time. Give yourself some time to do some editing of your materials, getting rid of the most boring bits and putting new ideas in. Perhaps even frighten yourself by deleting the old material and starting again from scratch.

- Try doing things differently yourself. Invent new in-lecture tasks for the students to do to get their heads around the content.

- Try to make sure that you've got at least some different content to work with, rather than just the same old workload.

- Start some team teaching going with the bits you're getting bored with – you may find that watching someone else handling these bits gives you new ideas and increases your own enthusiasm.

What can I do to stop the mobile phones that keep going off in my lecture?

The short answer is probably 'You can't!' However, the following tactics may reduce the occurrence of the problem.

- Say to the class at the start of a lecture 'Please leave your mobile phones *on* if you really need to be contacted, for example if you've got a seriously ill relative, or child, or a crisis in the family, and so on. I want you all the be relaxed enough to give your attention to the lecture, so remain possible to be contacted if needed. If your phone *does* go off, please slip out quietly and deal with the emergency'. Alternatively, 'Please set your phone to "silent" and do not answer it in class'. One result of this is that when someone's phone does go off, everyone wants to know what the emergency is, and students whose phones ring for no important reason are now quite embarrassed.

- Make sure *your* mobile phone doesn't go off!

- Alternatively, arrange that your mobile phone *does* go off, and pretend to have a seemingly long discussion with the (non-existent) caller, explaining that you're actually in the middle of giving a lecture just now, and so on! Sometimes, this makes the point you're wanting to get across.

- Stop the whole session and allow the student concerned to answer the call. It's quite uncomfortable answering a call with a large number of people listening in!

What can I do when a student asks 'will this be in the exam?'

A natural enough request. The following tactics can help.

- Always say 'Yes, it certainly could be' – if the answer was to have been 'no', students might well ask why they should be bothering to learn it.

- Expand a little on what exactly students should expect to become able to do, to illustrate their achievement of the learning outcomes relating to the topic.

- Avoid students having to ask the question by regularly reminding the class of the sort of things that you are expecting from them in the exam and any other modes of assessment.

- When something is not suitable to be in the exam, for example when a student asks a question about the topic which is off-target, it's sometimes worth responding along the lines 'This is very interesting, but you don't need this in the context of this particular course'.

What can I do when a student challenges my mark for an assignment?

This is sometimes a tricky situation, and one which needs to be handled sensitively, especially if the challenge occurs in a public context, such as in a large group session. The following tactics can help.

- Provide detailed explanations of how marks are awarded from the outset, ideally during the briefing for the assignment.

- Don't take offence. There might have been a problem with your marking of the assignment. More likely, the student may have a blind spot, and not yet see why marks had been lost in the answer submitted to you.

- Publish the marking scheme and assessment criteria in any case, written in language where students can see exactly how the marking has been done, so that it's less likely that any student will challenge your mark.

- Don't give the impression to all present that marks are not negotiable. Arrange a one-to-one session with the student concerned.

- At the one-to-one session, work through the marking scheme and assessment criteria with the student concerned, and (usually) show that the original mark was justified.

- Allow it to gradually become apparent to the whole group that you remain willing to renegotiate marks if there is a genuine case to be made, but that in practice it's extremely rare for a student to emerge with a better mark as a result of the process, and that sometimes they emerge with lower marks, if anything.

What can I do when all the students sit at the back and the front half of the room is empty?

This is a very common occurrence. It is human nature! Just watch lecturers themselves at conferences! One or more of the following tactics may be useful.

- Sometimes you can nip this in the bud by placing 'reserved' cards on back seats or using 'do not cross this line' ribbon for the back rows.

- Encourage students to sit in the central block rather than at the sides so you can at least see them all.

- Don't try to make the students move forwards. They actually resent quite strongly being made to sit anywhere.

- There could be some students who really do feel most comfortable at the back – not least anyone who might have to leave the room relatively suddenly, for example due to a panic attack which could be triggered by them being hemmed in in the middle of a row.

- Put out any handouts only on the seats you wish them to use.

- Offer a few 'prizes' for the first half-dozen students to come and sit in the front row – an extra handout, for example.

- Show a start-up slide with very small print on it, for example a shot of a newspaper cutting about the topic. This can cause students entering the room to move to where they can see the screen rather better (but don't continue to show small print to the class thereafter).

- Just continue as though you don't mind at all where they sit. If the atmosphere of the class becomes warmer and friendlier, they may well gravitate towards you on future occasions.

- Set a group activity for the students, and indicate that group 'A' is here, group 'B' here, etc., including locations at the front and back of the room. This can get at least some of them nearer to you.

- See if you can rearrange the session to a smaller room. The chances are that there will be a colleague with a large class who would like the larger room.

What can I do when asked at the last minute 'to cover a session' for a colleague who has not turned up?

Just about anything is better than simply cancelling a session – some students may have travelled a long way for it, and students remember cancellations when evaluation comes round. Being asked to cover a session is in fact sometimes a useful opportunity for you to illustrate how professional you are. It's worth always finding a way to meet the request, not least to enhance your reputation of being dependable and flexible. It also makes it more likely that someone will return the favour if you need to miss one of your sessions due to illness or an emergency.

One or more of the following tactics may help.

- Don't berate your absent colleague in front of the students (or to anyone else). It could be the case that the absence was quite unavoidable.

- If you have teaching sessions with the class concerned, you may be able to substitute one of your own sessions for the last-minute session, and make one of your future classes available to the colleague who did not turn up.

- If you really do need to try to cover your colleague's topic, you could run a revision session based on what the class had already covered, for example getting the class to generate questions about the topic on post-its, then facilitating a quiz of two or three teams of students, with a prize for the winning team.

- If it's a topic you know something about, you could give a session putting your own slant on the topic, keeping notes to pass on to your colleague to indicate what you had covered.

What can I do when I don't have a powerful voice, but don't like to be stuck behind the lectern near a microphone?

Lecturers need to be seen and heard. Ways of ensuring the latter include the following:

- See if you can get a radio mike. This normally allows you to walk around the room quite a lot, so long as you don't cause feedback loops by getting into the path of the linked loudspeakers. Using a microphone is good inclusive practice anyway, as hearing-impaired students will benefit if there is an audio loop in the room (and you may well not know that anyone has hearing difficulties, if they haven't declared them).

- Encourage the students to sit close enough to hear you. Admit that your voice is relatively quiet.

- Get some voice projection training. You may be amazed how much better you can project by due attention to breathing and stance.

- Don't try to be 'louder' than is comfortable for you – you may injure your voice, making the problem worse.

- Don't try to compete with students talking. Wait until it is quiet enough for you to be heard. Students' peer pressure usually causes them to stop talking if it is clear you are waiting for silence.

What can I do when I realize that I no longer understand the next point I'm about to teach?

This can be rather scary. Here are some thoughts.

- Celebrate! 'Understanding' dawns a little at a time, and we never stop deepening our understanding of something.

- As soon as you've done your best to explain the point to the students, get them explaining it to each other. Ask them 'What was the thing that helped you most to make sense of this idea?' and find out whether they've come up with better ways of explaining it than yours turned out to be.

- Take time before your next session with the group to have a good 'rethink' about the point concerned, and see if there's another better way you can get the point across to them.

What can I do when no one seems to be taking any notes?

Perhaps the question should be 'Is it important that students take notes, or are there better things I can get my students to do during the lecture?' There are plenty of *other* things that are *good* for students during lectures. These include the following:

- Jotting down their own thoughts and ideas in response to a question posed orally or on-screen.

- Comparing their ideas with those sitting next to them.

- Making a mind-map about what they've been hearing about for the last ten minutes.

- Writing down questions they need answered about the topic.

What can I do when nobody seems to listen at the end of my lecture because they are busy packing up?

A very common problem. It only takes one student to make 'packing up' noises and it spreads like wildfire. Try one or more of the following.

- End with something really important, such as a short explanation of the sort of exam question which could be based on what has been covered in the lecture.

- Make the close of the lecture so interesting that no one thinks of packing up.

- Avoid saying 'and finally...' too early, which is often the cue students take to start packing up.

- Avoid saying 'Right now, are there any questions?' This is widely interpreted by students as time to pack up. In any case, it's much better to seek questions in the middle of the lecture, or even at the very beginning.

- Some lecturers get away with ending each lecture with a joke or anecdote, and if this is engaging enough it prevents students from starting to pack up, or at least means those who do pack up are not missing anything important.

- Prepare yourself to close the lecture a few minutes before the students will begin to pack up. Continuing while they are packing up won't be of value to them in any case, so you may as well make the lecture that bit shorter.

What can I do when someone responds to my question with a totally wrong answer?

This is bound to happen from time to time, especially if you're successful at getting most students to contribute to answering your questions. The following tactics may help.

- Don't make the student giving the wrong answer look foolish. Thank them for their contribution, try to find something positive in what was said, then say 'Anyone got a different answer for this question?' and make it clear gently that the next answer is better (if, of course, it is better).

- Try to avoid picking the student who gave the totally wrong answer, when several students are offering to answer your next question.

- When a student gives a really good answer, be generous with your praise, for example 'Well done, that's great'.

What can I do if students are talking in my lecture?

Many lecturers get upset by this, and clearly if students can't hear you over each other's chatter, the situation becomes untenable.

- Don't just carry on trying to ignore it. That often makes the problem get worse. Pause, looking at the people who are talking until they stop – or until the other students shut them up for you.

- Don't necessarily assume they're just being rude. Sometimes, one will have asked another to explain or repeat something that has been missed. Sometimes they could be translating what you say into another language for each other.

- Acknowledge that you may have been talking for too long yourself, and give them something to talk about with near neighbours. In other words, *legitimize* their talking for a few minutes, and let them get the need to talk out of their system.

- Note any persistent 'talkers' but resist the temptation to confront them in front of the whole group. Instead, find a time to talk to them on their own, and explore how they're finding your lectures.

- Don't ask an 'offender' to leave! If they actually *refuse* to leave, you'll have a much more difficult problem to deal with. Never issue a threat that you would not be able to implement in practice.

What can I do when I come to the end and there are still 15 minutes to go?

Possibilities include:

- Say: 'This is a good place to stop this particular session' and revisit the intended learning outcomes for a moment or two, then wind up. Your students will not be terminally disappointed!

- Have with you a revision activity, for example a set of short, sharp quiz questions on your lectures to date with the group, and give them a quick-fire quiz until the time has been used up.

- Give out post-its and ask students to write any questions they would like to ask about the subject on them, and pass the post-its down to you. Choose which questions to answer to the whole group until the time is used up.

- Put up a slide of a past exam question on the topic you've been covering, and explain to students a little about what was expected in answers to that question.

- Ask the students to write down the two most important things they now know, that they didn't know when the lecture started. Then get them to compare with their neighbours, and invite volunteers to read out a few such things.

- Give a brief overview of what's coming next – for example, showing the students the intended learning outcomes for the next couple of lectures.

What can I do when students don't turn up for my small-group sessions?

In practice, there's little mileage in trying to 'force' students to turn up to any element in their programmes, and when students don't regard small-group teaching as particularly important, the problem of absenteeism increases. However, a combination of one or more of the following tactics can improve things sometimes.

- When the students who *are* present come away with something they would not have wanted to miss (be it handouts, the light dawning, tasks they found valuable doing, and so on), the word can get around and attendance can improve.

- If your institution has student liaison officers, or other staff who support the student experience, ask them to help you check up on absentees.

- Ask some regular absentees 'What's wrong?' Sometimes there could be a timetable clash you didn't know about, or travel difficulties relating to a particular time slot. Sometimes, of course, the answer can be 'I didn't find the sessions helpful' and we may need to probe gently into 'Why not exactly?' and remain ready to listen to the responses.

- Keep the assessment agenda on the table. When students can see that each small-group session has a bearing on helping them become ready for future exam questions, or helps them see what's being looked for in coursework assignments, students are less likely to miss them.

- Include at least *some* coursework mark for 'participation'. Don't just include it for *attendance*, however, or the odd student may come along but not join in!

What can I do when students refuse to do a task?

This is an awkward one. If *all* the students won't start your task, it's worse. The following tactics can help.

- Make sure the task briefing is really clear. Explain again exactly what you want them to do. It can be useful to say 'What it really means is...' and then put it into straightforward language.

- Show the task on a slide or overhead, or give it out as a handout. Sometimes, students can get the gist of a task rather better if they can see it and hear it at the same time.

- Try to find the block. For example, ask students 'Which part of the task are you having problems with?' and see if clarifying that part helps them to get started.

- Break the task into smaller bits. Ask students to just do the first bit now, and then explain the later stages one by one when they're properly under way.

- Ask them to work in pairs to start with. You can then go round any pairs who still seem reluctant to start the task, and find out more about what could be stopping them.

- Set a precise deadline for the first part of the task. Sometimes this is enough to get them started.

- Resist the temptation to keep talking. Give them some time when there's really nothing more going on, and it's clear that you expect them to get stuck into the task. A few seconds of solemn silence may seem interminable to you, but the resistance to getting started with the task may be fading away.

What can I do when one student dominates a group?

This is a frequent occurrence. Sometimes the causes are innocent enough – enthusiasm, knowing a lot about the topic, and so on. One or more of the following tactics may help you to balance things out.

- Set appropriate ground rules at the start of small-group work. It can be useful to say a little about leadership and followership – making the point that in many small-group situations in real life, too many leaders can militate against success and that everyone needs to be able to be a good follower for at least some of the time.

- Rearrange group membership regularly. This means that the domineering student moves on and doesn't dominate other students for too long.

- Intervene gently. For example, after the domineering student comes to a pause, ask: 'Would someone else now like to add to this please?'

- Have a quiet word. Do this with the domineering student outside the group context, for example giving suggestions about 'air time' and allowing everyone's views to be heard.

- Change the dynamic. Appoint the domineering student as chairperson for a particular activity, with the brief not to make any input on that task, but to co-ordinate everyone else's thinking.

- Don't fight it too hard. Recognize that domineering is a common human trait, and that domineering people often reach distinguished positions in the world around us and may be developing relevant skills in small-group contexts.

11

Reflective Observation

This final chapter is new for this edition. 'Reflection' is widely used and discussed in post-compulsory education in the context of a broad range of professional development programmes, and 'peer observation of teaching' is becoming ever more common *and powerful* in our attempts to make learning happen. Back in Chapter 2, you may have noticed the term 'reflective observation' in the context of the learning cycle which attracted critical comments. Indeed, I would argue that the combination of reflection and observation *may* contribute to successful learning, but more often these processes are likely to occur in an uncoupled way, and can then both be useful in the overall picture of making learning happen. However, both *can* be made to occur together, for example in the context of learning from peer observation of teaching. This is the main thrust of the present chapter.

Many institutions now have in place systems for the peer observation of teaching. These are often associated with the most public form of teaching – whole-class or large-group contexts. However, peer observation should not be restricted to the lecture room. There is much to be gained by observing teaching and learning in progress in each and every context in post-compulsory education, and also in extending observation to other aspects of higher education, as suggested by contributors in Gosling and Mason O'Connor (2009), not least assessment.

Sometimes, models of peer observation can be set up to be 'inspectorial', for example in many further education institutions in the UK, with observers making judgements on what they experience, resulting in grades or scores. In such schemes, observers are often 'armed' with detailed checklists, and make judgements on a series of particular aspects of the event they observe. Inspectorial approaches are often favoured by those wearing 'quality assurance' or 'quality management' hats, in their belief that the data gathered would be reliable and valid, and would warrant consideration in appraisal and promotion contexts, or as a basis for targeted development where shortfalls were identified. There is, however, usually an overall judgement. Are these informed judgements? Too often, observation is carried out where there has not been sufficient (or indeed any) training or rehearsal in the processes involved. Too often in 'inspectorial' models, no one observes the teaching of the observers. Sometimes they don't actually teach at all.

Sometimes they are completely external, and may know little about the bigger picture surrounding the particular snapshots they take of teaching.

The resultant wording following on from such judgements can be problematic. How would you feel, for example, if the result of you being observed was that your teaching was 'satisfactory'? Damned with faint praise? It would be fine if the judgement were to be 'excellent' or 'outstanding', but all teaching–learning events can't be 'outstanding'. What about the rest? Words such as 'adequate' or 'satisfactory' may be perfectly acceptable descriptors of the standard of operation of a vacuum cleaner, but should hardly be applied to human endeavours (this reservation also applies to the use of such words in feedback to students about their work).

My own view is that inspectorial approaches to peer observation do not bring out the best in teaching, nor maximize the benefits that can be realized from collegial or informal approaches where the main results are discussion, feedback and, above all, reflection – particularly reflection on the part of observers themselves. This indeed can justify the use of the term 'reflective observation' in this context. In this collegial approach to observation, observers gain a great deal of opportunity to see things they can emulate in their own approaches to teaching, as well as noticing things to strive to avoid in their own work. Gosling (2009: 9) usefully compares the characteristics of 'evaluation', 'development' and 'collaborative' models of peer observation, and prefers the word 'review' rather than 'observation'. It is this collaborative approach which I will expand upon in this chapter.

Later in this chapter, more detail is presented about the nuts and bolts of collegial approaches to the peer observation of teaching. First, we will think about the nature of the reflection that can accompany such processes. Then there is the wider picture of reflection, and the ways that reflection can help students deepen their learning. Finally there are the processes through which reflection can be evidenced – and even assessed.

Reflection and the factors underpinning successful learning

As long ago as 1933, Dewey defined reflection as 'an active persistent and careful consideration of any belief or supposed form of knowledge in the light of the grounds that support it and the further conclusion to which it tends' (Dewey, 1933: 6). In many disciplines and professions, the term 'reflective practitioner' is in widespread use. The work of Donald Schön is well known in this area, and commentators have differentiated between 'reflection on action' (looking back reflectively at events and happenings) and 'reflection in action' (interrogating one's present actions in a reflective way and making adjustments). Both of these processes can be useful in thinking about teaching, and both can help to deepen learning.

In the context of using reflection as an aid to making learning happen (and making teaching work better), we can think of reflection as linking to all seven of the factors underpinning successful learning, as follows.

1. **Wanting to learn**
   The fact that we engage in reflection is one form of our own evidence for wanting to (continue to) learn. It implies an intention to improve by finding out more about what is going on in an element of learning. Evidence of reflection is widely linked to continuing professional development in a variety of disciplines, not least that of teaching in post-compulsory education. But to become *skilled* at evidencing reflection depends on rehearsal and practice at doing so, and needs to be started as a normal part of the student experience from the outset of their higher education experience. We therefore need to become better at linking reflection to students' motivation, and work towards them *wanting* to provide good evidence of reflecting on their learning experience.

2. **Taking ownership of the need to learn**
   Engaging in the process of reflection shows at least some degree of willingness to find out more about what is going on. How well the need to learn is identified depends, of course, on the effectiveness of the reflection itself, and on how well it is used to analyse what is going on in the learning process. Well-designed opportunities for students to reflect on their learning can tell them (and us) a great deal about their perceptions of what they need to do to improve their learning, and help us to help them to learn successfully – in other words, to make learning happen.

3. **Learning by doing – practice, trial-and-error, repetition and so on**
   Reflection is itself a form of 'doing', albeit usually quite a cognitive one. However, reflection can be intensified if it involves making informed judgements about one's own actions, or about other people's actions and then applying or internalizing the judgements to one's own context. It is important to ensure that reflecting is not just another thing we require students to do – or indeed just another thing we require ourselves to do. It is one of the most important things – and we could argue that learning is never 'complete' without it.

4. **Making sense**
   Whether reflecting on our own practice or on observations of others' practice, reflection can be regarded as a natural part of the overall process of making sense of a situation, topic or context, helping us get our heads around it, deepening our awareness and understanding of the picture. Similarly, we need to help students not only to 'learn' something to the extent that they 'can do' things with it, but also to have increased their learning about themselves by reflecting on *how* they got to the stage of becoming able to demonstrate their evidence of achievement.

5. ***Learning through feedback***
   Reflection can involve gathering and analysing feedback on one's own actions and rethinking how those actions can be improved and developed by taking on board things learned from the feedback. Similarly, giving feedback to others on their actions can be regarded as reflection on our observations of what they do, and can also link to thinking inwards into our own parallel actions. Although, in essence, reflection can be thought of as a private process, it becomes much better developed if it is discussed and shared, not least in helping to develop better approaches to the process by learning from the practice of others.

6. ***Coaching, explaining, teaching***
   When we're directly engaged in any of these processes, it can be argued that we are necessarily reflecting on what is being taught or explained. However, if we're actually reflecting on the processes of coaching, explaining or teaching as well as on the subject matter involved, the reflections are all the deeper, and help us further in the *making sense* both of the topic and of our attempts to communicate the topic.

7. ***Making informed judgements***
   This is perhaps where some of the deepest forms of reflection occur – for example, when applying criteria to things we have done (reflection on action) or on things we are doing (reflection in action). In the context of peer observation of teaching, for example, we may be making informed judgements on others' actions, and on how well those actions are working in a given context, but we may also be reflecting on how we can apply our thinking to our own future actions in similar contexts.

Reflecting more deeply – the 'else' factor

Reflecting on a given event or process may well involve us interrogating it using the normal question words of why, what, how, where, when, who, which, and so on. There is a danger, however, that the *evidence* of reflection degenerates into a mere 'reflective log' in a rather low-key, narrative mode, just *describing* what is happening rather than analysing or interrogating the event. Reflective logs are widely used as evidence of reflection, and are often an assessed element in professional development programmes (not least in the teaching profession), but can be tedious to compile and are low-level to assess when they are predominantly descriptive. However, if we start using 'else' to include and address questions such as:

- What *else* was going on?
- Why *else* might this have happened?
- Where *else* may this be useful?
- Who *else* may be affected by this?

- Where *else* may this work well?

- How *else* can this be achieved?

- Where *else* are our students learning?

the reflections become much deeper, and more useful. In most instances, the response to an 'else' question is deeper, more interesting, and indeed more *reflective* than the response to the corresponding basic question under-pinning it. A reflective log becomes much deeper if the straightforward questions are answered deliberately precisely (i.e. the relatively obvious is stated concisely) and the 'else' questions are answered more expansively. Moreover, evidence of reflection is further deepened by extending the 'else' questions along the following lines:

- What *else* happened?

- What *else else* happened?

and so on. The deeper the 'else' questions probe, the deeper the level of reflection that they elicit from us – and from our students.

Putting word limits on reflection?

For several years until 2010 the website of Leeds Metropolitan University has carried a series of 200-word reflections from staff and students. The process was initiated by a former Vice-Chancellor, who for six years provided a daily reflection for the site, the topic ranging widely around academia, sport, management, and beyond. The 'game' was for each reflection to be *exactly* 200 words, and in two paragraphs (fitting nicely on to a computer screen). Before long, a series of 200-word reflections appeared on the website daily, written by other people, under such umbrella headings as 'International', 'Sporting', 'Assessment', 'Partnerships', and so on. Many colleagues and students who wrote these reflections noted that whittling the piece down to exactly 200 words invariably improved the quality of the piece (just about always, in practice, it turned into a matter of shortening a longer piece, rather than looking for words to expand a shorter one – 200 words is quite a short bit of writing). In shortening a piece to 200 words, decisions had to be made along the following lines:

- There are three ideas in this paragraph but there is only room for two ideas – which is the weakest idea?

- Which words in this sentence are not pulling their weight? How can I adjust the sentence to make the point I want to make, but more concisely?

- How can I make the first impression striking enough to draw readers in to the rest of this short piece?

- I want to end such a short piece with a bang rather than a whimper – how can I best achieve this?

In other words, the final 200-word reflections involved quite a lot more *reflection* than if there had not been a tight word constraint.

Teaching staff soon saw the benefits of setting students word-constrained tasks, such as:

- a 200-word reflection on a critical incident in their practice
- a 150-word summary of the main points a selected author said about a given topic
- a 300-word critique of the views of two authors on a given subject
- a 250-word proposal for a given course of action.

When assessing a pile of students' word-constrained work in such formats, several things increased the reliability, validity and authenticity of the assessment, not least:

- plagiarism is just about eliminated, as it would be very easy to spot it in a pile of one-pagers
- most students have necessarily drafted and redrafted their work to get it to the right length, and the work is therefore less rushed and more 'mature' as evidence of their thinking
- the quality of thinking behind the writing is much higher – less description, more analysis, more *making sense*, and so on
- it takes far less time to assess a batch of 158 one-page reflections than 158 3,000-word essays, and the reliability and the manageability of the assessment have increased very significantly
- students writing in English as a second language may well be less disadvantaged writing short pieces than when writing extended essays
- students can do a greater number of high-level, concise formative tasks, ranging their thinking much more widely than if they had to do just a single, big, low-level summative task
- the quality of students' evidence of their thinking is higher than if they were free to word-spin at length.

When 'reflective logs' are an assessed element of students' work, taking into account the factors mentioned above, free-ranging reflection, with the associated danger of word-spinning, seems far less attractive than focused, word-constrained reflection.

Benefits from peer observation of teaching

Why should we do it? What can we get out of having our teaching observed by our colleagues? As teachers in higher education, the benefits we can derive from peer observation include the following:

- opportunities, through both observing and being observed in our teaching sessions, to reflect on and review our teaching skills with the assistance of our colleagues

- identifying good practice, and needs which we can address, to ensure our ongoing personal and professional development

- helping to continue to learn from each other so that we develop shared understandings of best practices in relation not just to teaching, but to processes of assessment and feedback to students

- continuing opportunities to observe *students* as they learn in colleagues' teaching sessions, increasing our own awareness about how students learn well (and less well), allowing us to reflect on how we can enhance students' learning in our own sessions

- mutually beneficial learning experiences through both processes of observing colleagues and being observed ourselves

- getting to know a range of colleagues much better so that we have friends we can turn to when we are perplexed about difficult situations we may experience in our teaching

- learning new tricks from one another (experienced colleagues learn much from new staff and they in turn can teach new colleagues old tricks!)

- identifying generic development needs to feed into ongoing and future staff development activities

- increased confidence of all involved, derived from feedback on being observed and from picking up good ideas while observing others' teaching

- identifying really good practice so that this is more easily shared and built upon

- identifying commonly experienced problems and needs so that these can be made the basis of staff development opportunities

- focused 'learning conversations' between observees and observers, mutually helping everyone involved to continue to develop professional skills relating to teaching and learning.

Despite the many benefits associated with peer observation, Gosling comments: 'No scheme, no matter how flexible and respectful of staff autonomy, will be successful with all staff. That is a universal law of educational development!'

(Gosling, 2009: 13). Boyd (2009) summarizes four overlapping types of resistance towards peer review policies as follows:

- opposing 'managerialism': the policy is imposed and seeks to measure;
- opposing 'bureaucracy': yet another form to fill in;
- opposing 'intrusion': my teaching is part of my identity – back off!
- opposing 'reductionism': teaching is not as simple as that. (Boyd, 2009: 33)

Designing a framework for peer observation

Essentially, it is best when the processes of peer observation are entirely confidential between you and your observer. A reasonable expectation is that everyone who teaches should be observed at least twice per year – and observe someone else teach at least twice per year. It is natural that feedback from peer observation will be valuable evidence to put forward for appraisal or other forms of performance review. Later in this chapter you can see an example of a pro forma that you can use as the basis for your observation. You can use it to plan with your observer at a pre-meeting, and review at a post-meeting, where the form is returned to you to keep.

Ten steps in a peer observation framework

Below are details of ten steps which may be used as the basis of a peer observation scheme. These guidelines are written with 'you' being the observee. You can easily turn around steps 1–8 when it's your turn to be the observer – which may well be *before* you go in as an observee. There is no better training for being observed than to have had a go at observing two or three colleagues first. The intended processes are as follows:

1. *You choose your own peer observers and agree with them that you will observe their teaching too.* Normally, the intention is you choose a different peer observer for each session that is reviewed, to optimize the sharing of experience. In selecting observers, you might ask colleagues from your own subject groups or similar, but could also consider approaching staff from different areas or departments. If at all possible, you observe your observer (or others) before you yourself are observed. In this way you gain experience of the overall process.

2. *You decide what sort of teaching/learning is going to be observed.* All forms of teaching can be considered for review, not just lecturing. It may be intended that one observation should be of a classroom-based session, and the other could be a further similar session, or a tutorial,

a practice/work-based learning session or a review of learning materials, or whatever else you would like feedback upon. Ideally, the first session should take place in the earlier part of the academic year and the second at a later time. If you are teaching at a distance, virtual observation and review can be undertaken. Furthermore, there is nothing to prevent you having an *assessment* event observed, where the process of assessment is designed primarily *as* learning for students.

3. *You meet to set the scene.* You arrange a brief 'pre-meeting' with your chosen observer in advance of the session to be observed, to explain its context and objectives and to agree any particular focus for the observation. For lengthy sessions, for example teaching taking place in a studio or laboratory, you should negotiate the duration of the observation with your observer.

4. *You plan with your observer your feedback agenda.* At the 'pre-meeting' you plan the date, time and duration of the observation, and you also plan ahead for a 'post-meeting' after the observation so you can get feedback. Feedback should be constructive, focused, supportive and developmental. You choose with your observer a framework for the recording of appropriate observations for your session. Examples included later in this chapter show some possible frameworks for feedback, but these are only for illustration. The particular examples included in this chapter are designed primarily for observation of a classroom-based session. You (and your observer) can adapt these for other forms of teaching, as appropriate.

5. *You do your bit – your observation takes place.* Your observer uses the agreed agenda as a basis for recording observations and suggestions during your session, and prepares to bring this back to hand over to you at the 'post-meeting' referred to above.

6. *The two of you meet for the 'post-meeting'.* This might be immediately following the observed session or be planned deliberately to be a bit later, allowing both of you time to reflect informally on the session and the observation. During the feedback discussion, aspects of good practice and developmental needs are shared. It is your observer's role to assist you in the process of review and reflection with the aim of improving the quality of your teaching as well as highlighting good practice for wider dissemination. Remember you will be doing (or will already have done) exactly the same for your observer. Peer observation is a reciprocal process throughout.

7. *The two of you 'seal the deal' with your joint thoughts.* You could design a form along the lines of the example included later in this chapter for this purpose. Remember, no one else sees this form unless you choose to show it to them, so you can be frank and direct in your own comments about the session you taught. This makes it easier to revisit the form in future action planning.

8. *You send in the basic data of the observation.* After the 'post-meeting', you contact the person who oversees the overall process, simply supplying the date, location and nature of the observation session and the name of the observer, thereby recording that the observation has taken place. You are welcome to provide alongside the basic data any generic feedback points you would like to have disseminated more widely, and any training needs you have identified, to ensure relevant development opportunities can be provided.

9. *Reviewing managers do their bit.* At agreed points in the year, the reviewing managers collate a record of peer observations completed by staff. Records include:

   - dates of observations, locations
   - names of persons observing
   - names of observees
   - nature of sessions (e.g. lectures, seminars, tutorials, practicals, and so on).

   In addition, reviewing managers may compile and share an anonymous summary of general areas of good practice and development needs arising from the peer observations they oversee.

10. *Whoever is in charge of the overall scheme does their bit.* This could be producing an annual report on the implementation of peer observation of teaching for consideration by an appropriate committee.

Experiences of peer observation

What do you gain by being observed? Most importantly, you gain feedback both on your teaching and on how the students are responding to the way you teach. The following quotes from a range of staff in several institutions illustrate how beneficial peer observation can (and should) be.

- I have always found peer observation of teaching invaluable. I have learned a lot from watching other colleagues teaching. Consequently, I am able to be a better teacher with improved style of teaching and classroom practice. Likewise, others who had observed my teaching had commented how this experience had helped them. I have been teaching for 28 years and I continue to find each peer observation adding to my teaching skills.

- For me peer observation of my teaching is an invaluable and constructive way of ascertaining the extent to which I am achieving my stated aims. The feedback from observers enables me to identify areas that require further thought and also highlights existing good practice.

- The reward for me is the discovery of new approaches and constructive feedback on what I think I am doing. We think we are self-aware but you can't replace the reality of other people's observation. What a learning experience!

- I think that part of the value of peer observation is that it is a great prompt for reflective practice. It is sometimes easy to get complacent about teaching situations and to do it as you have always done it because it seems to go OK, but setting up an observation makes you reflect on the session from beginning to end, thinking 'What am I trying to do here?', 'Is what I normally do really the best way to do that?' And so on. Not wanting to show ourselves up [in front of the observer] is a great incentive to having a bit of a rethink!

Even greater benefits to observers

What do you gain by being an observer? The short answer is 'probably even more than through being observed!' A good scheme of peer observation is designed so that everyone is an observer as often as they are observed. But of course it's easy enough to gain even more practice at being an observer, not least when attending conferences and staff development sessions.

Here are some of the benefits you can gain from the opportunity to sit in others' classes and watch what happens. You may well be able to add to this list if you've already got some experience at watching how colleagues go about their teaching.

- *You see colleagues doing things that you can emulate.* Even very experienced observers comment that they continue to learn new things that they can take back and apply to their own teaching.

- *You may learn much from watching others use learning technologies, conferencing software or equipment unfamiliar to you.* It's often really helpful to watch someone else in action before you try something new yourself.

- *You see other ways of going about teaching.* The more the better. In a small circle of colleagues you might only see a limited range of approaches to helping students to learn. When you widen that circle, you're likely to experience different approaches you would not otherwise have met, some of which may well be worth trying out for yourself.

- *You may choose to observe colleagues who are renowned for their teaching.* This can feel a bit intimidating – 'However can I live up to how they approach it?' you might ask, and 'What will such an excellent teacher make of my attempts?' But it's still possible to selectively take away even just one or two of their techniques to try out for yourself. And when it's their turn to observe you, you may be surprised at how positive and reassuring they usually are. No one has been a 'renowned teacher' from day one, and they usually remember their relatively clumsy histories.

- *You get time out to watch and reflect.* For once, you don't have to say anything. You can watch, think, listen, reflect on your own teaching, and capture things in your notes to share later with your colleague. How often in your busy life do you get time to sit, watch and think for best part of an hour?

- *You can be a student for a while.* It's really useful to sit being a student. For some, it's a long time since we were *real* students. Watching the students as we observe helps us think about how our students feel in our own sessions. You can share the joy and excitement when your colleague generates such emotions with the class. You can also share the tensions when things are going less well. You can *watch* the students in a way you can't manage in your own classes when you're busy teaching.

- *You may see things to avoid doing yourself!* When you see something going wrong in a session you're observing, you can make a note to yourself to avoid that in your own teaching, or prevent a problem from occurring as you watch one developing. You may or may not choose to share all these things with the colleague you're observing. If they know they've got a problem, they don't need you to tell them. They might, however, welcome some feedback on alternative approaches which may have prevented the problem occurring, but let them tell you first that it was indeed a problem.

- *You get to know more and more colleagues.* Peer observation, and the discussions which follow it, are an excellent way of finding new friends and allies. They make teaching in higher education far less lonely than it can be when confined to one's own classrooms. You'll have more people to turn to when you need help or advice. In particular, it's good to build bridges with colleagues in other faculties.

- *You get the luxury of leading a 'learning conversation' with your colleague about teaching and learning.* Such conversations are extremely valuable, and in busy lives where time is precious it is good to take time out from all those other things and talk about learning and teaching. After all, the main part of most of our jobs is to do with these things.

- *The process of giving feedback to colleagues on their teaching helps you become more receptive to feedback on your own teaching.* For example, if something has gone really well, you will want to make sure that they know it has gone well so that they can build on it and repeat it. Or if something hasn't quite worked, you'll want to help them find ways of making it work better next time. In either case, you'll be choosing how best to be a supportive colleague to the person whose teaching you observed. All this pays dividends when it's your turn to be receptive to your own observers.

- *Being an observer is the best possible preparation for getting the most out of being observed.* Someone's got to go first, and in any reciprocal peer observation it could be you who is first to be observed. But when it's your turn to observe, it will still make future 'observation' occasions all the more productive.

Some nuts and bolts of a peer observation scheme

Let's flesh out the discussion above, regarding the rationale of having peer observation and the benefits which can accrue from it, with some of the finer detail of peer observation. The discussion which follows suggests how to go about designing the 'pre-meeting', the observation itself, the 'post-meeting' and some examples of the paperwork which might be used to make it all work in practice.

Preparing to be observed

It's best to have the pre-meeting within a few days of the observation, rather than try to squeeze it in ten minutes before the observation itself. This gives your observer more time to tune in to the nature of the session, and what you're planning to gain from the observation. The pre-meeting can address, for example, some of the following questions and issues:

- *What's the background?* For example, is this your fifth lecture in a series of ten, or a seminar following up a particular lecture, or a practical session based on previous lectures, and so on?

- *How do you feel about being observed on this occasion?* You may be very used to the experience, or it can be new and a bit scary for you. It can be worth sharing your feelings with your observer – you'll often get a lot of reassurance.

- *How long is the session to be observed?* If it's a long session, is observation just going to be for part of your session?

- *How is this particular group of students shaping up to date?* Any difficulties with them? Any particular strengths or characteristics that the observer could find useful to know?

- *What are the particular learning outcomes for the session?* For example, what exactly are the students intended to get out of the session? How (very briefly) do these outcomes fit into the bigger picture of their studies?

- *What, in particular, do you want to find out from the observation?* For example, are you trying out something new and would like feedback on how it works? Are you having some difficulties with this class and would like feedback on what seems to be happening to help you address these difficulties?

- *What pro forma would you like to be used by the observer during the observation?* Have you one of your own you'd prefer to be used? Is there one that's widely used in your own subject area or faculty? Would you like to rough out a specific one for this observation? If there's a particular form you'd like to be used to capture the observations, it is really useful to have this ready at the pre-meeting to give to your observer.

- *What do you want your observer to do at the session?* For example, 'be one of the students', 'sit in a particular place', and so on.

- *Will you explain to the students why someone else is in the room?* If so, how will you do this? At the time, or in advance?

- *Observing what exactly?* Do you want your observer to watch what your students are doing rather than just watch what you are doing?

- *What else might you want to find out as a result of the observation?* What *don't* you want to find out? For example, are there things you know already about your teaching in this particular context and would prefer not to be told?!

The observation event

There's a lot to be gained by both parties. Perhaps the most useful starting place is the form you choose to use at the session. An example of the sort of document which the observer might use during the observation is shown below. This form is quite detailed and may well need to be shortened to suit a particular observation context. My intention of including this example is to alert you to other things you might want to include in the agenda for an observation, or indeed to get you thinking about further things you might want to add. This form is quite specific to 'the lecture' as the observation event, but can be adapted readily for other teaching/learning contexts, such as tutorials, problems classes, practical sessions, and so on.

Example of an observation pro forma

Name of lecturer:		Name of observer:	
Date of lecture:		Time of lecture:	
Venue:		Topic of lecture:	
Date of report:		Approx no. of students:	

Aspects of the lecture	Responses, comments and suggestions
First impressions made by the lecturer:	
How the intended outcomes of the lecture were made clear to students at the beginning of the lecture:	
How this particular lecture was put into context regarding previous and forthcoming lectures:	
How intended evidence of achievement of the learning outcomes was clarified to students during the lecture:	
How the intended learning outcomes were revisited towards the end of the lecture:	
How the lecturer checked the extent to which the students felt they had achieved the intended learning outcomes:	
The general tone and style of the presentation:	
How visual aids were used to enhance students' learning:	
How student diversity (ethnic origin, disability, learning needs) was catered for during this particular lecture:	
How body language was used to enhance communication at the lecture:	
Tone of voice, clarity of diction, audibility, and so on:	
What students seemed to be doing during the lecture:	
The extent to which students were kept actively learning during the lecture:	
How students seemed to be using any handout materials during the lecture:	
How students' questions were invited and handled during the lecture:	
How well use was made of the available space as a learning environment:	
How links were made between the content of the lecture and how this would be assessed:	
Comments about the close of the lecture:	
Any further overall comments and suggestions:	

Aspects of the lecture	Responses, comments and suggestions
Further specific things on which the lecturer asked for feedback at the pre-meeting: 1 2 3	
The extent to which 'the lecture' was the most appropriate format to help students to achieve the learning outcomes:	
Action planning comments by observer, for example things to consider in own teaching:	

A shorter alternative observation format

A much more basic example than the one above can also be very effective in practice (see below). It is simply a log of the event observed, with the timescale down the left-hand side, a concise summary of what was happening in the next column, and observations and comments in the right-hand column.

Example of a simpler observation pro forma

Time	What was happening	Observations and comments

The post-meeting

Why is a post-meeting really useful? The main purposes of the post-meeting are as follows:

1. To enable you to gain feedback from your observer.

2. To enable you to receive your observer's notes and store them for your own information and use.

3. To enable your observer to explain things included in these notes.

4. To enable you to explain to your observer any things which need elaboration.

5. To complete, jointly, a summary record of the observation.

Why is it best to have this as a face-to-face meeting rather than paper-trail afterwards? After all, feedback can be dropped in your pigeon hole, sent via email, put through your letter box, or given by phone. But there's something about a face-to-face meeting, not least that you can both sign the documentation as a record for your own files. Most important, however, is that when you are face to face with your observer you've got tone of voice, eye contact, the chance to question-and-answer until you know exactly what your observer means, the chance to clarify things, the opportunity to explain why you did what you did instead of what your observer might have thought you might have done, and so on. The language of written feedback can sometimes look formal and cold on paper, but face-to-face explanation and discussion can be so much more natural and informal – that's often where the real learning and development takes place.

What comes out of the post-meeting?

The post-meeting usually takes a bit longer than the pre-meeting so it's best to allow for between 30 minutes and an hour. You also need to allow a few minutes to jointly draft a short, agreed record of the meeting, following on from your observer's comments. This record is based on your observer's feedback and your own thoughts about the session, and can be used in connection with appraisal if you choose to do so. You may also wish to quote directly from your observer's comments in an appraisal. A possible format is presented below to illustrate how you could design what suits you best.

Example of a formal record of an observation

Teaching observation joint notes	
Observee:	Observer:
Signature:	Signature:
Date of observation:	Date of these notes:
Observee: summary of main thoughts (e.g. what you got out of the observation, feedback from your observer and discussion)	Observer: summary comments (e.g. what impressed you about what you observed, things you may take back and put into your own teaching practice)
Agreed action points and any other matters arising	

Beyond peer observation

Good teachers reflect all the time, both during teaching and afterwards. However, a problem with reflecting is that unless some *record* of reflection is made at the time, one's best ideas can just evaporate away. It can be useful to design your own reflection template, and to spend say five minutes after particular teaching sessions jotting down your responses to various questions. You can then keep a file of your completed questionnaires. The actual questionnaire you use should develop over time as you find out more about what is most worthwhile to reflect upon. Indeed, as you find that you've developed your practice further as a result of reflecting frequently, some questions may no longer be needed.

To end this chapter on 'reflective observation' let's look at how you can do something on your own, in addition to the peer observation discussed already. This also goes right back to the factors underpinning successful learning, and in particular 'making informed judgements', by interrogating examples of your own teaching against various criteria, and planning what else you might plan to do next time you run a similar event. There follows quite a long 'reflective checklist' for a teaching element, which you may shorten or lengthen according to the nature of your own teaching, and the amount of time and energy you feel able to devote to such reflections. Ideally, it is worth using such a checklist regularly rather than rarely, so you can continually fine-tune the checklist to keep pace with the developing quality of your teaching.

What might you use as a starting point for designing your own reflective checklist? The following table is far too long to use as it stands, but is presented as food for thought. You can select those elements that you think will be worthwhile in the context of your own teaching and that will inspire you, or you can create better questions that are more relevant to your own discipline area. You may notice that some of the questions are about your own performance, while others are about the students themselves. It's worth reflecting about both sides of the picture.

Jotting down your thoughts as reflections on a session can sometimes be a relief! If you've had a session where things didn't go well, and it continues to prey on your mind, making a short, reflective analysis of the session can be a way of 'getting it out of your system', helping you to identify particular issues that you can address another time. This is better than the whole session continuing to creep into your thoughts.

It takes rather more self-discipline to make the time to reflect on a session which went splendidly – but the time is well spent as it may help you identify the features which made it go really well. You can then actively replicate them, rather than just hoping it will happen again.

In the checklist below, the order of the questions is not important. You'll notice that the questions are written in the first person, using 'I', 'my' and so on. This is meant to help the process become your reflection, and not an interrogation of your practice by someone else questioning you. In most cases, the main thrust of each checklist question is presented in bold print, with supplementary probing or deepening questions in plain print. It is worth spending a minute or two to record the basic details of the session – what sort of teaching/learning session it was, the date, time, number of students, topic taught, and so on. This prevents such things gradually becoming mixed up in our minds as time elapses.

Example of a self-reflective checklist

Main facts about the particular session	
Date:	Topic of session:
Place:	Time: Number of students:
Nature of session: Lecture, tutorial, etc?	
Overall, how I feel this session went: One of my very best. Fine. OK. Could have been better. Not at all happy about this one! Other:	
Checklist questions to capture my reflections	**My responses, reflections and planning ideas**
What is the thing about this session that is at the top of my mind at this moment?	
What did I like most about the way this session went? *Why is this?*	
What *else* worked really well at this session?	
What worked *least* well at this particular session? *Why was this? What can I do in future sessions to minimize the chance that similar things will happen again?*	
What surprised me most at this particular session? *Why was this unexpected? What would I now do, with hindsight, to address this, if it were to happen again at a future session?*	
How well do I now think that I *started* this particular session? *Have I learned anything about how best to start this particular kind of session? How may I now fine-tune the beginning of a future similar session?*	
How effectively did I explain the intended learning outcomes to students? *Which of these outcomes seemed tobe most important to them? With hindsight, can I adjust the intended learning outcomes to be more relevant to future students at similar sessions?*	
How well did the students seem to take ownership of the *need* to work towards achieving the outcomes? *Could the students see 'what's in it for me' regarding putting effort into the subject?*	

Checklist questions to capture my reflections	My responses, reflections and planning ideas
Did I let the students know what, in due course, they needed to do with the topic? How clearly did I explain to the students what exactly they would need to work towards to show they had achieved the learning outcomes?	
To what extent did the students seem to *want* to learn the topic? Is there anything I need to do to help them to increase their want to learn next time?	
How much did the students already know already about this topic, on average? Was this more than I expected or less than I expected? How would I adjust the content of a future session to fine-tune it better to what the students are likely to know already? How can I find out what they already know?	
What was the best thing about the teaching room at this particular session? Why did this really help the session? What can I do to try to ensure that this kind of venue feature will be put to good use in future sessions?	
What was the worst thing about the teaching room at this particular session? What can I do in future to minimize the risk of similar things spoiling a session?	
To what extent did I manage to get the students *learning by doing* during this session? Was this enough? If not, how could I have built in more student activity?	
Overall, how did the students behave at this session? Am I happy with this?	
Was there something I did at this session that I wished I hadn't done? If 'yes', what was this? What *else* could I have tried?	
What was my own best moment at this particular session? Why do I feel good about this particular aspect? What can I do to lead to more such moments at future sessions?	
What did the most 'difficult' student do at this particular session? What can I do to address such behaviours at future sessions, if they occur again?	

Checklist questions to capture my reflections	My responses, reflections and planning ideas
To what extent did teaching this session help me to _make sense_ of the topic better? What was the most important thing I learned about the topic?	
How much feedback did the students get on their learning during this session? How much of this feedback was from each other rather than just from me?	
Did I manage to include opportunities for students to deepen their learning by _explaining things to each other_ during the session? Could I do more of this next time?	
To what extent did I manage to help students to deepen their learning of the topic by making informed judgements during the session? (e.g. on their own work, or on things I gave them to judge).	
What, with hindsight, would I now miss out of the session? Why would I now choose to miss this out of similar session in future?	
What else, with hindsight, do I wish I had been able to include in this particular session? How best can I make time to include something along these lines in future similar sessions?	
How well do I think I closed the session? Did I end it with a whimper or a bang?! Was I rushed towards the end of the session, trying to get through everything on my agenda? What would I do next time round, with hindsight, to make sure that a future similar session ended really positively?	
What do I feel about the feedback I have received from students at this session? What will be the most important thing that I will do differently next time as a result of this feedback? What will be the most important thing I will do in exactly the same way because of this feedback?	
What was the most hurtful comment or grading in students' feedback? Why do I find this hurtful? Was it justified? Is it really important considering the feedback as a whole? Would it be useful for me to do something different next time round to address this particular aspect of critical feedback?	

Checklist questions to capture my reflections	My responses, reflections and planning ideas
What was the most pleasing comment or grading I received in students' feedback? Why does this please me so much? Will it be possible for me to get further similar feedback in future, and how will I adjust a future session to do so?	
How well did students feel that they had achieved the intended learning outcomes at the end of the session? Which outcomes had they achieved best? Were any of the intended outcomes less important than others? How would it be useful, with hindsight, to adjust the intended learning outcomes for a similar session next time round?	
What is the most important thing I have learned about teaching sessions of this kind from this particular experience? How will I put this learning to good use at future sessions?	
Any further thoughts? **Date completed:**	

Conclusions

This chapter is intended to help you to find out more about your teaching and about the nature of reflection so that you are better equipped to make learning happen effectively, efficiently and enjoyably with your own students. Einstein is reported to have said 'It is simply madness to keep doing the same things and expect different results'. Reflecting on our teaching and getting feedback on it from observers are two of the best tools we have for improving our performance. They allow us to go on to try *different* things to make our teaching even better, and to further enhance the learning experience of our students.

References and Further Reading

Anderson, D. and Race, P. (2002) *Effective Online Learning: The Trainer's Toolkit*. Ely: Fenman.

Ausubel, D.P. (1968) *Educational Psychology: A Cognitive View*. London: Holt, Rinehart and Winston.

Bandura, A. (1997) *Self-efficacy: The Exercise of Control*. New York: Freeman.

Bates, A.W. (1995) *Technology, Open Learning and Distance Education*. London: RoutledgeFalmer.

Bates, A.W. (2002) *National Strategies for e-Learning in Post-secondary Education and Training*. New York: UNESCO.

Biggs, J. (2003) *Teaching for Quality Learning at University: What the Student Does* (2nd edn). Maidenhead: Open University Press.

Biggs, J. and Tang, C. (2007) *Teaching for Quality Learning at University: What the Student Does* (3rd edn). Maidenhead: Open University Press/SRHE.

Blackwell, R. and McLean, M. (1996) 'Peer Observation of teaching and staff development', *Higher Education Quarterly*, 50(2): 156–71.

Boud, D. (1995) *Enhancing Learning through Self-assessment*. London: Routledge.

Bowl, M. (2003) *Non-traditional Entrants to Higher Education: 'They Talk about People Like Me'*. Stoke-on-Trent: Trentham Books.

Boyd, P. (2009) 'University of Cumbria: peer review of teaching, learning and assessment', in D. Gosling and K. Mason O'Connor (eds), *Beyond the Peer Observation of Teaching*. London: SEDA Publications.

Brown, S. (2009) *Assessing first year students effectively – right from the start*. Keynote at First Year Learning and Assessment Project Conference: Leeds Metropolitan University, 16 June.

Brown, S. and Knight, P. (1994) *Assessing Learners in Higher Education*. London: Kogan Page.

Brown, S. and Race, P. (2002) *Lecturing: A Practical Guide*. London: Routledge.

Brown, S., Jones, G. and Rawnsley, S. (eds) (1993) *Observing Teaching*. SEDA Paper 79 (A collection of articles on good practice, with example forms.) London: SEDA Publications.

Bryson, B. (2004) *A Short History of Nearly Everything*. London: Black Swan.

Burge, E.J. and Haughey, M. (eds) (2001) *Using Learning Technologies: International Perspectives on Practice*. London: RoutledgeFalmer.

Burgess, R. (2004) *Measuring and Recording Achievement*. The Burgess Report. London: Universities UK/Standing Conference of Principals.

Burgess, R. (2007) *Beyond the Honours Degree Classification*. The Burgess Group final report. London: UUK.

Claxton, G. (1998) *Hare Brain, Tortoise Mind*. London: Fourth Estate.

Claxton, J., Mathers, J. and Wetherell-Terry, D. (2004) 'Benefits of a 3-way collaborative learning system: action learning, continuous editing and peer assessment'. Paper presented at the conference 'Reflection on teaching: the impact on learning', Edinburgh.

Coffield, F., Moseley, D., Hall, E. and Ecclestone, K. (2004) *Learning Styles and Pedagogy in Post-16 Learning: A Systematic and Critical Review*. London: Learning and Skills Research Centre. (For a shorter review, see also Coffield, F., Moseley, D., Hall, E. and Ecclestone, K. (2004) *Should We Be Using Learning Styles? What Research Has to Say to Practice*. London: Learning and Skills Research Centre.)

Cotton, D. (2004) 'Essentials of training design. Part 5: adult learning theories and design', *Training Journal*, May 2004: 22–7.

Curry, L. (1990) 'A critique of the research on learning styles', *Educational Leadership*, 48(2): 50–6.

Denton, S. and Brown, S. (eds) (2009) *A Practical Guide to University and College Management: Beyond Bureaucracy*. London: Routledge.

Dewey, J. (1933) *How We Think*. New York: Dover.

Entwistle, N. (2009) *Teaching for Understanding at University*. London: Palgrave Macmillan.

Fleming, N. see http://www.vark-learn.com/english/index.asp (accessed December 2009).

Gardner, H. (1993) *Frames of Mind: The Theory of Multiple Intelligences*. New York: Basic Books.

Gardner, H. and Hatch, T. (1989) 'Multiple intelligences go to school: educational implications of the theory of multiple intelligences', *Educational Researcher*, 18(8): 4–9.

Gibbs, G. and Simpson, C. (2002) 'Does your assessment support your students' learning?', www.open.ac.uk/science/fdtl/documents/lit-review.pdf, Milton Keynes: Open University, accessed September 2004.

Gosling, D. (2009) 'A new approach to peer review of teaching', in D. Gosling and K. Mason O'Connor (eds), *Beyond the Peer Observation of Teaching*. London: SEDA Publications.

Gosling, D. and Mason O'Connor, K. (eds) (2009) *Beyond the Peer Observation of Teaching*. London: SEDA Publications.

Hammersley-Fletcher, L. and Orsmond, P. (2004) 'Evaluating our peers: is peer observation a meaningful process?', *Studies in Higher Education*, 29(4): 489–503.

Harper, S., Gray, S., North, S., Brown, S. with Ashton, K. (2009) 'Getting the most from staff', in S. Denton and S. Brown (eds), *A Practical Guide to University and College Management: Beyond Bureaucracy*. London: Routledge.

Hativa, N. (2000) *Teaching for Effective Learning in Higher Education*. Dordrecht, Boston, MA and London: Kluwer Academic.

Hodgkinson, M. (1994) 'Peer observation of teaching performance by action enquiry', *Quality Assurance in Education*, 2(2): 26–31.

Honey, P. and Mumford, A. (1982) *The Manual of Learning Styles*. Maidenhead: Peter Honey Publications.

JISC (2004) *Designing for Learning: An Update on the Pedagogy Strand of the JISC eLearning Programme*. Bristol: JISC.

Knight, P. and Yorke, M. (2003) *Assessment, Learning and Employability*. Maidenhead: Society for Research into Higher Education/Open University Press.

Kolb, D. (1984) *Experiential Learning: Experience as the Source of Learning and Development*. Englewood Cliffs, NJ: Prentice-Hall.

Kolb, D.A. (1999) *The Kolb Learning Style Inventory*, Version 3. Boston: Hay Group.

Laurillard, D. (2001) *Rethinking University Teaching: A Framework for the Effective Use of Educational Technology* (2nd edn). London: RoutledgeFalmer.

Lindsay, R. (2004) book review in *Studies in Higher Education*, 29(2): 279–86.

Litzinger, M.E. and Osif, B. (1993) 'Accommodating diverse learning styles: designing instruction for electronic information sources', in L. Shirato (ed.), *What Is Good Instruction Now? Library Instruction for the 90s*. Ann Arbor, MI: Pierian Press.

Meyer, J.H.F. and Land, R. (2003) 'Threshold Concepts and Troublesome Knowledge 1 – Linkages to Ways of Thinking and Practising within the Disciplines' in C. Rust (ed.) *Improving Student Learning – Ten years on*. Oxford: OCSLD.

Miller, C.M.L. and Parlett, M. (1974) *Up to the Mark: A Study of the Examinations Game*. Monograph 21. London: SRHE.

Overbye, D. (1991) *Lonely Hearts of the Cosmos: The Scientific Quest for the Secret of the Universe*. London: Macmillan.

Peelo, M. (2002) 'Setting the scene' in M. Peelo and T. Wareham (eds) *Failing Students in Higher Education*. Buckingham: SRHE/Open University Press.

Peelo, M. and Wareham, T. (eds) (2002) *Failing Students in Higher Education*. Buckingham: Society for Research into Higher Education/Open University Press.

Pellegrino, J., Chudowsky, N. and Glaser, R. (eds) (2003) *Knowing What Students Know: The Science and Design of Educational Assessment*. Washington, DC: National Academy Press.

Pratt, J.R. (2002) 'The manager's role in creating a blended learning environment', *Home Health Care Management & Practice*, 15(1): 76–9.

Race, P. (2005) *500 Tips on Open and Online Learning*. London: Routledge.

Race, P. (2006a) *The Lecturer's Toolkit* (3rd edn). London: Routledge.

Race, P. (2006b) *In at the Deep End*. Leeds: Leeds Metropolitan University Press.

Race, P. (2007) *How To Get a Good Degree* (2nd edn). Maidenhead: Open University Press.

Race, P. (2009) *In at the Deep End*; (2nd edn). Leeds: Leeds Metropolitan University Press.

Race, P. and Pickford, R. (2007) *Making Teaching Work*. London: Sage.

Reynolds, M. (1997) 'Learning styles: a critique', *Management Learning*, 28(2): 115–33.

Robinson, A. and Udall, M. (2003) 'Developing the independent learner: the Mexican hat approach', conference proceedings of the 3rd International Symposium on Engineering Education, Southampton.

Sadler, D.R. (1989) 'Formative assessment and the design of instructional systems', *Instructional Science*, 18: 119–44.

Sadler, D.R. (1998) 'Formative assessment: revisiting the territory', *Assessment in Education: Principles, Policy and Practice*, 5: 77–84.

Sadler, D.R. (2003) 'How criteria-based grading misses the point', Presentation to the Effective Teaching and Learning Conference, Griffith University, Australia.

Sadler, D.R. (2005) 'Interpretations of criteria-based assessment and grading in higher education', *Assessment and Evaluation in Higher Education*, 30: 175–94.

Sadler, D.R. (2007) 'Perils in the meticulous specification of goals and assessment criteria', *Assessment in Education: Principles, Policy and Practice*, 14: 387–92.

Sadler, D.R. (2009a) 'Grade integrity and the representation of academic achievement', *Studies in Higher Education*, 34 (7): 807–826.

Sadler, D.R. (2009b) 'Indeterminacy in the use of preset criteria for assessment and grading', *Assessment and Evaluation in Higher Education*, 34(2): 159–79.

Salmon, G. (2002) *E-tivities: The Key to Active Online Learning.* London: Routledge Falmer.

Salmon, G. (2004) *E-moderating: The Key to Teaching and Learning Online* (2nd edn). London: RoutledgeFalmer.

Schön, D. (1987) *Educating the Reflective Practitioner.* San Francisco: Jossey-Bass.

Smithers, R. (2004) 'Degree grading system faces axe', *The Guardian*, 4 November.

Stowell, N. (2001) 'Equity, justice and standards: assessment decision making in higher education', paper presented at the SRHE Annual Conference, University of Cambridge (*mimeo*).

Thorpe, M. (2003) 'Designing for reuse and versioning', Learning and Teaching Support Network Generic Centre, York, accessed via the Higher Education Academy website, December 2004.

Wierstra, R.F.A. and de Jong, J.A. (2002) 'A scaling theoretical evaluation of Kolb's Learning Style Inventory-2', in M. Valcke and D. Gombeir (eds), *Learning Styles: Reliability and Validity.* Proceedings of the 7th Annual European Learning Styles Information Network Conference, 26–28 June, Ghent: University of Ghent. pp. 431–40.

Yorke, M. (2002) 'Academic failure: a retrospective view from non-completing students', in M. Peelo and T. Wareham (eds), *Failing Students in Higher Education.* Buckingham: SRHE/Open University Press.

Seven factors underpinning successful learning: principal links

Index